'KNOW ME AS I AM'

An anthology

poetry and art by people with learning difficulties

Edited by
Dorothy Atkinson and Fiona Williams

Hodder & Stoughton
LONDON SYDNEY AUCKLAND TORONTO
in association with the Open University

Cover picture: *Self-portrait*, by Peter Reeder

ISBN 0 340 51329 2

First published 1990

Typeset by The Open University
Printed in Great Britain for Hodder and Stoughton Educational, a division of Hodder and Stoughton Ltd, Mill Road, Dunton Green, Sevenoaks, Kent, by M. & A. Thomson Litho Ltd, East Kilbride

Contents

Acknowledgements

Preparing this anthology for publication was, for us, an enjoyable and moving experience. However, the book represents the combined efforts of a great many people.First, we want to emphasize that it would not have been possible without the generosity of those people who sent us their contributions or allowed them to be sent to us on their behalf. Our only regret is that we could not use them all. Indeed, we could have prepared a book almost twice the size from the contributions we received.

We would like to thank the small group of people with learning difficulties who formed our editorial advisory group: Angela Davis, Alice Etherington, Gary Cruby, Anne Taylor, Frances Whelan and Robert Wise, and also Viv Parker, Viv Davies and Verity Maine who brought the group together for us. The group's insightful, sensitive and encouraging responses helped us resolve a number of editorial problems.

We are also indebted to those people who acted, where necessary, as intermediaries between us and the people whose contributions appear in the anthology. Their enthusiasm, co-operation and commitment were invaluable. In particular, we would like to thank Tom Hulley, upon whose idea the book was based, as well as Julia Allton, Carolyn Bew, Jacqui Billis, Mary Bodkin, Theresa Copsey, Jeff Davies, Hilary Dyter, Sharon Edmonds, Maria Edwards, Rosie Fooks, Ann Fuller, Elaine Green, Joan Greyer, Sue Hatton, John Hersov, Kim Holmes, Jan Howitt, Chris Hutchinson, Clare Jepson, Catherine Johoda, Beryl Kapp, Paul Lawrence, Sue Ledger, Dave Lewis, Loretta McLauchlan, David McLean, Jim McLean, Ann Mitchell, Gail O'Farrell, Jean Ollerton, Chris Pope, Maggie Potts, Nigel Pyart, Sheena Rolfe, Freda Ryans-Smith, Jane Sallis, Richard Shaw, Norah Smith, Liz Stancer, Jill Stern, Jeannie Sutcliffe, Joh Swain and David White.

Our thanks are also due to those who read through and offered constructive advice and encouraging comments on several drafts of the book. In addition to our colleagues from the Open Universiy – Ann Brechin, Jan Walmsley, Alyson Peberdy, Moyra Siddell and Will Swann – we would like to thank James Cummings, Chris Kiernan, Zenobia Nadirshaw, Oliver Russell and Paul Williams.

Finally, we express our thanks to Peter Lee, Rob Williams and Debbie Crouch from the Open University for helpful editorial and design advice, and to Christine Love who faced the task of typing a huge variety of manuscripts with cool and efficient equanimity.

Dorothy Atkinson and Fiona Williams
Department of Health and Social Welfare, The Open University

Introduction

'You have to know me as I am.'

(From a discussion on friendship, 'Speaking for Ourselves' class, City Lit, London)

An anthology: the origins of an idea

This book is unusual. It is, as far as we know, unique in its breadth and scope. It is a collection of 'life stories', but a very distinctive collection. The people whose lives are portrayed are people with learning difficulties. And the material compiled and presented here is 'theirs': their lives and their words, pictures, photographs and poems.

The idea for this anthology has its origins in the earliest meetings of the Course Team responsible for producing the Open University course K668 *Mental Handicap: Changing Perspectives.* Members of that team, which included the two editors of this book, made a dual commitment at the beginning of course development: to involve people with learning difficulties in planning the course, *and* to make their lives, experiences and views central to the whole course.

The question of how to meet this dual commitment proved taxing. How could the editors involve people actively in planning a complex and challenging course and one which would rely heavily on the written word? And how could people's lives and views form the centre-piece of a course designed for professionals, managers and others involved in planning and delivering services?

In response to a suggestion from Tom Hulley, the father of a young woman with learning difficulties, the idea of an anthology was conceived. An anthology of work by people with learning difficulties would enable the editors to meet both its commitments. These 'stories of people's lives' would become a set book for the course and, as such, would form the centre-piece of the course. In producing and submitting their 'stories', people with learning difficulties would be setting the agenda and providing the contents which would be central to the whole course. In addition, we decided to seek editorial advice from a separate group of people with learning difficulties who were not contributors to this book but some of whom had experience of their words being published. (See Etherington, *et al.* in Towell, 1988.)

The idea took root. People responded positively and hundreds of contributions were received. The anthology took on a life, and a momentum, of its own. And the product is far richer and wider ranging than was ever envisaged at the outset. The book became more than the central focus of the Open University course; it stands on its own as a testimony to the dignity and achievements of those people with learning difficulties whose lives are portrayed within its pages.

The process of enabling people to take part in this project and contribute their stories has proved challenging. It transpired that there was far more to this process then the mere provision of opportunities for people to 'have their say'. Before we indicate the main developments in that process, we outline briefly the place and significance that this anthology has in relation to other similar published literature on the lives of people with learning difficulties.

The development of autobiographical accounts from people with learning difficulties

This anthology should be seen as part of the important and growing development of presentations, contributions, written accounts and autobiographies from people with learning difficulties. Both in Britain and abroad there has been an increasing acknowledgement of the importance of listening to the voices and viewpoints of people with learning difficulties. It is this growing acknowledgement which has made this anthology possible, and it is the importance of this acknowledgement which this anthology reinforces.

Since the 1960s there has been a variety of different types of contribution to the area. Some have concentrated on revealing the creative talents of people with learning difficulties. These often challenge the assumptions that 'creativity' is part and parcel of 'intelligence' as measured by formal IQ tests. In 1964 David Holbrook published the writings of so-called 'backward' children in *English for the Rejected* (Holbrook, 1964). Since then MENCAP (The Royal Society for Mentally Handicapped Children and Adults) has also sponsored competitions and exhibitions. In 1988 The King's Fund in London organised an international symposium and festival on 'The Creative Arts in the Development of People with Mental and Multiple Handicaps'. Many colleges and centres sent us work which had been part of local exhibitions or college newsletters, or small unpublished pamphlets of poetry (see especially Chapter Five).

Other developments include written autobiographies by people with learning difficulties. In 1967 *The World of Nigel Hunt* appeared. This is an account, self-typewritten in diary form, of the life of Nigel Hunt, a 19-year-old boy with Down's Syndrome. Probably the most well-known autobiography is Joseph Deacon's *Tongue Tied* (Deacon, 1974) which was written collaboratively by four residents of an institution. Joseph told his story: one friend acted as interpreter, another friend wrote the interpretation and a third friend typed the written words.

In other works researchers have transcribed life histories told to them by people with learning difficulties. In *Inside Out: The Social Meaning of Mental Retardation* (Bogdan and Taylor, 1982) two American researchers tape-recorded the autobiographies of Ed and Pattie over a two-year period. In the following chapters in this book, some of the earlier memories of institutional life come from an oral history project by two researchers (Potts and Fido, 1990) which captures the experiences of institutional life in a mental deficiency colony of people now in their sixties, seventies and eighties. Other studies which have documented the experiences and viewpoints of people with learning difficulties include: from the United States, R. Edgerton's *Cloak of Competence* (1967), D. and B. Braginsky's *Hansels and Gretels: Studies of Children in Institutions for the Mentally Retarded* (1971); and from Britain, *Project '74: A Research Study in which Mentally Handicapped People Speak for Themselves* (1976) by Wandsworth Social Services Department and *We Can Speak for Ourselves: Self-advocacy by Mentally Handicapped People* (1982) by P. Williams and B. Schoultz. In 1987 an evaluation study was published by the Mental Handicap in Wales Applied Research Unit which documented *Clients' Views* of services for people with learning difficulties (K. Lowe *et al.*, 1987). Also there are two CMH (Campaign for People with Mental Handicaps) publications: *Beginning to Listen: A Study of the Views of Residents Living in a Hostel for Mentally Handicapped People* (1985) by D. Brandon and J. Ridley, and *Participation: Report of a Workshop Involving People with Mental Handicaps and Staff who Work with Them* (1986) by G. Harper and J. Dobson.

In common with this last publication, there are increasing numbers of transcribed accounts of the collective views of people with learning difficulties recorded at local and national day-schools and conferences arising from the self-advocacy 'People First' movement (see, for example, Ann Shearer's *Listen* and *Our Life*, 1972 and 1973, published by CMH). We too received a number of original transcriptions, from ATCs and colleges, of group discussions on various aspects of life, including one from a women's group on their experiences as women with learning difficulties.

This book contains contributions which reflect the influence of all these different strands. We include poetry, art, photography, and story-telling, as well as transcribed, word-processed and sometimes self-written memories of the past, experiences of the present and wishes for the future. Some are short, vivid vignettes of life, or flashes of insight, or moments of reflection, others are flowing life-histories. Some are by individuals, some by groups, some interpreted through a friend. Thus, whilst this anthology arises from the growing acknowledgement of subjective accounts of people with learning difficulties, its contribution to this development lies in the breadth and scope of its coverage.

The importance of the development of autobiographical accounts

The opportunity to understand the world from the point of view of someone with learning difficulties is extremely important. It challenges our assumptions and stereotypes, even when we think we have none. It was mentioned earlier that some writers had focused on the creative potential of people with learning difficulties and challenged ideas about monolithic forms of intelligence. The accounts which follow in this book challenge most fundamentally the idea that people with learning difficulties have no capacity for understanding their own situation, or their own feelings, or their own deprivations. Many of the writings of oppressed or marginalised groups (black people, women, disabled people) have given the lie to the idea that those who know no better life wish for no better life. This is also the case when we listen to what people with learning difficulties have to say. Furthermore, there is an added importance in this, for it has often been assumed not simply that the opinions of people with learning difficulties did not matter, but that they did not exist.

Accounts of their lives which come directly from people with learning difficulties provide an important antidote to accounts which come from other quarters. The presentation of people with learning difficulties in everyday life – in newspapers, on television, in charity advertisements – usually centres upon their impairment and all else is secondary. This extracts our pity. In professional life we get to know people and their histories through the distorted and exaggerated perceptions of case records. This reinforces our distance from the 'client'. Even though the well-intentioned and perceptive accounts of the worst aspects of institutionalised life by scholars and researchers extract our shame and arouse our conscience, they still only allow us to see the residents as victims. We don't see them as people reflecting and choosing, enacting, rather than acted upon. The importance of accounts by the people themselves is that they give us a quite different perspective from the first two viewpoints and an important balance to the third.

In the accounts and contributions which follow, people give us a rounded picture of themselves. They describe themselves in terms of the cultures they come from – London's East End street market life, rural Wales or rural Jamaica. They describe themselves in terms of their past relationships, their present work or routines or friendships, their future hopes. They are individuals with a personal history, a culture, a class, a gender, as well as an impairment. *Their own* accounts therefore arouse our sympathy, our anger, our humour, our admiration, our wonder, our solidarity, as well as our shame.

The following accounts are represented in written or pictorial form. As such they carry the disadvantage of allowing us to underestimate the effort and co-operation involved in getting them realised. At the same time there is an advantage. By presenting these experiences in this rather formal medium, readers 'without learning difficulties' can take the opportunity of time and distance to reflect upon their own preconceived ideas and assumptions.

Last but not least there is the value of such accounts to other people with learning difficulties. Autobiographies and life histories create the opportunity for experiences to be shared, for common interests to be fostered, for common understandings to be forged and for consciousness to be raised. In this way they help to shift the burden of problems away from the individual who suffers them and on to the society that imposes them.

Background to this anthology

This anthology came into being through the work of four different groups of people. Most central and crucial have been, of course, *the contributors* themselves. Their contributions have, for the most part, reached us through the work of the second group – *the intermediaries* – people who work or live with people with learning difficulties. Contact was made with both these groups by the editors, who are both members of the Department of Health and Social Welfare at the Open University, and, as such, members of a *Course Team* engaged in the production of a distance-learning course – K668 *Mental Handicap: Changing Perspectives.* The editors also received valuable advice from the fourth set of people involved – an *Editorial Advisory Group*, who are a small group of people with learning difficulties from Camden in London. This group included Alice Etherington, Frances Whelan, Anne Taylor, Gary Gruby, Angela Davis and Robert Wise.

A detailed account of the relationship between these groups and the process of creating the anthology is contained in the Conclusion of this book. For the moment we simply sketch the main developments.

The Open University is well placed to undertake the compilation of an anthology of this kind. As a national organisation it has links with all parts of the United Kingdom. More specifically, the Department of Health and Social Welfare is nationally known to people in the field through its successful introductory course, P555 *Mental Handicap: Patterns for Living*. The course has generated its own network of students, trainers and enthusiasts. This network proved a good starting point in the search for contributors.

At the time that the idea of an anthology was taking root, the introductory course (P555 *Mental Handicap: Patterns for Living*) was being 'transformed' into a course for use directly by people with learning difficulties (P555M *Patterns for Living: Working Together*). This new course was already attracting people in large numbers as would-be 'testers' and pilot students, and eventual trainers and students. These people formed a second nationwide network of enthusiasts who also proved receptive to the idea of contributing to a new anthology.

Other sources were tapped. The Open University's own Regional Centres were circulated. Personal contacts were approached. An item was specially written for the People First newsletter. Letters were sent to *Community Care* and *Nursing Times.* Contact was made with theatre, music and arts groups.

As individuals and organisations heard about the proposed anthology, so word began to spread informally. The idea seemed 'right'. It struck a chord. As first contacts were made, and word got round, so the editors became inundated with replies. People from all over the country, in different settings and social situations, liked the idea; they wanted their 'clients' or 'students' to have the opportunity of taking part.

The people who replied, then, were not actually people with learning difficulties but those who worked or lived alongside them.

This was not really surprising as most of the networks tapped were made up of people who could act as intermediaries rather than likely contributors. Attempts to make direct contact with possible contributors through the pages of the People First newsletter and by letters to magazines drew replies, but again from intermediaries rather than from the people themselves. Constrained by the written word, the editors made contact with those people who had the easiest and most direct access to its invitation to participate, such as tutors, teachers, lecturers, social workers, instructors, therapists, nurses and relatives.

From the outset, most of the work has been carried out locally. Contributors have produced their work in their usual setting, working with a person familiar to them. The editors, in most circumstances, have been involved in the discussion, planning and production of people's stories but not in their actual 'telling'. The telling and writing of stories in most, though not all, cases has involved the individual or group working alongside an instructor, teacher, nurse, social worker or other intermediary.

Part of the rationale for compiling the anthology was the editors' commitment to involving people with learning difficulties in planning and developing the course. An early decision was made, therefore, to establish a *personal link* between a member of the team and each potential contributor. Initial contact was made through intermediaries, whose enthusiasm was striking. As one instructor working with a group of students in London put it: 'I think my group is important and the work they do matters. I want their work to have an outlet'. Appointments were made through the intermediaries and a six-week intensive programme of around 60 visits to all parts of the country was undertaken.

This decision was made before the true level of response was known. In the event, the deluge of enquiries and actual invitations to the editors to make a personal visit made it impossible to honour the commitment in absolutely every case. Nevertheless, strenuous efforts were made to link with contributors.

Time, and energy, eventually ran out. But only a handful of latecomers missed out on the personal contact. Some links were made with individuals and couples, but in most cases visits were made to organisations, centres, institutions and classes where groups of up to 20 and 30 people were involved. In this way, contact was made with most of the 200 or so contributors.

The idea of making a personal link with contributors was based on five considerations:

- it would give potential contributors the opportunity to meet one of the people involved in looking at their work; it would personalise the link between the individual and the Open University
- it would give people a chance to hear a first-hand account of the proposed book, and its place within the Open University course

- it would give the intermediaries an opportunity to check on what was involved, the shape and format of the stories sought, and their own role in the process of 'story-telling'
- it would give contributors and/or intermediaries a chance to ask questions about the selection procedure and presentation of material, and the use of people's real names or otherwise
- it would give the editors a first-hand opportunity to meet and talk with likely contributors and their intermediaries; to put faces to names and, where needed, to help initiate the story-telling process.

In addition, the editors kept diaries of the visits made to contributors and intermediaries as reference points for later selection and editing work.

The contributors included people of all ages (except young children) and both men and women. Intermediaries included people working and/or living in Social Services Departments, hospitals, hostels, ATCs, colleges, adult education classes and family homes. The contributors with whom they put us in touch lived in various situations and social circumstances: in hospitals, including secure wards and units; in hostels; in family homes; in convents; in flats, houses and group homes.

Contributors came from various social, cultural and ethnic backgrounds. Most were single, but some were married. Most people attended centres, but some had jobs or were involved in voluntary work. Most stories were produced by individuals, but sometimes groups produced their own joint contributions.

In our selection we have used a broad definition of 'learning difficulties' with the result that we have contributions from a range of people with many different kinds of 'impairment': from dyslexia, epilepsy and lack of literacy and numeracy skills, to severe and multiple handicaps.

The structure of the anthology

The contributions in the anthology have been divided up into nine different chapters with nine different themes. These themes emerged from the nature of the contributions themselves. The themes of the first four chapters all focus on aspects of personal identity.

The first chapter, 'A sense of self', is made up of personal reflections from people about themselves. These reflections suggest that most of the contributors do *not* identify themselves first and foremost in terms of their impairments, nor do they consider themselves as essentially different from other people. This aspect is echoed throughout the book.

The second chapter focuses on 'Memories', and the way identity is built up through sad and happy memories. This is followed by Chapter Three 'Relationships', which is made up of descriptions and accounts of significant relationships in people's lives with family, friends, lovers and spouses. Chapter Four, 'Transitions', covers accounts of major changes, turning points and developments in people's lives – bereavement, home to hospital, home to hostel, hostel to community, marriage and adulthood.

The fifth chapter separates the first four chapters on *personal* identity from the second four chapters on *social* identity. Chapter Five acts as a bridge between these two sets of themes and is called 'Creativity, imagination and fantasy'. It brings together poetry, stories, plays, photographs and coloured and black and white illustrations.

Chapters Six to Nine step into the social world of people with learning difficulties. Chapter Six, 'My daily life' is made up of accounts of daily routines: getting up, shopping, housework, paid work and leisure. Chapters Seven and Eight represent two sides of an important aspect in the lives of people with learning difficulties. The first (Chapter Seven) is called 'Experiences of oppression' and covers experiences of sexual harassment, violence, prejudice and harassment from neighbours, workmates and in the street. It also reveals forms of control and punishment exercised by those in authority and 'care', as well as feelings of inner frustration and despair. By contrast, Chapter Eight on 'Struggle and self-determination' shows, movingly, how the human will to struggle and survive still persists, in spite of these oppressive experiences.

The final chapter is a collection of three *life histories*, two dictated and one self-written. These cover many of the aspects of the previous eight chapters but within the more coherent and flowing context of an autobiography.

In the 'Conclusion' we have described our thoughts and experiences during the process of compiling this anthology. This includes information on the problems, successes and limitations of the methods of our research. In addition it points to issues which have been thrown up by our anthology that deserve further research and inquiry.

One final point concerns our use of the word 'stories' in the text to refer to the contributions. The point has been made before now by those concerned to give space and respect to the experiences of people with learning difficulties that the use of the word 'stories' is inappropriate. It could imply that we are not taking those accounts of experiences seriously, as issues of fact, but are reducing them to 'stories' as if they were 'childish'. We considered this question and the variety of other available terms – 'accounts', 'descriptions', etc. – and none of them seem to convey quite the range of oral, written, and illustrated story-telling that takes place in the following pages. 'Stories' seemed to convey better the wide range of communication skills the contributions utilised, so we have from time to time used that word in the hope that it does not diminish the contents of the contributions.

Chapter One
A sense of self

Much of the emphasis in the literature on the lives of people with learning difficulties has concentrated, importantly, on the process of stigmatisation. Part of this process has meant, especially for those living in institutions, a stripping away of personal and social identity, and the imposition of a label, or a 'spoiled' identity – a lens through which the person's identity is given distorted and often unwanted meanings.

In an attempt to remedy the consequences of these processes many of those who spend their time with people with learning difficulties concentrate on retrieving personal history and identity. Some of the contributions in this chapter have emerged from such attempts.

Many of the following accounts point, on the one hand, to a very fragile and tenuous link with the conventional forces that shape and reinforce adult identity – paid work, parenthood, leisure pursuits. On the other hand (and in spite of this), they indicate a very tenacious hold on a sense of self. Whilst identity can be spoiled or damaged, a sense of self, it would seem, remains stubbornly resistant to assault.

In these accounts we can see how different identities are forged between the 'self' and the person's immediate environment, particularly her or his own family life. Parents feature particularly prominently: they appear to continue to mould and reflect identities long after they have died. Although this is true for most adults, it must especially be so for adults with learning difficulties who are denied many of the avenues in adulthood which reinforce identity – work, parenthood or social activities. Perhaps it is also the consequence of trying to assert a positive identity in a world that effectively denies one. When we want to establish more firmly who we are, we often return in our minds to the more fixed areas of our lives: our families, our cultures, our past, our roots. One of the contributors remembers her 'best time' as being the one time her mother was able to read her a story; another remembers her father who was a miner, tall and thin, who used to rock her and sing to her and who had a 'smiley face'; someone else remembers his father: 'Back home in Jamaica he eat ackie and saltfish'. Not all memories of family life are happy: some people had brothers who would bully them. The poem 'I go home' conveys a complex mixture of distress, loneliness and a need for love. In contrast, for Edward Bradley his family represents a strong source of confirmation of his normality and a counterbalance to his marginalization in the outside world. He says: 'I don't think I'm disabled at all. I'm just a normal person. That's what my mum says and I agree with her'.

Significantly few of the contributors find their senses of self reinforced in paid work. Indeed, several people bemoan the boredom and low pay of the work they are given (a point reiterated in Chapters Six and Seven). One exception is George Coleman who, after a life in institutional care, went to Little Plumstead Hospital 'to learn a trade'.

The forging of our identity through relationships in the family is mediated by other factors: our gender, our culture, our class. Several contributors describe themselves in terms of their parents' class background. Gerard Ward describes with neat accuracy the background of a London skilled working-class family: his grandfather worked at Bryant and May, his father was a 'first-class bricklayer' and his mother worked in Harrods and Fortnum and Mason 'on clothes'. The importance of place and country of birth comes through strongly in the contributions by people from Irish, Ugandan Asian and Jamaican origins. Mangla Jethwa's account of her life evokes not only her strong cultural identity but also the experience of being Asian, disabled and an unmarried and childless woman in a white able-bodied society where most women get married and have children, and from a culture where these attributes are even more highly valued. Aspirations to marriage and motherhood are echoed tentatively in the accounts of the four women discussants from the William Brinson Centre. The exception here is Winnie Ward who celebrates being a grandmother. She is one of the very few contributors in the whole book who is a parent.

Not all the contributors offer a presentation of self through the conventions of family and home. In a beautiful account, Brian Southee describes his childhood and adult life in terms of famous national events – amongst them the Coronation in 1953, Churchill's funeral in 1964, the cold winter of 1963, England winning the World Cup in 1966: a presentation of self not in terms of homes, hostels, hospitals or centres, but in terms of his social and political environment. The chapter ends with a remarkable fantasy presentation of self. Under the pen-name of 'Georgette', Sandy Marshall shifts his gender identity and puts himself in the shoes of an attractive and able young woman, and describes her innermost thoughts, feelings, hopes and fears.

Contents

Self-portrait *(Peter Reeder: Adult Education Centre, Little Plumstead Hospital, Norwich).*

Peter Reeder.

Edward Bradley.

Eddie's life story

I was born at Wainstalls in 1942. I was born next door to a farm, on the 24th of March. When I was a little boy, I went from Slack Farm to 'The Spring' up the road. It was alright but we should never have left Wainstalls. I was in an old-fashioned farm house and we had geese there, round the back of the house.

When I was six or seven, I moved to Cousin Lane. Around that time, I went outside to play and got under somebody called Tommy Beaumont's wagon and my dad had to drag me out. That is my earliest memory.

Cousin Lane is a right long place, with a pub at the end of Ovenden Way. There are houses on both sides. One of my memories there is falling off a wall. I'm very accident prone. Oh, and I have three sisters and a brother. I didn't like it there much because the other boys were always fighting me. We used to play fire on the banking, setting the grass alight nearly.

From Cousin Lane to near the Queen's Head pub. It was round the back of the pub and quite near a farm and fields, but the farmer there told us off when we went on them.

They left when we went to Kirkstall. When I was 23 my dad died and I had a nervous breakdown. I was in a hostel for five years, only coming out for good at Christmas. My mum and brother got me out in the end. I hated the hostel. I got a CB Alpha mike off my uncle and when I came legal, I used to talk to truckers every morning, from six o'clock. I liked doing it very much. I was living at Abbey Park, Kirkstall then. It was alright but it's been pulled down. The houses are still there but the flats I lived in are not. Imagine it! I got in the papers to give £4 to Chatham Street to buy a CB with. I earned it, the money.

I don't think I'm disabled at all. I'm just a normal person. That's what my mum says and I agree with her.

When I was 30, I think, I moved to a cul-de-sac on the Keighley Road to Bolton.

I was about 41 when I moved to where I live now: Heather Bank, Mixenden Lane Farm, Underhill Road, near Illingworth. I am now 46. I live with my mum and next door to Margaret, my sister, and Melvyn, my brother-in-law, and their two girls, Zoe and Lindsey.

We may be moving again. My mum wants the whole family to put all of its money together and buy one big house for everyone, with a horse.

Edward Bradley: Queen's Road Community Centre, Halifax (Dictated)

In the olden days

IN THE OLDEN DAYS MY PARENTS USE TO THROW STONES AT WINDOWS,THEY USE TO TAKE BIKES.IF MY GRANDAD CAUGHT THEM THEY WOULD GET HIT WITH THE STICK. I DONT THINK MY MUM AND HER BROTHER AND SISTER LIKED THAT TIME.ONE OF MY GRANMOTHERS DIED WHEN I WAS A BABY. I DID NOT SEE HER IN IRELAND.I WENT AWAY FOR A WEEK TO SEE MY UNCLE.

In the olden days my parents used to throw stones at windows. They used to take bikes. If my grandad caught them they would get hit with the stick. I don't think my mum and her brother and sister liked that time. One of my grandmothers died when I was a baby. I did not see her in Ireland. I went away for a week to see my uncle. When I came back my brother used to pick on me - he still does. My parents came from Ireland. When I was young I went away with my uncle to Cornwall. In the olden days my mum wore the same clothes as us. They did not have television, telephone, fridges. They used to read newspapers and listen to the radio. The house that they lived in was cold and frosty, they did not have a fire. They ate the same food as us. When I was young my brother pulled me out of the cot and took my bottle. I can remember going to the zoo and I saw a monkey. I am going away in August. Last night I saw dad and he gave me money.

When my grandparents were young they used to live in Ireland. They ate carrots, bread and milk. My grandmother did not like it when the war was on. My grandmother is very old. She was born in Ireland. When she sings I like her voice. When my grandfather was young he had an accident - he was standing too near the edge of the platform when a train came by. He had an artificial leg and only one hand. My grandad has two walking sticks. He can tell fun jokes. He can sing as well. They still wear the same clothes as us. I like my grandparents very much. Their names are Billy, Emma, Joseph and Theresa.

My brother is a bully. He is nice looking, he goes out most nights. My sister is very good. Sometimes she is kind to me when she wants to be. My sister is moody sometimes when she has drink inside her.

In Ireland, when it is hot, you can go down to the sea. You can see lots of cows, dogs, and sheep. My grandad owns his own farm. There are no pavements over there, you have to walk on the road. They don't have a bathroom or toilet where my grandad lives so you have to wash yourselves in the sink.

Theresa: Hammersmith and West London College
(Self-written on to a word-processor)

They used to play games in Jamaica when it was a hot day

When I was a young boy I used to play with my cat a lot. My cat used to teach me how to walk down the street, but it was fun to go outside in the sun. My mum and dad did meet in Jamaica when they were younger. They used to play about in the class room. They get hit with the stick. My grandad used to go swimming when he was small; when they come from swimming they have their dinner. After, they play records. When I was small I used to play with a train set. My grandmother used to hold me when I was small. My grandad used to buy a racing car set for me. My mum did ride a donkey in Jamaica when she was small. My gran feed me when I was small. My grandad did take me shopping when I was small. I did play with my dad's record-player when my dad was at work.

When they were small they used to play cricket in Jamaica when it was hot, and fly their kites in the wind.

They have to cook their dinner, wash up. They used to climb the coconut tree when it was warm. They were born in Jamaica. When they wake up in the morning they make their own breakfast. In Jamaica they had plantain and green banana to eat, they drink coconut water for a drink. They make their own beds. It was very hot in Jamaica and warm. They used to go to school. They used to go out on outings. They have a bath. They have to clean their own bedroom all the time. Lincoln used to boss me about when I was small. When I was a little boy my mum used to take me to Littlehampton fun fair. My mum used to give me breakfast. When my dad was young he was in the war. He had to fight for his life. When grandfather was small he used to go to school. My dad used to teach me how to read and write. My dad has got grey hair because he is very old. When he was in Jamaica he was young and fat because he had lots of food to eat. My mum have to bath me when I was little baby and also she did have to dress me and put me to bed when I was young. She did have curly hair when I was small.

I did wear shorts and T-shirt when I was a little boy.

Maurice: Hammersmith and West London College
(Originally handwritten and then transferred to a word-processor)

My dad went to school in Jamaica

My Dad Went to School in Jamka
MY Dad had to Make his own bed
ANd he had to Make his own breakFast
and brush his own teeth
and get up in the Morning
My dad ues to climb the Mango
trees My Dad ues to play Football
in Jamaica They ues to Drink Rum
They ues to eat yams in Jamaca
My dad ues to climb the Coconut tree
AND Make coconut cake

My dad went to school in Jamaica. My dad had to make his own bed and he had to make his own breakfast and brush his own teeth and get up in the morning. My dad used to climb the mango trees, my dad used to play football in Jamaica. They used to drink rum. They used to eat yams in Jamaica. My dad used to climb the coconut tree and make coconut cake.

He wore different clothes because it was hot.

Back home in Jamaica he eat ackie and saltfish.

The weather is very beautiful. My grandfather was flying to Jamaica. They used to wear old clothes; they wore shoes and socks then they play cricket. They listen to Jamaica records. They did not watch television, they had a swimming pool. They had to keep the room nice and tidy. They wore pyjamas, then they did a little bit of shopping, then they wash the new window curtains, then they came out of the pool. They play games together. My grandmother looked a bit younger. She was black. She is small. But my brother used to bully me about, he used to ask for my money, he tell me to make the beds. He tells you to stay inside. He tells me to put the TV on. He tells me to buy the records. He takes my money away from me. My mum teach me to walk. I couldn't talk, I used to run out in the road, I used to wear Batman and Robin T-shirt. I used to be small. I chasing a balloon, I used to play with toys. I used to play with a train set at Christmas time. I used to go to the fun fair with my mum. I went on all the rides with my brother. Then it was time to go home.

My grandmother used to live with me in the house. I used to blow bubbles when I was small. I used to play football. When I was a little boy I miss my grandfather in Jamaica. My mum used to feed me, she used to look after me.

I used to get lost in the funfair. She couldn't find me anywhere. I was born in my mother's belly. I turn over my dad's tea. He used to give me some homework; I show him and he went to bed. He was very pleased with my work, used to tell me to stay inside the house. My mum took me out with my brother to buy fish and chips for all of us. We all live in the same house together. I used to play snooker with Lincoln. Lincoln, he is very fat, he is. He eats a lot of chips and he tells me to buy them for him, but does give me no chips. My mum says he is mean.

I used to have a cat. It scared of my sister Marline. She used to throw him outside the door. My grandmother used to feed the cat a lot. She used to sit on the window sill. My sister got the same colour as me but doesn't live with me, she live in a hotel. She has big black hair and she wears digital watch, comes to my granny every Sunday. She is pretty. She took all her clothes and things to the hotel and a car come for her. She is 23, she had records big one and small one. She had an argument with my mum. She spends money in the arcade in the machines. Sometimes I like her. I used to wet the bed but I don't any more. I read the *Daily Mirror* before I come to college. I gives me money to dad.

Derek: Hammersmith and West London College (Maurice's brother) (Handwritten)

My father was a baker

My father was a baker, he died in Manor Park Hospital. He met my mother at the paper mills. He had a bald patch, blue eyes. He used a walking stick and wore a cap. He used to take me on a few trips when I went home from hospital. He took me to Swanage and Exmouth. My favourite trip was to Swanage. I went by coach. My mother died from cancer at Manor Park Hospital. She had it on the neck of the womb. She was short. She used to take snuff and drink beer. She didn't go out to work, she worked at home. I miss our dad because I liked being with him.

Audrey Hall: Portway Centre, Bristol
(Dictated)

Pearl Chilcott.

Mum and dad are dead now

My mum and dad are dead now. They were nice – dad and mum.

My dad had white hair and he had a nice face. He had brown eyes.

He was tall and thin. He worked in a coal-mine. He used to sit me on his knee and rock me. He used to sing to me. He had a smiley face.

My mum had black hair and brown eyes. She was nice. She had a nice face. My mum used to do the washing at home – I was too small to help her.

I was small when they died so it's difficult to remember them, but I've got a photograph.

My dad died in Southmead with shingles – he got out of bed and fell on the floor and died.

My mum died in bed at home. She died first, my dad afterwards.

My mum and dad – I miss them. I used to go with my sister for a walk in the pram. I fell out of the pram and on to the floor. I couldn't talk properly because I was deaf in one ear when I was a child, but I'm alright now.

Pearl Chilcott: Portway Centre, Bristol
(Dictated)

I went to Butlins

I went to Butlins every two years with daddy and mummy. One time we were there some youths threw chairs out of the window. We were having our tea before going to the theatre when they started shouting and throwing chairs around. The police caught them. I was frightened. The police came and ask if I was alright. Mum and dad just carried on. We still went to the theatre. We went on a monorail. At the theatre they had knobbly knees competition and ballroom dancing.

We used to play games like cricket, football and bowling. Dad won a plaque for bowling. He played for Canford Park and when he died his name was put on a plaque at the club.

Mary Lander.

I used to tidy up his shirts for him. Dad fell on the floor and Mr Stone came over who is a neighbour. The Vicar and Baptist Minister came to talk in the evening.

Mum and dad used to go bowling and I used to help with teas. Dad used to take me to the Rovers Ground to watch the football. Dad used to take me on the Downs and we had an ice-cream. Dad was the Headmaster at Westbury Park School. He was always pleased to see me at home time when I would wait for him after I finished at St Christopher School. Dad always said thank you when I met him.

Mary Lander: Portway Centre, Bristol
(Dictated)

I go home

I go home, I sit down
slowly, slowly, sleep -
All the pictures and memories come back,
some good, some bad -
Sitting there in an old house
I went to my father's chair
I sit in it for half an hour
When I fall asleep I say to my father:
'Please please please don't touch me'
and he never laid a finger on me
but he laid a finger on my mother...
My darling sister crying tears
Me – I was in the middle
waiting to hear, to come back home
He buy me a house
where we be good, happy and kind
Then sadness -
Mother by the blue chair, holding hands
upstairs, helping my poor sister
Me – I just lonely; lonely, sad
'What has gone wrong?'
'I don't know, I must be dreaming.'
I went out shopping with my father.
He comes and goes, he comes...
And now it all comes back.

Group poem: Lanercost Centre
(Dictated)

Me and Sarah

This is me and Sarah, girl and boy. That is us in Nursery School. Me and Sarah with our arms around. That's our teacher there, the top one, I've forgotten her name now. All the kiddies sat down on the floor, we would play with toys. After, we had a drink of milk and a biscuit, and we had our lunch together, me and Sarah. We were four year old. There are two boys who are looking at me and Sarah.

We went out to the park, little Sarah and me.

It was a long time ago. We were young and we were friends, and still friends now.

Alan Marshall: Portway Centre, Bristol
(Dictated)

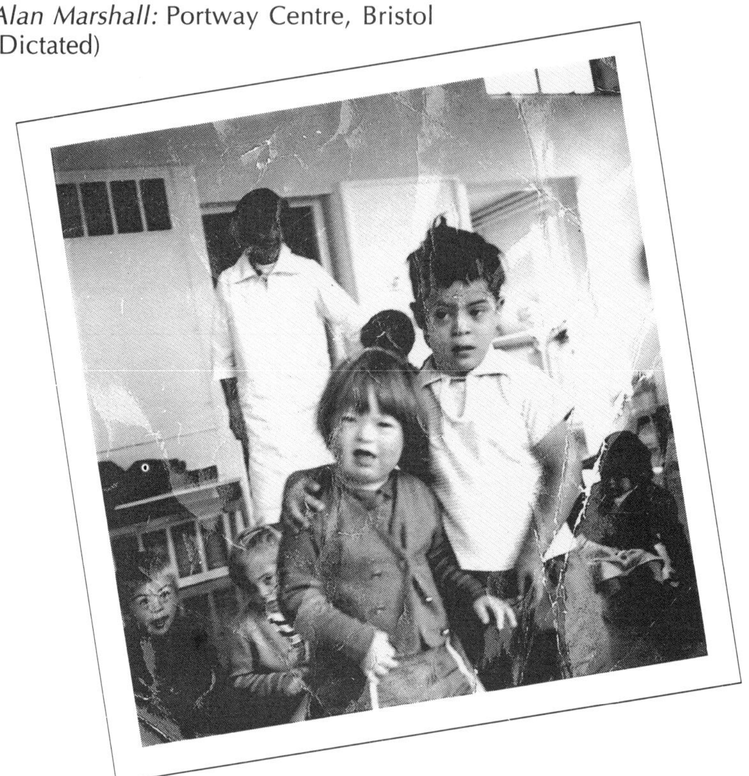

Alan Marshall and Sarah.

My dad was a first-class bricklayer

My dad was a first-class bricklayer; he worked in every street in the City and West End of London and Bedford College in Regent's Park.

My mother worked in Harrods and Fortnum and Mason on clothes.

My grandad worked in Bryant and May's for 25 years, and all through the war, he got a certificate.

Gerard Ward: Coborn Street SEC, Bow
(Dictated)

Baptism

These notes are just a few thoughts of what I want to put in my book.

Last night I was lying in my bed thinking of something short and sweet to give to you. The Light of the World made me think of baptism, and I am really truly getting baptised. God is helping me do this.

There was a garden that made me think of the baptism service. The Lord is being baptised in the River of Jordan. The Lord said, 'I am the Way, the Truth and the Light'.

I hope you can understand some of what I have written, because being baptised is so important to me. I have to go to a different church because my church do not do baptisms. My church is at sevens and eights at the moment because we have had vandals and it was burnt down inside. So I did not go yesterday, but I was still praying.

Mary Elizabeth Hayes: Cheshire Homes, Hitchin
(Dictated and transcribed)

Mangla's story

I was born in India. Then we went to Uganda, near Kampala, because we had a gents' clothing shop there.

In Uganda I had my accident when I was nine years old. I was going to play with my friends and I did not know a car was coming. He didn't sound his horn, so I ran, and he collided with me and broke my leg. I was in hospital for a long time. My leg was getting better slowly, slowly, then a Ugandan doctor suggested that I come to an English doctor to make me walk.

Then I came to England, but the hospital couldn't help. At first I lived at home with my sister and went to a day centre from nine to three. Afterwards I went to a home for the handicapped, John Grooms in the Edgeware Road in London. They took me there for a month, then they wrote here to the Cheshire Home.

When I first came here, I didn't like it. For the first three weeks I didn't eat, I wouldn't tell my name, wouldn't speak English. Since I've been here I know fully English now. When I came here I would say 'yes', 'no', 'please' and 'goodbye', and now I can talk fully English.

They say, 'When you first came you never said anything, and now you never stop talking!' It was English, English, English all day, until my sister and mother came. Then I spoke my own language, Gujerati.

The first teacher I had taught me English, reading and writing. The second teacher lived in Bedford, and my third teacher has got a full-time teaching job now, so she can't come to teach me any more. I like the English language but I also like my own language very much.

My hobby is going to church on Sunday morning and listening to the programme *Songs of Praise*. I like to read religious books. I like to do something, I don't like to do nothing.

My family is in London and my four sisters are married. I didn't get married because of my handicap. I have got two brothers who are working now and also married. I've got a mother but have lost my father. This is my story.

Mangla Jethwa: Cheshire Homes, Hitchin
(Dictated and transcribed)

Brenda Cook.

The best time

It was on a Saturday afternoon and my dad bought me a new book of *Jimmy Johnny's Journey*. I said to my mum I wants this book reading seeing as it was new and it was special because it was the first book I had in my life and I treasured that. So I sat on my mum's lap and she read the story to me and that was the only time ever she had time to spare with me to read that book, and I really made the most of that afternoon. She was always busy working – she was a hard working woman, and I know dad didn't have much money as he was a student and saving up to go to Canada to get a better job. That was why that book meant so much to me.

Brenda Cook: Portway Centre, Bristol
(Dictated)

Headlines

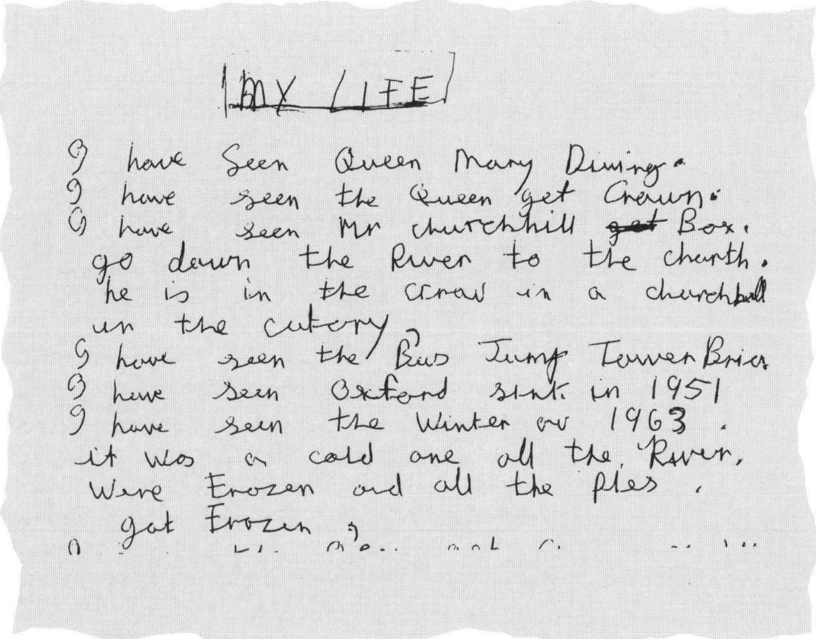

MY LIFE

I have Seen Queen Mary Diwing.
I have seen the Queen get Crawn.
I have seen Mr churchhill ~~get~~ Box.
go dewn the River to the charth.
he is in the craw in a church
un the cutery.
I have seen the Bus Jump Tower Bric.
I have seen Oxford sint. in 1951
I have seen the Winter ov 1963.
it was a cold one all the River,
Were Erozen and all the ples.
got Erozen.

I have seen Queen Mary dying.
I have seen the Queen get crown.
I have seen Mr Churchill Box,
go down the river to the church.
He is in the grave in a churchyard in the country.
I have seen the bus jump Tower Bridge.
I have seen Oxford sink in 1951,
I have seen the Winter of 1963.
It was a cold one: all the river were frozen and all the pipes
got frozen.
I saw the Queen get crown on TV.
I was the only one to have a TV in my street.

I have seen Stan Matthews play for Blackpool in the cup.
I have seen the Word Cup in 1966 when England won the cup
by 4-2, Spurs won the cup in 1961 and 1982 and the League,
and in 1971 Arsenal done the same.
I have seen the captain of the *Free Enterprise* which sink, he
stayed on it and went down with the ship.

I can remember when George Formby died.
He made a book on films.

Brian Southee: Southwark Adult Education Institute
(Handwritten)

Miss Eleanor Mary Hearn

Eleanor Mary Hearn.

My name is Miss Eleanor Mary Hearn. I live in an old people's home, I have my own bedroom and I go to the Baptist church every Sunday night. I like going to church and saying prayers to my family. My family that's gone. I go to my sister's every Sunday morning for dinner and tea.

I was born outside of Badminton and I'm 67 and 68 next August. I used to live with my sister. I was with my people – mum and dad – 30 years, and my sister 23 years, and now I'm in an old people's home.

I got blue eyes, black glasses, white teeth I'm white and grey now but I used to be fair.

Eleanor Mary Hearn: Portway Centre
(Dictated)

The story of my life

My place of birth was the West of Ireland and I come from a big family. I had five sisters and 10 brothers. My mother died when I was 14, so I looked after my father and my two younger brothers until I was 15. Then I went out to work for a vicar, his wife and two daughters. They lived near me at home. I trained as a parlour maid. I also scrubbed, polished, cleaned. Sometimes I went to the stables to feed his two horses because he was too skimpy to pay a man. My salary was £2 per week and my hours was from 6 a.m. until 8 at

Winnie Ward.

night. When I think back it was really shocking but we had to do it, it was the same all over Ireland, there was plenty of work but no money, what you call cheap labour. I stayed there until I was 18 then I came to South Wing hospital, Bedford, as a ward maid. The first week I was on my own; I was so homesick I went home again. My father didn't know what to say, he was shocked. Four weeks later I was sent back to the hospital to my job. I made friends with the rest of the girls, then I felt happy.

I enjoyed working on the wards, talking to the patients and helping the nurses. I would like to do better but I didn't have a lot of education. The nursing staff and matron was very nice. We had every afternoon off from 2 p.m. to 5 p.m. Some afternoons I cleaned out my room and did my washing. Other times I went to the pictures with the girls.

I didn't go out much at night, I was too scared to begin with. I met my husband at a dance at the Corn Exchange and he asked if he could take me out. So I said 'yes'. So we went to the pictures to see *Gone with the Wind!* He came from the West of Ireland too. I went out with him for two years, then we went home to get married in Dublin. So we had a week in Ireland and returned to Bedford. We had a lovely flat in St Michael's Avenue, Bedford. We lived there two months, then we came to Luton and took a mortgage out on a house.

Five years married I had my first son, now I have three sons, a daughter and one grand-daughter.

I like Luton very much and the people. My family grew up and went to school here. But at times I still miss home. I shall be going back in August for a week.

Winnie Ward: Bedfordshire Special Adult Learning Programme, Luton (Dictated)

June Morris.

My name is...

'My name is June Morris. I live at Hightown, Wrexham, with my mother. I work at Marchwiel Training Centre making sink plugs and doing sewing.

I have a dog, a poodle called Sherry.

I am an only child. I like coming to the Community Studies Centre to the art class on a Monday.

I like shopping for food at the weekends. We are growing potatoes, peas, radishes and flowers in our garden.

I like going to Morecambe and staying at my auntie's caravan for holidays.

I go to Prices Lane Community Centre to help to serve the meals to the old people on Fridays.

I like taking my dog for a walk.'

Jonathan Griffiths.

'My name is David Lawton. I live in Pentre Maelor, Wrexham. I have a dog, a retriever called Ollie.

I have one brother called Andrew, who is older than me.

I like canoeing, horse riding and photographing people and animals.'

'My name is Jonathan Griffiths. I live in Rhosllanerchrugog and I have one brother and one sister. My sister is the eldest. Their names are David and Sian.

I keep eight chickens from which I get five eggs a week. I also have an Alsatian dog, Iona, who is six years old.

I enjoy going to Spain for holidays with my parents.

I like trees, particularly their colours.'

June Morris, David Lawton, Jonathan Griffiths: Community Studies Centre, Wrexham, Wales
(Dictated)

Dog *(Linocut, Frazer Bartlett: Queen's Road Centre, Halifax).*

Patrick's life

They were the good old days. People were better to talk to – more sociable and more polite than they are today.

Once my stepsister and my mother died, they wouldn't let me stay in the council flat at Hither Green. They offered me a couple of places, but they were top-floor places and I couldn't walk up all them stairs because of my spine problem. Then my social worker got me a place at a hostel over in Sydenham – Holmbury Dean. It was a place for people with learning difficulties. I didn't have a learning difficulty but there wasn't room anywhere else. They were all young people at the hostel and I wasn't all that keen. My social worker promised me a place at the Blackheath group home as soon as the conversion was finished. I've been there two years now. I've lost touch with all the friends I used to know but I get on alright with everyone at the home. I'd like to get in touch with my old friends. They must all be settled down with families growing up and having their own children now.

The most important thing in life is being secure, and I am secure, comfortable and I'm not lonely. I've always been a jolly, happy, contented person. I think my friends would be surprised to learn that I'm living in a 'group' home.

Since I've been at Blackheath I've had to go to Leemore. I don't think I should be there because they reckon I'm more educated. I used to work for the LCC and then the GLC, as a painter and decorator. So I'm better off since we started to come to the flat at Brandran Road. I'd be happy to come here every day.

Patrick: Leemore Day Centre
(Dictated)

About me

What makes me really happy is playing my music centre – playing all my Abba tapes and the *EastEnders* record I've got. I like to lie on my bed to listen to my music. Sometimes I watch the telly. I bought it myself. I don't know how much money I've got. Mum does it for me. I like to be in my room and shut the door. Sometimes, I've been doing my scrapbook – I put in all my programmes.

Christine: Leemore Day Centre
(Dictated)

'Life'

(From a discussion between four women.)

'We are here in this world to be happy and life at the moment is a little bit good. It would be better if I did not have so much work to do at the hostel, because I would not get so very worn out.

In 10 years' time I will be 42. I hope things will have changed. I would like to live in a flat with my boyfriend. We would be sharing the housework.'

'Life is where you find it. I'm really a mature girl. I dream of happier things to come in my life.

I would very much like to get married; life would be much happier with the one I love.

I was born later in life (late in my mum's life), so that means I'm not perfect.

My life will be the same in the next 10 years. I'd never change the friends I have known from the past.

I would like a job as a beautician, which will take me two years' study. I would like to be Joan Collins.'

'I'm happy with my life because I've got a boyfriend. Without him I'd be miserable.

Friends are important, otherwise you'd be lonely. People are more important than money.'

'I can't remember what it was like to be a child. Everything is the same. I feel the same. But as a grown-up I can have a baby.'

Women's Group: William Brinson Centre
(Dictated)

My life

My name is Gerry Cleary and I came to Kirkdale Centre because I couldn't read. The woman in the dole office, she started me off to come up here like. She said, 'Would you like to learn to read, Gerry?' and I said, 'I would'. She said, 'I'll phone up Kirkdale and fix a time for them to see you'.

I feel more happier now because I can read a bit and I never could when I was young. Well, I had no interest and if I had I would have learned how to read.

When I went to school, the teachers were very rough and they wouldn't have no time with you. If you didn't know the word, they wouldn't tell you. They didn't give a hoot if you never learned, but these days it's different.

This was in Ireland, in the south of it. I left school early when I was 14, in the third class, so I never got the stick, neither did my brother because he was brainy.

It has all changed in Ireland now, more like the English schools. If you are English there, you don't have to learn any Gaelic. They only use that in bank jobs, most people don't speak it, you would never hear it used much.

My grandmother was the most important person in my life. My mother died young, 37 or 40. My dad spent most of his life in England so my grandmother brought us up. There were five of us. There were two girls, Tess and Ann, and three boys, me, Thomas and Brendan.

Gerry Cleary: South Lewisham Institute
(Dictated)

I was born outside Norwich

I went to East Dereham
Childrens home I think I
was I was Eleven or twelve
I wasn't there very long

I was born outside Norwich. Mum told me I had rickets. Mum had a hard time when I was being born. We lived in Hanworth and lots of places. I went to a children's home. I used to be a little devil. I used to fight with the other children. I used to nick the plums and apples, pears from the orchard. I went to East Dereham children's home. I think I was 11 or 12. I wasn't there very long. I was at Sidestrand Hall for several years. I remember the food was lovely, the food was well cooked – fresh every day. I learnt to ride a bike on the playground and the playing field. I liked it on cold windy days in winter, it was dark and dull, it was black as the ace of spades. We had lessons, I taught myself to write using a pen that I dipped in an inkwell. We help to pick fruit in the summer. We went for walks together. We could buy things. When we were good we could walk out on parole. I left Sidestrand Hall when I could leave school. Then I went to Overstand, it was a children's home. I helped to clean and polish and do washing up, went to church and went for walks; we went on the cliffs down on the beach and in the country. I enjoyed myself; I was about 20 when I went to the YMCA in Norwich. I worked in hotels. I did washing up.

George William Leonard Coleman.

I came to Little Plumstead to learn a trade. I learnt to work hard at M8. I work hard in the gardens.

I come to Adult Education two days a week. I like writing. I am good at spelling.

George William Leonard Coleman: Little Plumstead, Norwich
(Self-written)

They said I was unteachable

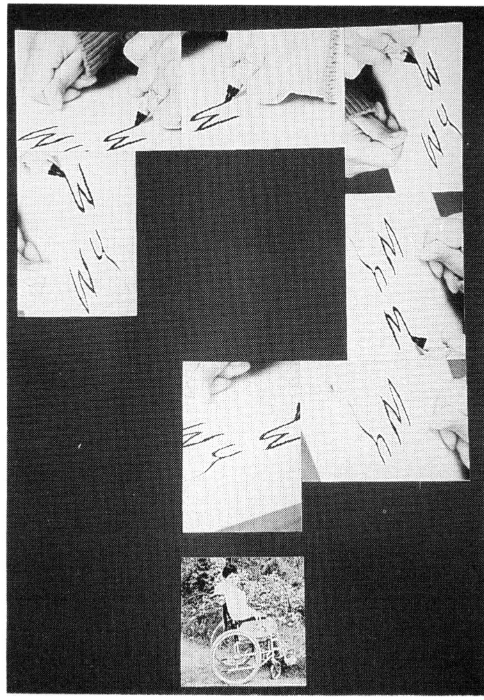

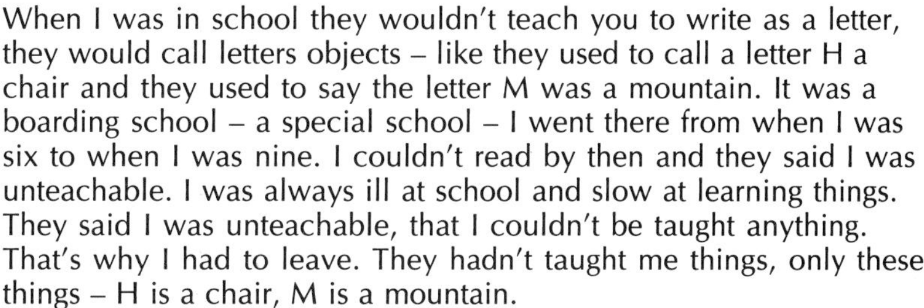

When I was in school they wouldn't teach you to write as a letter, they would call letters objects – like they used to call a letter H a chair and they used to say the letter M was a mountain. It was a boarding school – a special school – I went there from when I was six to when I was nine. I couldn't read by then and they said I was unteachable. I was always ill at school and slow at learning things. They said I was unteachable, that I couldn't be taught anything. That's why I had to leave. They hadn't taught me things, only these things – H is a chair, M is a mountain.

When I left I was only tiny, and I was sorry because I'd made some friends there. I was confused because I didn't know why I was leaving, I didn't understand that I hadn't learned anything. I left school on the Friday and I thought 'Oh, I'll be back on Sunday', but I didn't go back...I didn't understand until my mother said, 'You've left school, they've taken you out of school, they said you were unteachable'.

She was very hurt, she didn't understand either. I had to have a home tutor for two years. They couldn't find a school for me. Then, when I was about 11 I went to another special school – a day school.

Michelle Thomas: Llwynypia Day Centre, Wales
(Dictated)
(From a group project called 'Snapped Lives', run jointly by Rhondda Vanguard Service and Rhondda Community Arts)

Michelle Thomas.

About a non-existent girl

Were I a boy
I might be spending
Most of my time squabbling
Instead of which I get on with tending
To my garden in my spare time,
Of which I haven't much
Because the rest is taken up
Working as a waitress in a coffee shop.

And as I like singing at work,
I'm known to some as the new
Kim Wilde - a view
Not held by others
Who can go and stew
Themselves, because I'm not going to be intimidated
Into doing what they want.

As I am a girl
I get on with working
At my job, and not playing
Around, as some of my mates do;
And I like to sing
During it, which makes people remark
That I'm like Kim Wilde and not Bing
Hitler, and I'm not stark
raving mad, as some people make me out to be.

I am a slim lass
Am 25, am 5 ft 2 inches
And come from the Minches
And have got blonde hair.
I like writing poetry - but alas!
I haven't got anything published yet
But maybe my pal Dorothy will set
Me on the right tracks.
As I am only a mere girl
(And non-existent at that)

Not knowing the proper outlets
Like all young ladies
Who have something to sell.

And I like riding as well
Showing off my equestrian prowess
At the weekends
When I sally forth
On Humphrey, my invisible pony
To get a breath of fresh air.
And being on him
Gives me a sense of exhilaration
Getting away from the shop
Where other people lend me an ear
And tell me their worries, when they pop
In, for a while.

Considering I'm an innocent, attractive (popular)
lass
Whom the lads queue to see
It's surprising I've not become visible
Before now.
But anyway, I would rather stay single
And wear my new Pringle
Jersey just now,
But I may want to get in to white later.

Because I am invisible human lady
And don't try to squabble or fight
At work, where I sing,
I'm known to be queer, and I string
The boys and girls along.

'Georgette', also known as Sandy Marshall: Thomas Fortune Centre, Glasgow
(Self-typed)

Chapter Two
Memories

The focus in this chapter is on memories. It is not a comprehensive collection of the memories contributed to the book; one chapter could not contain such richness, depth and diversity. This is a partial account; a collage of personal and social memories on a range of issues.

Other memories are included elsewhere in the book, placed according to their theme. The chapter on 'Transitions', for example, contains people's accounts of changes in their lives, a process which necessitates their looking back. The 'life histories' in Chapter Nine are largely based on memories.

Memories matter. They are our links with our own personal pasts. They are ways of saying this is who I am. Numerous contributors to this book have chosen to share their memories. In looking back on their experiences, and remembering how life was for them, they are saying a lot about who they are now. They are people with a past, a past that has helped shape them. So often the pasts of people with learning difficulties have been discounted. Here they are celebrated.

The focus on memories continues the theme of 'A sense of self'. A sense of self develops through life experiences and interactions with others. In this chapter, contributors share their memories of their childhood and adolescence. There are happy and unhappy memories, containing details of people, events and experiences which mattered *then* and which have helped shape the person of today.

Several early memories are about people who mattered during the formative years of childhood; including parents, grandparents and a favourite brother. These are fond and generous memories. The authors pay tribute to the important role played by some significant people in their early lives.

Some events and experiences of childhood have a lasting impact, and are always remembered. We include some memories of happy and unhappy events. They range from 'Happy time' to 'I screamed...'.

Schooldays are remembered but are not, on the whole, recaptured with great fondness or happiness. There are memories of fear, of isolation and separation. For some people, this was their first remembered experience of being different and 'special'. However, memories of schooldays were not universally unhappy ones as C. Price and John Symes make clear in their contributions.

Some memories recapture a particular time and context, and give a rich account of the period in which the author was a child. These are 'period pieces', conveying the social customs and family practices of that remembered time. These memories have a lot in common with most children's lives: street games, conkers, dressing up, outings and special events like hop-picking.

Some people placed their lives in a wider social and historical context. Their memories include social changes and major world events. Rich cultural and historical detail is recaptured in these accounts. There are memories of London and Kirkcaldy and how they used to be in years gone by, and there are personal and family war-time memories.

Finally, we include some longer stories of people's lives. Three authors pick out those people, events and times which they remember as significant in their lives. Two of the stories include schooldays, and an early awareness of feeling different. The third contributor, G. E. Wilkins, vividly recalls the stormy period of his adolescent years. Some of his behaviour might, in other settings, be described as 'challenging'. In a sense it was, in that a young man was actively challenging authority. There is nothing unusual in this, except that this was a young man with Down's Syndrome. Not only did his behaviour challenge authority at that time, it may challenge our assumptions about people with Down's Syndrome and their expected compliance.

Contents

Alan Marshall.

Early memories of people who mattered

I was born a baby

I was born a baby. My mum used to sing songs to send me to sleep. *Hush-a-bye Baby*. And she would rock me. She was nice and I had baby food. I used to suck my thumb when I went to sleep, and I dirtied my nappy. Mum used to change it for me. When I got older I used to wash my face. I got soap in my eyes. I screamed, 'Wah! Mum!', and she came and washed the soap out. Afterwards she took me for a walk to aunty's in the pram. I went to sleep. She pushed the pram round the shops. Those are happy memories, and now I'm grown-up.

Alan Marshall: Portway Centre, Bristol
(Dictated)

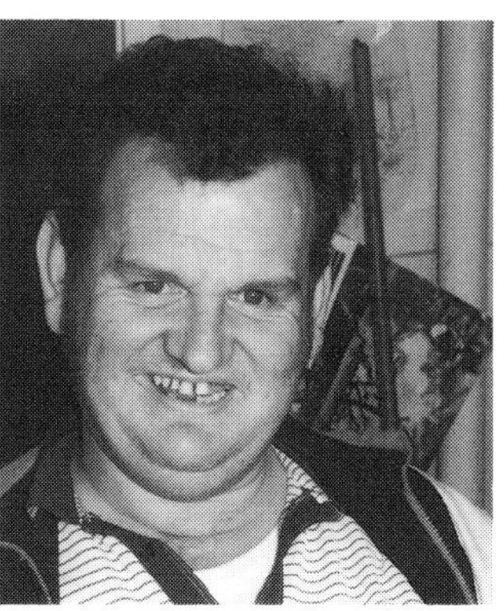

John Symes.

John's memories

When I was two years old I was in a pram with my clothes on and I was going for a walk with our ma. Mum took me out of the pram and she carried me upstairs to go to the toilet. She was young my ma, about 34 years old. After the toilet I said to ma, 'Let me walk down the stairs'. She said it was all right. I missed one step and I went down 24 steps to the bottom, and hit my head, and I was in a coma for 48 hours. I woke up in hospital and I had a lot of trouble after this. 'Where am I to?', I said. 'In hospital', they said. It shocked me when my mum told me about it. This is a sad memory.

When I got better, I can always remember my dad. He had a motor bike called a Corgi. He took me to school on the tank. That was a happy time and I remember going to see my first football match with dad, to see Bristol City play Walsall. I had a corduroy suit, jacket and trousers, woolly hat, and City scarf as well. I walked away from my dad and got lost. A copper found me; he put it out on the tannoy: 'A little boy has been found wearing corduroy trousers and jacket'. Dad picked me up and played hell. After that I started school. I followed a horse and cart – a rag-and-bone man – around, which made me late for dinner. I was supposed to be back at one. My mum was cross to start with, but she was all right in the end. These are some sad and happy memories.

John Symes: Portway Centre, Bristol
(Dictated)

My brother Roy just before he got killed in the army

My brother Roy always cleaned his bike outside. He had fair hair and blue eyes. He was about 5 ft 4 in. He used to have a girlfriend called Marj and she practically lived in our home – it was called her second home. He used to look after me on Saturdays. One Saturday I went off and got lost. Roy went riding all over the place to look for me. He asked a lot of people because he was concerned. Suddenly someone told him they had seen me getting in a baker's van. The baker dropped me off at the Police Station, and when I was in the Police Station it was on teatime and they were having rice and that – I didn't want any rice so I had biscuits. There were two other children came to join me as they were lost as well. The policeman was quite funny; he said it was like a play hour with all these children coming in. By the time I had got settled in with the children, my brother came to fetch me as he had found out where I was. He did not get cross, he was pleased I was safe. He just said, 'I won't let you out of my sight again'.

Brenda Cook: Portway Centre, Bristol
(Dictated)

My gramp and nan

We went down to Weymouth. We took the cases in the Consul car. We got to Weymouth and were in the caravan that day. We unpacked the cases and I made teas for us lot. We went to Bingo – the first day we didn't win anything, the second day we won something, the third day I won £27 on the machine. I said to our ma we are all going out for a meal so we went.

We took gramps fishing; when we came back to the caravan I sold the fish for 10p each.

Gramps had grey hair, brown eyes. Nan was in a wheelchair, she had arthritis in the legs all over. When we came back gramps had a sharp pain in the chest; he told his wife he was going to bed as he had a headache, and he died. Soon after my nan died. She had a stroke which made her paralysed. I used to go down and see her before she died.

Gramps had a brown suit. He kept chickens up by Walton Road where Jim O'Neil is now. I used to go down and pinch apples off the tree and pinch the eggs. Gramps never used to say anything because he did it himself.

Gramps smoked a lot. That's all I want to say.

John Symes: Portway Centre, Bristol
(Dictated)

Grandpa and grandma

Grandma was short and grandpa was short, and he had a moustache and he was a shepherd who looked after sheep. He had a white dog called Rover and when that one died he got another one, a black one called Rover.

My grandma made old-fashioned wine, parsnip wine. She made it in the boiler, boiled it up. She used to put her washing up on a pulley in the kitchen, up to the ceiling. My mum used to do that and help grandma with the washing.

My grandma had an old-fashioned iron which was a saucepan, which she put greens, potatoes and bacon in, all at once. It used to taste nice in those days. My grandma used to cook on the range, and my mum did, and she had an old-fashioned poker to poke the fire in the range.

I went upstairs to get the cat, and I fell downstairs. My grandma said, 'What are you after the cat for?' 'I wanted him downstairs', I said. I was a bit hurt and grandma put some ointment on. My grandma had old-fashioned dresses, and she hung them on hooks. She had old-fashioned dishes and she saved cigarette cards.

I used to go out with grandpa sometimes to look after the sheep. Sometimes he used to stay out all night. He took his lunch with him, bread and cheese and onion, and he used to drink cider. Sometimes he wouldn't have dinner, just a glass of cider. My grandpa had a moustache, and my Uncle Joe. Grandpa and Uncle Harry smoked pipes, and my dad.

I stood on a chair to pull the curtains, and fell off and broke my arm. They said, 'What did you get on the chair for?' I didn't realise I'd broken my arm till after. The District Nurse came down, called Nurse Bees. She said I was a tomboy because I fell down. My grandparents were upset. They were good grandparents and so was my mother and father.

Eleanor Mary Hearn: Portway Centre, Bristol
(Dictated)

Experiences that mattered

Happy time

When I went on holiday, I used to go up to Badminton to my aunty's. I had a girlfriend and she had a shoe box with a doll in. I used to remember this shoe box and go around with it. It was a bit of fun. I used to go around the garden with it and around the well with the water in it. I used to go there every holiday and stay with different uncles and aunties out in the country. I used to go to Badminton and Overton in Wiltshire. I used to go to a fair show in Badminton. They used to have roundabouts, dodgems and side shows. I used to have an aunty up there in Badminton. When I used to stay in Overton, some people over the road put jelly on the toilet seat as a joke. I said what did they put that there for, they said so someone would sit on it. I thought that it was funny.

When I came back from Wiltshire, my relations moved to a new house. I was happy because I was out in the country, I like the country best. I was pleased to go on holiday. We had a field at the back of our house and we used to play in the field. We had races around the field, it was happy times.

Eleanor Mary Hearn: Portway Centre, Bristol
(Dictated)

Collected memories

I remember when I was born
Nobody wanted me...

I remember being whipped when I was small
I remember living in a noisy building...

I remember the Watney Street Market,
It was very busy,
Lots of stalls selling things,
People shouting, pushing and shoving.
I was born there.

I can remember my dad hitting me when I was four.

Coborn Street SEC, London
(Handwritten)

I can remember my Dad
hitting me when I was 4

Paul I remember When
I was
born no body wanted

Linda
I remember being whipped when
I was Small I remember
living in a noisu builing

I screamed...

I screamed because my mum and dad wouldn't let me
light the candles. In the end they let me but I dropped
the lit match on the table.
'You might have had the whole room on fire', said my dad.
'It would have cost your dad at least a thousand pounds to have
the room repaired', said my mum.
It was a bit weird in the dark. Five unlit candles.

Lanercost Poetry Workshop, Bristol
(Group composition)

Snippets

'I used to fight with my brother. My brother got mair than I got. "That's a gannet, he's eaten all my sweeties", and I only got one. At that time you got a muckle bag of sweets for a penny.

Me and my brother played truant twice. We didnae go to school, we went someplace else. We hid in the air-raid shelter and then later slipped up to the railway station. I was ten and my brother was nine. We went to Edinburgh for the day.' (Jean Stewart)

'At school one time I asked the teacher if I could go to the little girl's room, and I went there and never went back to the classroom. I disappeared home. Mum said: "Where's your schoolbag?" I left it at school. I didn't like that school. I didn't like the dinners either.' (Susan Keddie)

'I had a fight with my brother. My wee brother ducked when I threw the shoe and it went through the bloody window; I got a row from my mother when she came home. "Who broke the bloody window?"

When I was a baby my mum didn't have a dummy tit, she didn't even have a bottle. I had to be fed by her breast.' (Ronnie Gray)

Jean Stewart, Susan Keddie, Ronnie Gray: St Clair ATC, Kirkcaldy
(Group discussion)

Our memories of childhood

'My dad was in the army overseas all the time when I was a child.'

'I walked around the streets in Ballymun (Dublin), and I was late for school and the headmaster Mr Molloy told me off.'

'I had curly hair when I was a child. The other children in the school had long hair.'

'When I was a baby, my brother picked me out of my pram and dropped me on the floor. It hurt my back. I went to a boarding school. It was horrible. The kids there picked on me and poked me in the chest.'

'When I was seven or eight, a car went over my legs. I also banged the kettle and the hot water went down my leg.'

'When I was little I didn't use to wear glasses. Now I do. People used to call me "goggle eyes". When I was washing up once, the plate hit my forehead and I had to have stitches. The nurses had to hold me down.'

'When I was a baby, I fell down the stairs. They were going to send me to hospital. When I was a bit older, I started having fits. When my mum couldn't look after me, I had to go to a mental hospital in Banstead. We used to go to a church service in the evenings there.'

'At Assembly Hall once at school, some children knocked me over and I cut my right eye which needed stitches. I also fell down and broke my nose.'

'I can remember being frightened of going to bed because of daddy-long-legs in my bedroom.'

'My mum took me out shopping on weekends to buy some food.'

'I was a little fat baby with curly hair. When I was five, mum threw some fat on the stove and the flat went up in flames. Our cat died in the blaze. I cried like anything.'

'When I was little I got my head stuck in the railings at Regent's Park, and the fire brigade had to come and get me out. When I was at school I wore short trousers and people called me "matchsticks" because of my skinny knees.'

'A Chance to Speak' class: City Lit, London
(Group discussion)

In Redfield

I was living with my gran in her house and her house was by the river. Her garden looked right over the river and the swimming pool and the school. We used to play outside quite a lot, and when the children came out of school we used to ask them what they'd been doing. I was too young to go to school myself.

My gran brought some drinks outside to us. She had coffee and we had lemon and orange. She had a little table and a bench in the garden. We all sat out on the bench having a drink. We'd been running around and hiding from each other, my sister and me. It was a very hot summer like it always seemed to be. The drink was cooling. There were biscuits, but they were not enough for me, so when my Gran went to clean the bedrooms, I nipped in and took a banana out of the cupboard. I unpeeled the banana, took the banana out, and folded the skin back so it looked as if the banana was there inside. I put it back in the cupboard. My gran said later, 'I'm sure I had a banana'. She picked it up, and the banana was all loose. She thought it was one of my brothers. I enjoyed eating the banana, and I enjoyed the boys getting told off for it. I always remember the banana, and the cupboard where the banana was, and it makes me laugh.

Brenda Cook: Portway Centre, Bristol
(Dictated)

Memories of schooldays

Fear

When I was small, about eight or nine, I was at school, and these boys threatened to get a gang on me when I came out of school in the playground. That was all because I went with this girl who was my best friend. This boy didn't like it because he thought I'd taken her away from him, but she was my best friend and she wanted to stay with me. He wanted to go out with her but she didn't want to go out with him.

I dreaded to go out in the playground; I was frightened inside and it was all bottled up. I knew something awful was going to happen. I just dreaded to go out in the playground. I didn't tell the teacher or nobody. I thought if I did it would just make it worse for me. Then it came to the bell time. The bell went and we all had to go out. All I wanted to do was stay in. My poor stomach went over like anything. As I got out to the playground, they were waiting for me. Bernard, the boy, sent this girl up to me. She said, 'Oh there you are, so you're the one that's taking our friend off of us'. I said, 'Before you start this, why don't you ask her how she feels about it?' So they asked Grace (she was one of twins), 'No way I want to go with you two. If you sets on her, you'll have my dad to answer to'. Her dad was a copper.

That was fair enough for the time being, then come towards dinner time they waited until she went in. They thought she wouldn't know about it, seeing her going in first. They grabbed hold of me, pulled my ribbon off, and also pulled and dragged from behind and broke my belt off. I then was filled with outrage. I turned round and slashed him round the face and made his mouth and nose bleed. Then his gang went away because they got frightened when they saw the blood. I can take so much and then I lets myself go.

My friend still sitting in the class was saying, 'I wonder how Brenda is?'. She's worrying about me while I'm sorting them out. We were close friends and she didn't like anything happening to me. Then I gets back in the class. Bernard and the gang have gone in in front of me. Grace sees them: 'What happened?', she says, 'Oh yeah', and guessed what had happened. She's seen the nose and mouth bleeding. I can only take so much and then I lets them know it.

I told the teacher why I did it because she wanted to know what had happened. She kept them back and said, 'I gather you asked for this'. She'd heard them so often say they were going to get me one of these days and she felt sorry for me. The headmistress said, 'I'm sure she can sort herself out', and I did as well.

Brenda Cook: Portway Centre, Bristol
(Dictated)

Schooldays

'I was sent away to a residential school. It was terrible. They used to cane us on our hands. They said I was there to learn.'

'I went to a special school. I don't know why it was called special.'

'I went to a special school with nuns. Because I couldn't read and write. I liked it. I liked saying my prayers every morning.'

'My mum couldn't cope with me so I was sent to St Lawrence's Hospital. There was a school there. They said I could get on alright. The food was terrible.'

Gary, Violet, Marion, Carol: Camden Institute, London
(Transcribed extracts from discussion)

Schooldays

When I was at school we always used to have to go in lines – like the army does. When the classes were finished we had to line up in two's.

We got up at seven o'clock and made our own beds. The dormitories weren't brilliant. The food was mainly salads. Some of the girls were quite spiteful. Some of the time I spent in bed with a bad ear infection through one of the girls hitting me on the ear. A lot of the girls weren't handicapped – they had mainly eye problems. We weren't taught arithmetic, reading or writing. My mum taught me to read after I left this school. We were taught mainly religion. We were in assembly, singing hymns and praying until 10.30. Then we'd have to go in two's to classes after assembly.

I was confirmed when I was at school, when I was about nine years old. We were taught religion all day long – and I hated it!

The uniforms were horrible – blue skirt, white blouse, blue blazer and white socks. We never had much free time. My mum and dad never came to see me because my mother was ill. We had a rotten headmistress who was always drinking.

I didn't like it there at all. I was at school there from nine to fourteen. Then one or two girls left and I was brought away when I was 14 as my mum and dad did not like the way I was treated.

I have learned more in the last two years than I ever did at school. I've been going to Adult Literacy classes, where I've caught up on everything. Now I can manage my money because I can add up, subtract and multiply, which I could not do before.

Susan Campbell: Cheshire Homes, Hitchin
(Dictated)

Schooldays

Weston-super-Mare
Clevedon camp. Shopping. Walks.
Spending money. Sleeping at school.
Running away. Climbing walls.
Going to school. Having
Parcels, letters, postcards.
Visits to jumble sales at school.

C. Price: Portway Centre, Bristol
(Handwritten)

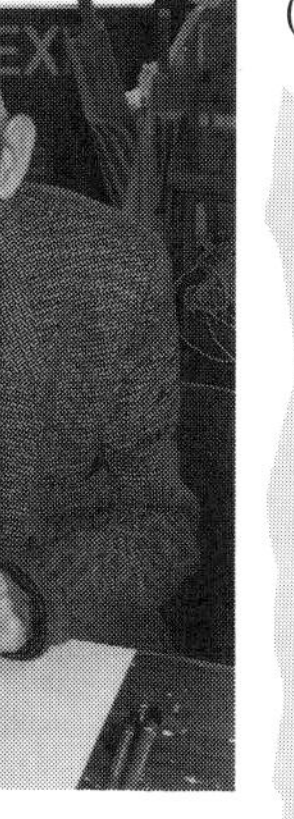

C. Price.

weston soopurmer
kleepun kamp shopin wollks
shendin muney sleepin at skool
runing away kliming wolls
gowing To skooll having
pasils letturs parsills powskards
visits To Gumboll sells at skooll

About 14 years old

This photo is when I was at school at Russell Town Avenue, and we went out for a day trip. I was about 14. The teacher's name was Mr Foster. He decided to put the trip on to Coventry. Coventry for a day, just me and him and his mate. I carried his briefcase up, because it was too heavy for him. I was a short, stocky bugger, he had long legs it was difficult to keep up with him. The picking-up point was Old Market, by the Artillery ground. That's Mr Foster, the middle one. I'm carrying the case. I can't remember the other one's name. I think it was John someone-or-other. He had burn marks over his arms and body where he got scalded. We went up there for the day. We really enjoyed ourselves. Mr Foster told jokes on the way up. We went by train. It took four-and-a-half hours to get up there. It was a long journey; I was tired when I got home. When we went up there he bought us a cup of tea, and on the way back he bought us one. He was singing.

This photo was taken in the park in Coventry. I'd like to see that teacher again.

John Symes: Portway Centre, Bristol
(Dictated)

Memories of a particular time and context: period pieces

Childhood memories

Me and Peter (brother) went to Haseltime School during the war. We stayed in London. They didn't teach me anything. Me mum said, 'Why aren't you learning anything?'.I left school at 16 and I couldn't read or write. I'm learning now, though, at Holbeach Road (Ravensbourne Adult Education Institute). At school I used to sit there doing little baby exercises and that. I was fed up. I'm happy where I am now at Leemore and Holbeach, learning to read and write.

We used to play hopscotch and *Clearly round the lamp-post* with a bit of string. We used to have a game called *I've come to learn the trade*. We used to stand in the gutter and they would say, 'What are you doing there?'.We'd say 'We've come to learn the trade.' They'd say 'Set to work and do it then!' We'd say, 'We're stuck in a jampot'. Then they'd try to catch us before we got over the other side.

Hop-picking memories

I didn't like picking the hops. My brother'd say, 'Go and get the sandwiches'. We used to get our feet stuck in the mud. We used to go down to the gate to get the milk. We'd take a jug and the milkman would fill it from an old-fashioned can.

We started going hop-picking when I was about five. I went with my five older brothers and my mum. I remember we used to have a straw bed with a sheet. We used to have an old-fashioned paraffin lamp at night. I didn't like it (hop-picking) much because the smell of the hops got on food when you ate bread or anything.

Peggy Riches: Ravensbourne Institute, London
(Tape transcript)

Conkers

One conquers the other
My mum with my aunty – put string through and hit it -
I feel with my hands they are conkers – shiny -
They're warmer now, holding them -
They feel like nuts -
They are full of memories -
The white pithy bit smells, the shells stain your hands -
Long summer evenings, crowds of gnats
Short trousers and Startrite shoes -
Tony played conkers, so he says -
Soak 'em in vinegar, stick 'em in the oven
An alleybomper, a oner, a twoer, a tenner -
Impatient boys fling sticks -
Smells cold -
Marcia makes eyeballs.

Lanercost Poetry Workshop, Bristol
(Group composition)

My life

I Let the Gun off and the old,
Women went dow the R d like.,
a Bat out or hell, -
I used to help the Milk-man and
I used to pull the cart sometimes.
And we had a factre down the
Road and the Lorrys Lorries ~~com~~ used to.
come down, my Road and I wed.

I used to play *Look down ginger*. I used to play out in the street and down the road there was an old bomb site and there was an old woman who came down the road and one of my mates had a toy gun. He lent it to me, and I put two stones in it and when she came down the road I let the gun off and the old woman went down the road like a bat out of hell.

I used to help the milkman and I used to pull the cart sometimes and we had a factory down the road and the lorries used to come down my road and I used to throw bricks at them. There used to be an old wall at the side of the road and that is where we got the bricks.

I used to go up Camberwell Gardens; there was a tunnel and the steam trains.

I used to go past two doors down from my house and see the horses bring the beer to the pub, cellar doors open. And I used to see old Steptoe and I used to go up to the baker's horse and get out my cap gun and the horse went mad.

The end.

Brian Southee: Southwark Adult Education Institute, London
(Handwritten)

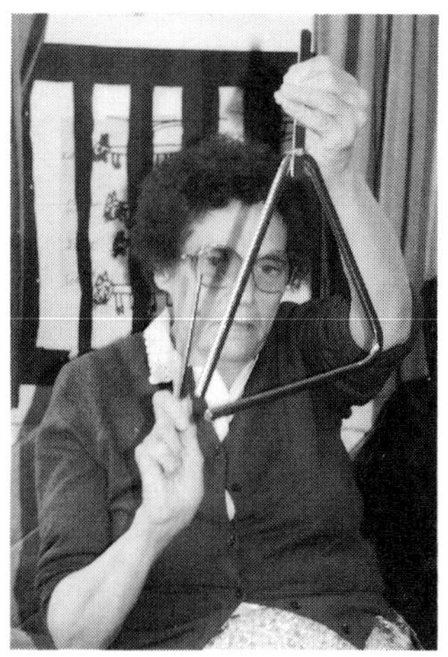

Doreen Randall.

I remember when...

I remember when I played with my dolls and pram. I used to go up my gran's at the weekend to Barton Hill. We used to go to the old-fashioned pictures. They used to show old-fashioned films which used to wind round with candles for light. We used to pay 2d to go in. I went with my sisters, Betty and Beryl; we used to go to Avonmouth pictures down by the docks. It was called the bughouse. We used to take sweets and chocolate to eat, and drinks.

My mother used to have old-fashioned teapots and I've still got my aunty's old-fashioned stool. It's got old-fashioned handles and you can open the seat like a chest, and little drawers, and we used to keep pins and sewing stuff in there. The lid and drawers are all done up now, you can't open them any more. We used to go to Temple Meads on the train. Along the Feeder was gran's house. We used to visit her at weekends. She lived on Marsh Lane. Gran used to take me out round Barton Hill swimming pool. They were happy memories.

Doreen Randall: Portway Centre, Bristol
(Dictated)

Dressing up

Me and my sister were playing round the rubbish tip in my grandmother's garden. She kept her rubbish in old sacks in the shed, and she wanted us to go through it all and sort it out. There were no windows in the shed. There were all sorts of things, old handbags, dresses, old socks, old shirts, trousers, old jerseys. We folded them all up and put them back again. We played dressing up in the shed. I wore a long dress that used to belong to my aunty. My sister put on an old dress as well. We tried on old shoes. When we were dressed up, we went to show what we looked like. My grandmother was next door. She laughed.

'Why did you put that rubbish on for?'

We showed mum and dad and made them laugh. They said, 'What did you put that rubbish on for?'

We had put it on for a bit for fun.

Eleanor Mary Hearn: Portway Centre, Bristol
(Dictated)

Toy dog

When I was young I washed a toy dog and it went out of shape. I ran out, and before I went my mother was cussing because I left water on the table. 'Bloody water on the table!' I went to someone else's house. I was scared of the dog because the face had gone out of shape. It was frightening because it had a haunted look. Mother moved it when I went out. It was gone from the table when I got back home. I don't know what happened to it after, someone threw it out. Lots of years have gone by since then. I was scared of the dog, I'd never wash a toy dog again.

Audrey Hall: Portway Centre, Bristol
(Dictated)

I used to live in Brighton Street...

George Grimster.

I used to live in Brighton Street near Muller Road coach depot. I lived with my Uncle Ken, my Aunty Nellie and my mother in a pub right on the corner of the street. It was when I was a little boy and I was wearing sandals.

We had an old-fashioned gramophone which we used to play records on. We played Al Jolson. I've got a photograph of me standing next to a coach with a cigarette in my mouth, which was a long time ago. I used to smoke Woodbines a long time ago but I gave up also a long time ago – I used to smoke eight a day. Somebody used to light them for me with a match.

We used to go down the road and down some steps to visit a cake shop. We had post boxes on the corner on Ashley Down Road. A lady called Mrs Davis used to look after me – on City Road. I used to go there on the bus. My Aunty Ida, Edna and Isabel used to have a pub on the Bath Road a long time ago. We used to go over there for a drink. I used to play darts in a pub on Ashley Down Road. I used to go to school on Park Row.

We used to go to the Metropole cinema. There were pink curtains.

I used to watch Max Bygraves – he sang all my favourite songs. He's a big man. My favourite singer is Al Jolson who wears lots of make-up – last Christmas I was given a tape of Al Jolson.

My sister Gwen is living in the United States – she came over to see me a long time ago. She's got a son.

When we lived at Ashley Down Road – we kept records downstairs and we had puzzles on the tables. We had a gramophone with a handle which we used to wind to play records on.

Aunty Mabel, Mrs Davis and Aunty Nellie used to come for tea and cakes – and Uncle Ken.

Someone came to the house with an accordion and used to play it to us.

George Grimster: Lanercost Centre, Bristol
(Dictated as part of a group reminiscence project)

Memories within a wider social context

Memories

I was with my foster aunt in Clapham Common; she died and the house was supposed to be left for me.

I went to my mum when I was 21. I brought my cat with me, Timmy.

Cable Street was not like it is now, there used to be a lot of old houses, it is changed a lot now with new houses.

There were women with overalls, they were called washerwomen with their hair tied up in a turban.

When I first came to mum's they had trams running down Leman Street, they were just about to take them away then. We used to live near the Royal Mint but they knocked the old houses down. We didn't have any bath...so we had to go the Aldgate Public Baths. My mum used to bath Georgie, Andrew and Tony in the tin bath, we had to keep it hanging up in the toilet. They've got lovely houses with gardens now. My mum always wanted to go back there.

I have a lovely flat now, nobody don't interfere with you, everyone keeps themselves to themselves. You've got everything there, with a green to sit on.

My dad came back to my mum three times. But mum needed him when we were young, we were fostered out. There were nine of us, so mum could only keep the little ones.

Margaret Martin: Coborn Street SEC
(Dictated, written by staff, copied by author)

My father's name was John

My father's name was John. He was in the army. He was in the 1914 war, and my Uncle Shughie, in France. My Uncle Shughie was in that regiment that wore kilts, but I couldn't tell you the regiment my father was in. The two of them were passing in line one day in France, in their separate regiments, and they were not allowed to speak to each other, and they never saw each other again because my Uncle Shughie was killed in battle just a couple of weeks later. My dad got his legs off during the war and he was invalided out.

I was born after the war but there are older ones than me. My brother Donald is 70, then there is my brother John. There's eight years between Donald and him. They both live down the south side now. I'm going down to visit them on Saturday. Because I was the baby and I was born after the war I only remember father with no legs. He couldn't work because of this.

My mom had to earn the money; she worked in an office. My father stayed at home and looked after us. My big sister Phyllis helped look after me. She's seven years older than me. She lives in Bellshill now.

My sister used to be in charge of a grocer's shop when I was a girl, before she got married. My oldest brother had a boy, Donald. He had eight in his family, four boys and four girls. There is six left, two died.

My other brother, John, he had a boy and a girl; and my sister, do you know how many she had? She had 17 altogether. She lost four and she raised the rest. Her man was working. That's him that died a couple of weeks ago.

We had a Green Lady – used to come in three days a week when I was a girl – to bath my father in a tin bath. Then they got us a house low down facing the dog track, for the sake of my father and mother. It had an ordinary bath in it.

My oldest brother is going into hospital on Tuesday. He has to go for an operation on Wednesday to try to remove shrapnel from between his spine and his lungs. The stuff from the shrapnel is going into his eyes and he can hardly see now. You have to take his hand and speak to him before he recognises you. He got the shrapnel in the Second World War. He's coming up for his golden wedding anniversary.

Susan McIsaac: Whiteinch Centre, Glasgow
(Dictated)

Memories

Kirkcaldy's changed a lot now – it used to be called Auld Reekie. Old Kirkcaldy had all different shops and tram cars. There were an old granny across the road and she used to make home-made toffee – we used to get a bag of toffee for two pennies. At that time you got a muckle bag of sweets for one penny.

I mind the war. We went to Edinburgh and the war was coming and there was an air-raid shelter and we had to go down to the shelter. The shelter was all crowded. There were a lot of folk – men, women, bairns, old folk, young folk. They sat all amongst themselves and blethered. The planes flew about right overhead, we heard them – and when they were all clear we came out. Me and my brother were evacuated when the war was on. We got sent to a camp with tags on our jackets. We took our gas masks and everything with us. That was in East Lothian.

I mind the Coronation. All the school ones got a silver penny and a poke of goodies. I like the olden days. When the war was on we had one of these old-fashioned gramophones, and we used to open the window and everyone was dancing out in the street. I liked it better afore – now you never get nothing like that. It's bingo and fighting.

Jean Stewart: St Clair ATC, Kirkcaldy
(Dictated)

Longer stories of people's lives

When I was young...

Mary McLean.

The first thing I remember was that I was epileptic. I'd been going to school down in Eastville. I was playing in the playground. I fell forward and knocked my teeth. I'd been having fits since I was three months old. When I was 12 years old, I went to Lingfield Colony for epileptics in Surrey, near the race course, and I stayed there for four years. We had a teacher called Mrs Parrot. We used to call her 'parrot nose'! It made her angry and she ran after us.

When I was 16, I went to Hortham Hospital.

Before I went away, I lived with my mother and father, my sister and brother. My father died last weekend. He was a famous footballer, captain of Bristol Rovers, Blackburn and Rob Roy, and he got a gold medal.

My brother isn't very well, he's got a bad heart. Today is my birthday and my sister brought me a birthday cake. I get on well with her. My cousin, Grace, is at Purdown, the same as me. I left Hortham a long time ago and went home. I was taken into Purdown as an emergency when my mother went into the old folk's home.

When I was a little girl, I went to school at Bannerman Road Primary School. I was a real tomboy, I liked doing what the boys did – football, jumping in puddles, playing with slings and arrows. I used to go to St George's Park and I fell in twice, fishing for tiddlers!

My brother used to be a coastguard at Minehead in the summer, and in the winter he worked with old people. I used to go to Townsend Youth Club on a Thursday night. My mum used to work as a helper on the coach on a Thursday night. When my mum stopped going because of her heart, I stopped going.

When I was 16, I had a black and white spaniel called Twink, but he got distemper and had to be put down. He was about six years old. I used to take him to St George's Park for walks. We also had a cat that we called Whisky because it was Black and White! The cat wouldn't let me have my tea in peace. It didn't like milk, it liked warm tea.

My cousin Peter used to go and shoot rabbits. He let me shoot the gun. He was a gamekeeper on an estate in Scotland. He once put a baby ferret up my jumper! We used to go to Scotland four times a year, by car; first of all a Morris Traveller and then a Singer. It was a 13-hour journey to reach Blantyre, which was quite near Paisley. We stayed with my Uncle Willy. My cousin was on night shift, so I slept in the 'hole in the wall' with a curtain going across. It was crowded in the house. It was a back-to-back terrace. We were on the lower level.

When Rudolph Hesse came to Scotland, I saw him. I was only five at the time. He came to the house next door as a prisoner of war. My uncle thought he was violent, so he took me away quickly. They took him to a Women's Club in Blantyre and held him there until the military police came for him.

We were in Blantyre during the war. My mother wanted to go back to Bristol but my uncle insisted that I stay in Blantyre. Bristol Cathedral had been bombed and some of the hospitals. I stayed there up to age five and didn't go to school. I used to help my mum. My uncle was away most of the time as he was in the army, helping to construct aircraft.

My cousin was a gamekeeper on Lord Weim's estate. So we were there from 1940 to 1945. I am now 48 years old. My brother was in the marines during the war. He was stationed in Haifa in Cyprus. My sister went to Eastville Girls' School. My dad worked in Rolls-Royce during the war, helping on the military aircraft. He lost his eye there – a piece of metal penetrated his eye. He had to have an operation but it wasn't successful. He could see with his left eye but not his right, but he carried on playing football for Bristol Rovers. He was injured playing football; a kick made a deep hole in his leg.

When my sister was little an iron gate shut on her finger and cut the top joint off.

I enjoy knitting and watching TV. My favourite programmes are horror films, *Come Dancing, Dallas, Sherlock Holmes* and the news. When I'm not watching TV, I read thrillers. I get my books from Stapleton Library...

Mary McLean: Lanercost Centre, Bristol
(Dictated as part of a reminiscence group project)

My life story

I was born in Chippenham, Wiltshire, in 1952. My father was a Sergeant in the RAF. He was stationed in Yatesbury. He became Flight Sergeant later on. We went to Easterton Sands for six months. We also stayed in Easton, near Portland Bill in Dorset. We stayed there for three months, then we moved to Worcester for one year. We moved to Stafford in 1954. We stayed there for three years. We then moved to Geilenkirchen in Germany and stayed there for two years.

The school was just across the road. I couldn't do lessons so I had to stay at home. I should have started school in 1957. I've tried to do lessons but I couldn't do them. Then I was told I had to 'consider the others'. In 1956 I should have been in my second class at school. When I learned my alphabet, I couldn't say it properly. I could only say it backwards.

We were posted to RAF Leuchars. We lived at 39 Meteor Row. We stayed there for five years.

When I started school I went to school in Cupar. I was in an old building in St Catherine Street. It was called Marathon House and we had to walk up three flights of stairs. There were two classes there. We were in the same room all the time for lessons. And we were in another room for dinner. When the pupils reach a certain age they moved up to another class. They were in the same room until they reached 16. The school was called a Junior Occupational Centre. The pupils who left there had to stay at home, because there wasn't a senior one in Cupar. They wouldn't have got a job. One of the pupils used to take the milk crate downstairs in the afternoon. At one time those who left the Junior Occupational Centre in Cupar had to stay at home or go to the nearest one. One of the pupils used to go to the one in Kirkcaldy. He used to travel from Newburgh. Another used to travel from Auchtermuchty.

In 1962 I transferred to the Special Class at The Burgh Secondary School. In 1964 we moved to Barnstaple. Dad was stationed at Chivenor. We lived at 23 Abbey Road, Pilton, Barnstaple in North Devon. I went to an ordinary school. I went to Barnstaple Girls' Secondary School. It was a modern building. There were 500 pupils there. I was in a C stream, which was a Remedial Stream. We wore navy blue and white at St Andrew's. We had to wear bottle green and white. The school was twice the size of the one I went to in St Andrews. The Burgh School had 250 pupils. The gym was an old one. It was also a dining hall. In Barnstaple, the gym was a modern one. The floor was made of parquet. The other pupils in my form had one year at that school and they were in the second year. Whereas I was in my first year. In a way, I was a little different and I was thrust among them. They were in 1C. I was in 2C.

I found the writing difficult, because the others started learning to write earlier than I did. And we had to read out to the class. Whereas before, I only read to the teacher. The others would have learnt to read out to the whole class a lot earlier on. In 1965 I was in 3C. We learnt Cookery. In 1966, there was a new head teacher. There were some changes in the school...

In April 1967 we were sent to Singapore. Dad was at Tengah for two-and-a-half years. We lived at a guest house in Kim Yam Road, in Singapore Town, for a while, then we moved to the Pacific Mansions. We lived in 11K. I went to St John's school. It was a Senior Comprehensive School. It was very big. There were 1,000 pupils. I was in the fourth form. I was in 4N8. In September that year I was in 5N7. In 1968 I was still in 5N7. We left in 1969.

I could have left school when I was 15. I had to stay on when I was 17. But it didn't do any good. I had to leave school without any qualifications. The ones I was at school with were in 1C before I joined them. Then they were in 2C when I joined them.

We went to Kinloss, near Forres, Morayshire. We stayed there for a year and a bit. I couldn't get a job so I had to stay at home. We were in our second year at Kinloss when we moved to Marham, near King's Lynn, Norfolk, in 1970. I still couldn't get a job. So I had to stay at home all the time. When we were at Tengah, we lived at 20 Meteor Row. When we were at Kinloss, we were at 2 Grange Road. When we were in Marham, we lived at 260 Pine Avenue.

We went to Cyprus in March 1972. Dad was stationed at Akrotiri. We stayed at Limassol for one month. We stayed at 28 Patch Crescent when we moved to Akrotiri. We had three years in Cyprus. We had to have evacuees staying in the camps when the coup started. It was a bit of a nuisance. We had people staying with us for weeks. We had 10 days of everything back to normal, and the evacuees went back to the camps and they had to wait until they were told the time of their flights back home to the UK. It was a nuisance. Some people came home earlier because of the coup.

We still had to stay until 1975. We left in March that year. We went back to Leuchars. This time, we lived at 19 Hamden Court. I had to go to an adult training centre. I went to the one at Cupar. The centre was at the Corn Exchange. It was in St Catherine Street. In July, the pupils at Castlehill Primary School moved into a new building. We moved into their old one.

In 1976, we left Leuchars. We moved to Glenrothes in November that year. The new building at Cupar was built. We went up to see it and have a look round. We moved into the new building at Bank Street in November that year. It is next to Adamson's Hospital. I still went to Dalgairn.

I started to go to Elmwood College for English in 1976. In 1978 I still went to Cupar. In 1979 I still went to Cupar. In 1980 I still went to Cupar, until June. I left in June. I started going to St Clair on Monday 23 June. I had to go to St Clair ever since.

I felt set apart from other people since I was 12. Even before that.

Moira A. McCandlish.

Moira McClandlish: St Clair ATC, Kirkcaldy
(Self-typewritten)

My life story according to me

WHEN I WAS YOUNGER I WAS A MISCHEIF
THIS MEANS I DROVE A MILK CART CRASH IN-
TO A HEDGE AND EVERY TIME ANYONE SELE
-CTED I.T.V. CHANNEL 8 I FLEW INTO A SHOC
-KING TEMPER THESE HAPPENED WHEN I WAS
14 YEARS OLD. LATER ON I RAN UP THE RAI
-LWAY TRACK WHERE I WAS LATER FOUND
OUT IN A SIGNAL CABIN LONG BEFORE BEING
QUESTIONNED BY THE POLICE WHO LATER TOOK
ME BACK HOME FOR WHITCH OFFENCE I WAS
TOLD TO COMMENCE HOOVING AS PUNISHMENT

When I was younger I was a mischief. This means I drove a milk cart crash into a hedge and every time anyone selected ITV Channel 8 I flew into a shocking temper. These happened when I was 14 years old.

Later on I ran up the railway track where I was later found out in a signal cabin long before being questioned by the police who later took me home, for which offence I was told to commence hoovering as punishment. Later on I drew pictures on my bedroom wallpaper and later on I threw a pear crash into a window and my mum told me: 'Here young man, you will pay for that!' My father was that annoyed that much he made me pay for the broken window and obtained a fresh piece of glass, 20 by 30 inches of course.

And later on I once fiddled with a floor-standing plug in radio and my father told me: 'You will make the radio crackle'. And later on I did pull up the floor-boards in my bedroom and saw the hall from upstairs. And later on I got into a grocer's van without his noticing anything happening. My father told me off severely like: 'Hey you, get out of that you Arab!'

Later on I was found out making a cake with a mixture of ground ginger, flour and pepper, and my teaching sister caught me and made me eat the offence as punishment. And later on I disgraced myself in plugging a wind-up Hornby train set into a mains socket and nearly but not quite died of an electric shock, and later on I almost hurt myself with first a piece of burning paper then a bottle of Sloans linament which burned a hole down to the bone. Mum found me out and wound a bandage on my offended right hand after washing it all out.

And later on I annoyed a policeman in dialling a false 999 call for which offence I was severely punished by my teaching sister who said: 'You naughty boy, don't ever never do that again!' Later on I posted two addressed unstamped postcards and my nursing sister caught me out and told me: 'You naughty boy, never do that again!' And later on I once switched the mains power out for having broken a water heater cable contact by accident.

Later on I started doing man-like things like laying the table before mealtimes and cooking the meals ready on a mains pipe gas cooker oven, and later on I once made toast light brown every breakfast time, including cereals and milk, and the Sunday lunch and pudding also. And later on I covered the beds over ready for sleeping in, and later on I stayed in bed with chicken pox and later downstairs with measles. And later on I poked a pencil in my throat and had to go straight into hospital with tonsilitis. Poor old mum nearly lost me. And later on I got mumps similar to meningitis, and later I got severe gout in Cannock Chase.

G.E. Wilkins: Waterside Day Centre, Burton-on-Trent
(Extract from self-handwritten account)

Chapter Three
Relationships

This chapter continues our central theme of identity. People establish who they are, and where they belong, through their relationships with others. This chapter contains a selection of relationship stories, across the spectrum of family, friends and partners. These are accounts of close relationships, and what these meant to the authors.

Many contributors focused on relationships, though not all of their stories appear here. Some also reflected other themes, such as 'transitions', and their stories appear elsewhere. The accounts in this chapter take us across the range of close relationships. They involve detailed observation of the people who mattered to contributors, and their feelings in relation to them. The stories present a multi-dimensional view of human life. There are heart-warming accounts of relationships, told with affection and warmth; and there are more chilling expositions of neglect, abuse and violence.

Most of the stories in this chapter are by women. There is a contrast between the accounts presented here, which are mostly 'women's stories', and those in Chapter Nine, which are entirely 'men's stories'. The selection was not based on gender. The focus of the stories, however, showed a gender bias. Men, it seemed, were more at ease with the chronological life-story approach which chronicled the main changes in their lives and how they felt about them; whereas women's stories often seemed to be about people who mattered and their relationships with them, rather than a systematic account of life events.

The chapter is in two main parts: 'families' and 'friends'. In the families section, we start with some short 'pen pictures' of individual family members – mother, father, sister, brother and niece. Then we look at what their family meant to our contributors. For some it's a story of positive experiences, and a feeling of belonging. We include a selection of positive statements, including a detailed description of her family life by Samantha Hulley. This account was compiled with the help of her father, Samantha using signs and sounds to convey her meaning.

Often families have a supportive role to play in adult life. Kinship, and one's kin network, can be the strongest and most enduring form of human support available. The accounts by Ann Henderson and Ian Meechan illustrate this theme. The loss of parents is coped with in both instances through the help of a supportive sister. To illustrate the theme of the supportive family network, we also include here Alison's pictures of her own family. This features aunts and uncles as well as her immediate family.

Family life is not always positive and supportive. Four young people write candidly about their more mixed experiences of family life. These stories are of strained relationships, the break-up of marriages, divided loyalties, foster homes and children's homes, separation, rejection, abuse and violence. And yet, the young authors write with a warmth and understanding that belies their years – and their apparent 'handicaps'.

The second main section of this chapter is called 'friends'. We start with two group submissions on the theme of friendship and making friends. These short statements say a lot! Feelings, wisdom and insight can be, and is, captured in two or three lines. Two actual friendships are celebrated by two women authors; one in prose and the other as a poem.

The focus then moves to boyfriends, girlfriends and partnerships. A few short statements about 'boyfriends' set the scene. Then four couples talk about their relationships. Again they pull no punches. These close relationships offer much in terms of personal identity and a sense of belonging. But they also bring with them doubts, jealousy and anger. None of the couples is married but there is considerable speculation about getting married, especially by the women partners.

Contents

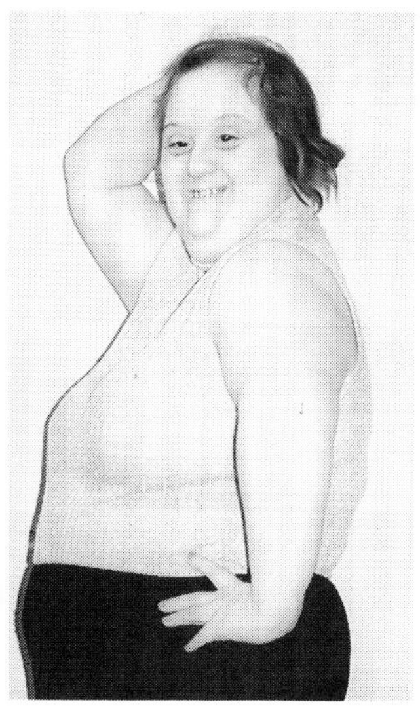

Linda Collins.

Families

(i) Pen pictures of individual family members

I've got a lot of love for mum

I've got a lot of love for mum. She's part of my life. She always says she doesn't know why I come here to the centre. She'd like me to have a job. She thinks that because she loves me...

Linda Collins: William Brinson Centre, London
(Handwritten, then transferred to word-processor)

Carol Smith.

I love my mum

I love my mum
I want her to walk again.

I love my aunt and my uncle
and my cousin and her family...

Carol Smith: William Brinson Centre, London
(Dictated, then transferred to word-processor)

Pamela Reynolds.

My dad was six foot tall

My dad was six foot tall, with white curly hair and blue eyes and he had a small moustache. He was an engineer and could do anything in the house, and he could mend everything too. We used to have parties sometimes on the lawn at Grange Court Road when the weather was nice and he used to take us out for meals quite often. He used to like treacle tart and always teased my mum by asking for it every day.

Pamela Reynolds: Portway Centre, Bristol
(Self-typewritten)

My sister Mandy

My sister is Mandy. Mandy is nice. Her hair is alright, it is black. She has brown eyes. She has a baby and she is married. Her husband is Alan – he is my brother-in-law. He has a mum called Margaret Palmer and a sister called Tracey Palmer.

My sister is nice. She buys me sweets. Me and Sean have them. When I am off to work she kisses me, and Sean when I'm in the car says, 'Ta ta Uncle Alan', and waves to me.

My mum had an electric shock when she was moving a parcel from the Christmas lights and burned her hand which made her wedding ring go black. I cried and my sister was upset. My mum's sister was upset.

Alan Marshall: Portway Centre, Bristol
(Dictated)

Rose Neale.

My brother Ken

My brother Ken does the washing and the ironing, and he buys the presents.

He has fair hair, he wears glasses and he's tall and thin.

He watches TV and his favourite programme is *Coronation Street.*

Rose Neale: William Brinson Centre, London
(Handwritten)

My niece Vicky

My niece Vicky is Beryl's daughter. She had dollies and prams and all that when she was a little girl, and her daughter's got them now. She used to work down near the docks in a hairdresser's shop down by the traffic lights. She has two dogs and rabbits and she had two horses. She is blonde and she wears glasses now. She had a nice mother and father, that's Beryl and her husband. She's taller than Beryl. She used to do typewriting, and she's got three children, Sarah, Natalie and Charlie, and her husband is Steve. I'm going round tonight. She will say, 'Hello, Aunty Doreen'. I go round there every Wednesday night after Keep Fit, and she's nice, all right for me.

Doreen Randall: Portway Centre, Bristol
(Dictated)

(ii) Positive experiences of families

Love

I love my mum and dad very much because they are my family. They love me too because they had me as a baby.

I loved my brother because when it was my birthday, and at Christmas, he liked parties and he danced with me.

I loved my nan because she used to make bread pudding and Ovaltine when I slept at her house...

Susan Bonshall: William Brinson Centre, London
(Handwritten, then transferred to word-processor)

In my family there was me

In my family there was me, my mum and dad, my pop and nan.

I remember my pop and nan having a row about horse-racing. They shouted at each other.

I used to help my nan with the cooking.

I used to play with my dad. We hit each other with pillows and wrestled.

Carol Smith: William Brinson Centre, London
(Dictated, then transferred to word-processor)

My mum's done a lot for me

My mum's done a lot for me. I always think I'm the worst one of the lot, but I'm not. I'm a great help to my mum with the cooking and the washing-up.

My family means a lot to me. They torment me with food at Christmas time, telling me to have more.

I think of my dad at Christmas wishing he was here. It brings a lump to my throat.

Linda Collins: William Brinson Centre, London
(Handwritten, then transferred to word-processor)

My family is very important to me

My family is very important to me. I wouldn't like my parents to get hurt - there are too many violent people out there in the street. I don't like accidents. My dad had a heart attack in his lorry. My brother had an accident and he died. I wish my brother was alive now. He would be a grandad.

I've got cousins in America. They've been to see me and I'd like to see them in America, but I think it's too much money to get there.

I've got uncles and aunts, nieces and nephews, and the best sister in the world.

Susan Bonshall: William Brinson Centre, London
(Handwritten, then transferred to word-processor)

Tomorrow will be my dancing day

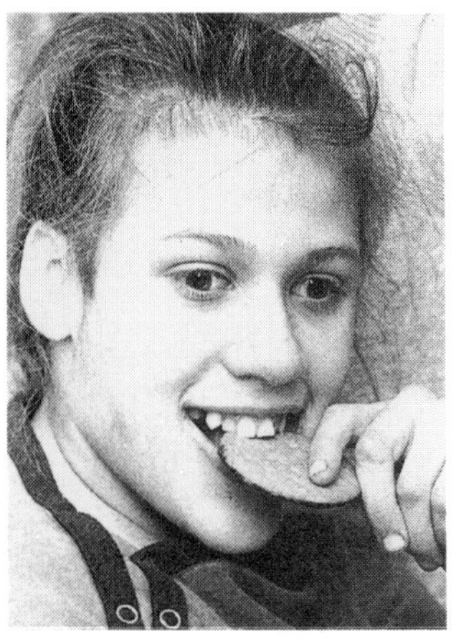

Samantha Hulley.

Tomorrow, school is shut. I want to have a picnic at home in the garden with granny. I am asking daddy to take her out there. I like sitting with granny and looking after her. Mummy and daddy can go shopping.

Granny talks about swimming. When she is finished she talks about my friends and cooking and school. I drink my coffee in her room. When it is finished I take my cup into the kitchen and tell everybody that I have had coffee.

I like helping granny. I fetch her bedpan and tell mummy or daddy that she needs the toilet. I wish I could do it myself. Sometimes I tell them that granny wants a cup of tea. I help to make it. Granny reminds me what is happening later because I always want to know.

On Saturday night my dad takes me out to the *Bell*. I make sure that my brother, Lenny, stays with granny and talks about swimming. Then it is all right for me to go out. I phone Lenny from the pub and he tells me what sort of crisps he wants.

It is good when people talk to me. I tell dad that I am finished with him. I want to stay on my own. At school I like some help in the lessons but it is really nice to stay with my friends at lunchtime. I send the adults away.

Scott and Greg are my friends. I want to phone them tonight about swimming next Wednesday. I get somebody to help me use the phone. I wish school was open. I go there to see my friends. My class is 3 Akeman.

At school I like drama best. Now I enjoy maths and science more than humanities and English. My friends do trampolining and dance with me. We do cooking on Wednesdays. My friends went on a school trip with me to Alton Towers. I had lots of rides. I didn't bother to eat my picnic even.

Each night I talk about tomorrow. The arrangements are important to me so I ask until I understand. On Monday, Tuesday and Wednesday I take my brother to school. He sits on my lap in the wheelchair. I put his shoes in the bag at school and get his trainers. I went to his school when I was little.

I check if my uniform is ready. I really like my school uniform. I need to know who will do my hair in the morning. It is important to look nice. Sometimes I ask for my earrings. I wore my nicest clothes and dangly earrings at the school disco. My friends all came to see me.

People matter to me. Gil and Linsey help me at school. Sometimes my mum and dad come instead. I like going out and having visits from friends. I enjoy my food, my listening, and swimming, but I like being with people the best.

It is time for physio now. When I go to bed I will listen to *Heidi* or *Tyke Tiler* on my cassette. I shout when it needs turning over. I can practise my kneeling up dance movements tomorrow. We might go to the woods or the garden centre.

Samantha Hulley: Stevenage
(Interpreted from signs and sounds)

(iii) Kinship and family support

I've got one brother, Sid

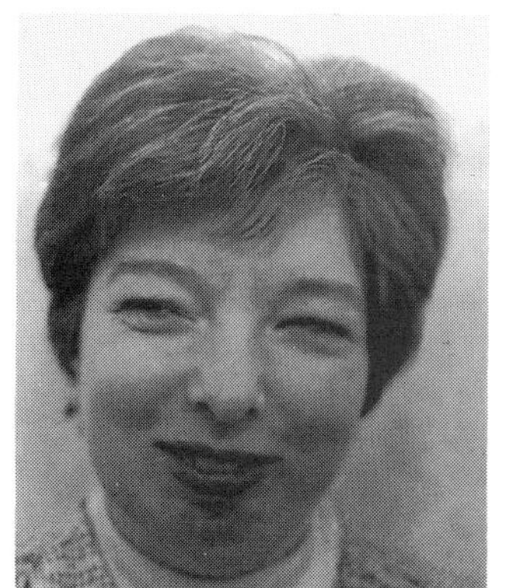

Ann Henderson.

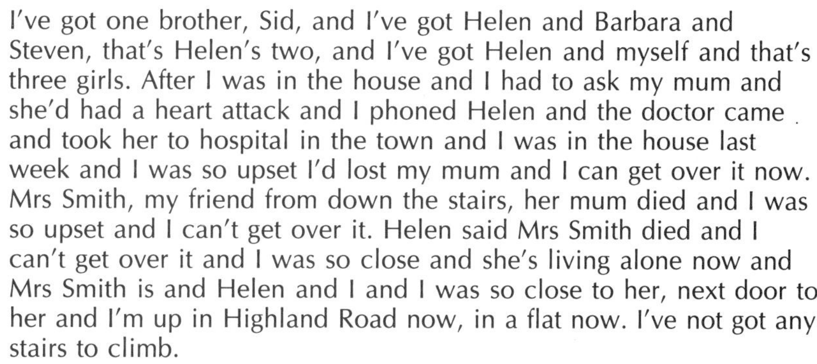

I've got one brother, Sid, and I've got Helen and Barbara and Steven, that's Helen's two, and I've got Helen and myself and that's three girls. After I was in the house and I had to ask my mum and she'd had a heart attack and I phoned Helen and the doctor came and took her to hospital in the town and I was in the house last week and I was so upset I'd lost my mum and I can get over it now. Mrs Smith, my friend from down the stairs, her mum died and I was so upset and I can't get over it. Helen said Mrs Smith died and I can't get over it and I was so close and she's living alone now and Mrs Smith is and Helen and I and I was so close to her, next door to her and I'm up in Highland Road now, in a flat now. I've not got any stairs to climb.

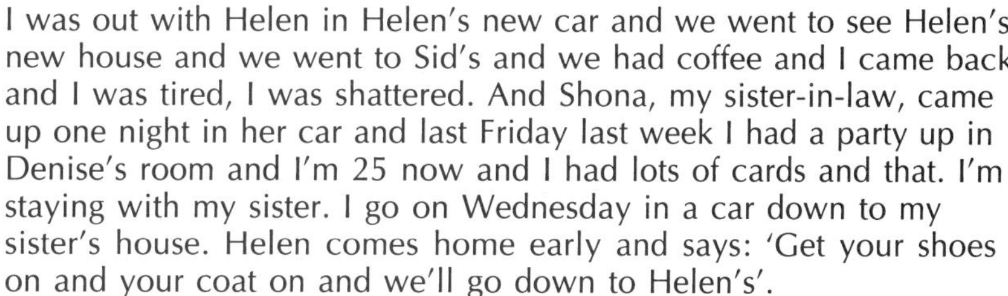

I was out with Helen in Helen's new car and we went to see Helen's new house and we went to Sid's and we had coffee and I came back and I was tired, I was shattered. And Shona, my sister-in-law, came up one night in her car and last Friday last week I had a party up in Denise's room and I'm 25 now and I had lots of cards and that. I'm staying with my sister. I go on Wednesday in a car down to my sister's house. Helen comes home early and says: 'Get your shoes on and your coat on and we'll go down to Helen's'.

Steven, my sister's boy, is coming home this weekend. He's staying with his mum and dad, he's got red hair. He's alright, I can get on fine with him.

Ann Henderson: Whiteinch Centre, Glasgow
(Dictated)

My name is Ian

My name is Ian. I have three brothers and two sisters. One brother is married and lives in England. My two sisters are married, one lives in America and the other lives locally.

Two brothers and me went to a special school and when we left, we went to an adult training centre. I remember going to school on a grey bus which often broke down.

When we were young we went to clubs – I remember it only cost 3d – that's just over 1p in decimal money. When we were young, we went with our parents every year to a rented house in Rothesay for a fortnight. We went from Upper Greenock Station by train to Wemyss Bay, then by the boat (paddle steamer) to Rothesay. We went for walks to the parks, and up the High Street. Sometimes we got the bus outside the post office – near the pier – and we would take sandwiches and ginger – and go to Kilchattan Bay, Ettrick Bay or Port Bannatyne. We had good times. There was always plenty to do. When the Highland Games were on, there were pipe bands and accordion bands and there were Highland dancers, and these folks played and danced and entertained us on the sail over to Rothesay. After the games, the pipers would spend the evening in the pub, and sometimes they would forget the time and miss the boat and they'd have to stay overnight. We went to the pictures and to shows where there were singers and dancers, and we joined in sing-songs in the pub with mum and dad and we always enjoyed ourselves.

Dad used to make most of our meals because mummy had difficulty walking as she suffered from arthritis for many years. Our sisters helped dad to prepare the food.

We were always out and about doing something. Rothesay is not the same anymore, there's not so much to do.

Mum and dad are both dead now. We three brothers still live in our family home. When mum was alive, but very ill, we did the shopping and the housework, and our sisters would pop in now and again to see that everything was alright.

Now that we are on our own, one sister comes in several times a week just to see that everything is OK. She brings in our shopping and pays our bills for us. She helps us to keep the house well organised, and her husband paints and decorates to keep the house looking smart. We helped him to strip off the old paper and to keep the room clear.

We have a home help who does the washing and ironing and prepares our food, so that we just have to heat it up – then eat it. We have a rota system for doing the dishes and the kitchen floor. We do other housework too. Mainly at the weekend. Thomas does a lot of the shopping and our sister writes the list. He is at an adult training centre. Robert has a voluntary job in a painter and decorator's shop clearing up rubbish, and keeping the store tidy. I work in a voluntary job too in a community centre lunch club. I wash dishes and make tea. I work there Monday to Friday. I used to have problems in a job I had previously. I worked in a sawmill, but sometimes the men would make fun of me and call me names. The boss would tell them off but it didn't do much good. Eventually I got the job I'm doing now, in the lunch club. Robert's only problem in work is that they won't provide him with boots with steel toecaps!!! Otherwise he gets on well with his workmates.

Last January I was in Spain – Majorca – for a holiday. We stayed in a hotel and enjoyed ourselves. It was the first time I'd been on a plane. It was great. I had my breakfast before I left home – then had another on the plane.

Robert is saving up for a holiday in Florida, USA, next summer. Our sister says he's almost got enough money saved. Our other sister lives there with her American husband and two children. We are very fond of our niece and nephew.

Thomas, Robert and I are quite happy living together. We get on well most of the time. The only time we were really unhappy was after mum died, but eventually when we got over the worst of it we all pulled together and, with other people's help, we got down to organising our lives and everything is fine now.

Ian Meechan: Strathclyde Outreach Project
(Dictated)

This was a hot time in Dominica. *(Alison, Hammersmith and West London College)*

(iv) Mixed experiences of family life

During the Easter holidays

During the Easter Holidays I was doing the house work for the whole two weels, doing the shopping, cleaning and it was good it wash't boring it was Something to do in the holidays, my Dad is not, Fat Shot and till is meel shie fat and my Mum is med till and is skinny - is Bluond hair and my Sister is darker than me, my sister is middle size tall she is a little bit chubby she is nineteen she is a trainee chef in a hotel in Ireland, she has the same bad temper that I have she hates housework.

During the Easter holidays I was doing the housework for the whole two weeks, doing the shopping and cleaning, and it was good. It wasn't boring, it was something to do.

My dad is not fat, short or tall. He is medium-size fat, and my mum is medium tall and is skinny. She has blonde hair. My sister is darker than me. She is middle-size tall. She is a little bit chubby. She is 19 and she is a trainee chef in an hotel in Ireland. She has the same bad temper that I have, and she hates housework. I tripped my sister over by accident in the grass and cow's muck. She was cross at me and went crying to my mum. I laughed at her. My Uncle Percy stood up for me, and my cousins.

The children went to a market with my nan. It had loads of clothes and holy stuff; Jesus, Mary, Joseph, pictures, necklaces, rings, statues, crosses and so on, and different foods like vegetables. My grandmother makes loads of bread, it's nice. She is small and curvy. She is very strict. She has a stick which she whacks me with when I am cheeky to my mum. She has a pale face with rosy cheeks and blue eyes. She has short black hair. The only jewellery she wears is a wedding ring.

My grandad does the gardening and grows vegetables. He has chickens and a dog. There is no drinking water in the house; we have to go to a special well. It is five miles' walk to the stream where we get the water from. My grandad died not long ago. My uncles get the water for my grandmother. Her cottage has four rooms. There is no upstairs. There is a big water butt outside, the roof is of slate. It is nice there.

My cousins and my sister like discos, and my aunty and uncle like discos. They want me to go to the disco, they want to fix me up with some boys. I don't like them, nor will my sister who likes cooking a lot. When we lived together in Ireland we used to fight. She used to take my clothes and we would hit each other. I think that now we are older we will be friends.

My mum got married again last December. I am going to see her in Ireland at the end of July. I shall see all my family – uncle, aunty and cousins – that I haven't seen since I was little. And my nan too. I live with my dad in Neasden. It's alright in London except for the mugging and stabbing. My step-mum got mugged.

My step-sister passed her exam and is a hairdresser. My step-cousin lives with me. He's got a dog called Toby. I take him out everywhere I go. He is always on my bed. I've got a cat called Boops.

Anne Marie: Hammersmith and West London College (Handwritten)

I got a mum and dad

I GOT A MUM AND DAD . THEY LIVES AT SOUTHEND. MY NAN TELLS ME OFF SOME TIMES. WHEN I LIVED AT SOUTHEND I WENT OFF TO THE SHOPS WITH MY BROTHER. MY GRAN PARENTS WERE GOOD TO ME WHEN I WAS LITTLE. WHEN I WAS LITTLE I COULD NOT WALK SO I WENT TO HOSPITAL WERE I WAS BORN. I WENT TO IRELAND TO SEE MY GRAN DAD AND NAN . MY NAN IS SCOTISH AND MY GRAN DAD IS IRISH. WHEN I WENT TO SEE MY GRAN DAD HE USED TO TELL ME OFF BECAUSE I USED TO SHOUT AND THROW THINGS. MY REAL DAD WAS KIND TO US BUT A DONT LIKE MY STEP DAD. I HATE HIM VERY MUCH. MY REAL DAD IS NICER THEN MY STEP DAD. IRELAND WAS SO GREEN

I got a mum and dad. They lived at Southend. My nan tells me off sometimes. When I lived at Southend I went off to the shops with my brother.

My real dad was kind to us. My dad died of cancer. He was 54 years old when he died. It was on my brother's birthday.

My grandparents were good to me when I was little. When I was little I could not walk, so I went to the hospital where I was born.

I went to Ireland to see my grandad and nan. My nan is Scottish and my grandad is Irish. When I went to see my grandad he used to tell me off because I used to shout and throw things.

Ireland was so green and sunny, and sometimes rainy. The last time I went to Ireland it was my cousin's birthday party. He was four years old then. I put him to bed and went back to London.

My grandad is big and tall, with small hands. His face is small and his voice is deep. My aunty is nice looking. Her face is small, the same as my

grandad. Her voice is soft. She wears glasses. She has a cat called Tabby. My nan is a nice lady. She's got brown eyes. She likes me very much because she used to give me sweets every day. She's got a dog named Patsi and a cat called Taddy.

My sister is having a baby. My brother is 14 years old. My sister is 23. I've got a dog and a cat and a cockatoo. My sister is at college, she is 18 now. My sister was nice to me a lot. I hope she does not lose that baby. My elder sister has got a boyfriend, his name is Richard. My other sister has got a boyfriend, his name is Andrew. He's got brown eyes and he's got light hair, and he's a nice boy. My mum met his mum, and his mum likes me very much. She thinks that I am very nice too.

My aunt has got lovely blue eyes and dark hair. She wears glasses. My aunt works in a pub, she is a bar man. She has got the pub by herself. I like her very much.

When I lived in Southend my friend lived next door, she was called Tracy. Peter was also my friend. I've got one best friend. He is called Bunmi, he comes from Nigeria. My best friend is Marvin. Marvin was good to me, he used to let me play with his toys. He goes to school every day. He calls for me sometimes. He has a cat in his house. He lives at No. 84, yellow door. In his flat near me he's got a sister called Helen.

My friend when I was at school was Jason, and Roy, and my girlfriend was Jackie. She was 15 years old. Jason was a good boy all the time. He's got nice brown eyes. I like my friend very much. I wish he was still at school. I miss them very much at school. I like all the teachers. I missed them a lot. They used to be nice to me all the time.

Outside at school one day I had a fit when I was running, and I banged into the wall. I had to go to hospital for a week, then I came out.

I was living in a children's home at White City, and it was good there. My best friend was a boy called Dennis. He is 13 years old. He was a good boy. He goes to school at Hammersmith School. My brother goes to the same school. My friend lives near me, by my house. My brother called for my friend on Sunday, and we went there. His mum said that he will not be back until four weeks, from his holiday in Jamaica.

My friend has got a girlfriend, her name is Judy. She is 14 years old. She is a white person. Dennis has got black eyes and black hair. He said he would be my friend for ever.

John: Hammersmith and West London College
(Self-handwritten, and transferred to word-processor by author)

I went to the seaside

I went to the seaside. It was very nice, I enjoyed myself. I went in the sea and played on the sand. My mum and aunty and uncle came with me. They liked it as well.

And then I got bigger and went to a school called Wood Lane School. I was in Class One. My teacher's name was Mrs Harwood. I liked the school.

I like my mum, she is very pretty. She takes me to the seaside and she used to give me pocket money. My aunty used to come at the weekend. My aunty was very kind, she gives me presents. I used to play with my friends where my aunty used to live.

Now I live with Kay. Kay is a very kind person, she buys me presents and takes me away for holidays.

I like it where I used to live. I used to go to my friend's house, and go to the park and play in the park. I used to take my friend's dog for a walk. I liked my old school very much. I did not want to leave there, but I knew I had to leave.

I like where I live now. I like my Aunty Mag, she is very nice; I wish I could see her more times. I can't get to see her very much, only when she comes to stay with my other aunty and uncle. I like my aunty and uncle, they are very nice to me. I like my Aunty Joan, she was very nice and I miss her a lot. I wish she hadn't died.

I like where I used to live. If I get a nice job I would like to be by myself and get a flat.

I like going to Kathy and John's. John makes me laugh and Kathy is nice to me. I like when I go to see my cousins. I like going to Bournemouth. I play games with my cousins. I like it when they come to see me. I like family, they are nice to me and I like going to see them.

I like Kay's sister's children, they are nice. On my birthday they bring me presents and I have a party, and all the family comes to it. I like it when Aunty Rosemary makes all the nice puddings for my birthday.

Every year when I was little I went to the zoo and saw lots of different animals. I like it at the zoo. When I was a baby I used to fall over a lot. When I was little I used to have asthma. I did not like to have asthma. When I was little I had trouble with my walking, and now I am glad I can walk better.

When I was little my uncle used to be a bus driver. He used to take people to work. I used to go and see him with my mum on the train. My aunty and uncle used to meet us at the station and we went to his house to see aunty, and I used to go to the goose fair every year.

I have an Uncle Leon who lives in France. My mum met him in France when she was over there on a day trip. He wanted to marry my mum, but she did not want to live in France. She wants to live in London and she did not want to marry my uncle. My uncle comes to London to see me and my mum. My uncle likes London. I have not seen him for a long time. I wish I could see him more that I do now.

I like taking my cousin's dog for a walk. I like going to see my aunty and uncle. I like my aunty's daughter, she is very nice; I wish I could see her more than I do. I like going to see Keith and Denise. I like it when they come to stay with Kay and me.

I went to Spain with my mum, and to Jersey and to Lourdes. I went swimming with my mum and my aunty.

Amanda: Hammersmith and West London College
(Tape transcript, transferred to word-processor by author)

This is about my love life

I've got a half-sister who can't speak any English because she comes from Spain. My dad divorced my mum and got married again to a Spanish woman, called Isabel.

My dad is half Scottish. My grandad is Italian. I have one sister who lives with me called Ruth. My mum lives with me, her colour hair is red, maroon colour. My sister likes to stay out all night and go to parties and discos.

My mum was married at 18 years old. My dad was 17 when he married my mum. My mum used to have a lot of worry with me in the hospital. My mum has a cleaner's job, she works as a cleaner.

My nan, when she was a little girl, used to live in Blantyre Street. They only had rations of food, and didn't have much money in them days. My grandad, when he was a little boy, it was during the war-time.

My uncle got married to Pamela then he got divorced. One Christmas, Pamela just left him with the dog, Amy. My uncle was just a big kid when he got married to her.

My Aunty Jean is always drunk when she's had a few. When she goes out to parties and things, she falls over and hurts her knees.

When I was a little girl I tipped a gallon of paint in Lunar Street. I was caught downstairs nicking all the strawberries off the trifle.

I went to see my Aunty Liz. She couldn't come out because she couldn't walk, so we used to go and see her every day when I was little. We used to go and make dinners for her. My mum did. And when we weren't well we had to go over and stay with our Aunty Liz, because my mum worked. And our aunty gives special stuff, some special medicine that she used to make.

Me and my mum and my dad were hippies when we were little. I had a hippy dress. My dad had hippy trousers and a shirt. My mum had a hippy dress. And then I grew out of them, and after a while we stayed at our nan's till we got our own place.

We went to live in Lunar Street, not very far from Blantyre Street. Blantyre Street was only down where the pub is, not very far from there, and it was very quiet in them days. The kids looked like right little scruffs in them days. It was the old days, and I used to go down Blantyre Street when I was little. I was a right little villain, up to mischief. We used to get caught getting really dirty when I was little. I was a right little scruff.

We used to go dancing with our Scottish nan, the cancan, when she was still alive. My Uncle Frank used to take us over the bridge where the pub was, and play on the machines. We used to get spoilt, me and my sister. We had loads of sweets. Aunt Lou used to come round every Saturday. And me and Naomi used to go over the club with my Aunty Lou and Uncle Bert. And then Great Uncle David came, and Aunty Cath, and Aunty Winnie from Doncaster. My Uncle Ian is my dad's brother. Shamlet, my Uncle Ian's girlfriend, is always drunk.

My sister's got a boyfriend. She fancies him. He's called Dean Kurd; he's just come out of prison. He was my boyfriend – we were going to get engaged. I used to go with my Uncle John on his motor bike sometimes and my ex boyfriend, Dean Kurd, didn't like it. One time he came to my school and left me a message. He said Dean Kurd is here to see you, he wants to go to Bishops Park at 4 p.m. So I met him. He said I'll come and meet you from school one day. He said I'll see you later.

My mum doesn't want to get married. She wants to stay where she is. Jim is a scientist, my mum's a cleaner. When Jim comes home very late at night – he's my mum's boyfriend – he's always drunk and falling over. He keeps nicking all her fags and everything. My sister's the same.

My Uncle Frank was so funny, it feels so strange without him around. And my aunty, my nan, Cath and Sade. I remember her when she was alive and I miss her around now. She died too young.

My dad used to beat us up when we were little. We didn't have any money. Me and my sister used to go to work with my mum when we were little as there was no one to look after us. And when I started getting ill, very ill, my nan rushed me to hospital. I was in a terrible state. I was nearly born dead. I was born premature and I am epileptic, I have fits. I was born with brain damage and I can't read or write. I feel I sound funny on the tape.

Sally: Hammersmith and West London College
(Tape transcript, then handwritten.)

Friends

(i) Friendship, and making friends

Friendship

'Most of my friends I've had for 20 years and they've become part of my life. We've been through life together and have got common points of interest. Sometimes you make new friends, when your friends from school move away to get married, etc.' (Terry)

'My friend is Janet. We like writing up notes. I like looking at her face. I see her in the group with the children. I like to go for a walk with her in the park.' (Florence)

'I've known my friend Diane since I was little, at school. We go out together at lunchtimes. Sometimes she treats me and sometimes I treat her...' (Kim)

'I used to have a friend, Helen, at William Brinson. When you've known someone a long time and you leave the centre, you think about them a lot. Once I moved to Coborn Street, it had to end. Another boy has got her. At first I felt lost without her, but gradually I got used to it...' (Stephen)

'I've got friends like Florence and Tracey and Richard, from my centre. I like to talk to them and cheer them up when they look sad.' (Sylvia)

'I've got loads and loads of friends – a thousand! My special friends are Stephen, Ray and John. They go to football with me at the gym on Monday nights. We like playing football and hockey. All these of my friends are men.' (Julian)

'I've got plenty of friends at the church, plus a friend who takes me out to the theatre. They keep you company (I've got no parents) and cheer me up as well.' (Sylvia D.)

'As I've got older, I've got few friends and lots of acquaintances. A friend is one who knows all about you and loves you just the same. A friend to me is someone really special. Even if we don't see each other for years we can pick up where we've left off. I've got one friend I've known for 34 years!' (Margaret)

'I've got Irish friends up in London. I like to drink with them in the pubs. My friends are not important really. You make your own way in the world and find out for yourself where you stand.' (Mark)

'I don't have many friends I've known a very long time. I like going out with friends to do things we both want to do. I don't think I have very many close friends.' (John).

'A Chance to Speak' class: City Lit, London
(Transcribed extracts from discussion)

Friendship, and making friends

'I've got friends where I live, at the hostel. When I move I'll still visit them.'

'I have a best friend; she helps me do things. Best friends are closer to you; you can speak to them openly.'

'I knew my friend for 15 years. We were at the centre together.'

'I've got friends that I go out with. My special friend moved away to the seaside without leaving her new address.'

'Sometimes people don't stay in touch. Sometimes you can't stay in touch when you leave.'

'You need to try and keep in touch, by writing or by phoning. This can be expensive if they are in America or Australia!'

'Sometimes you don't know who you choose or what they are going to be like.'

'You can tell by their body language.'

'Choosing friends is a chance in a million – whether they are going to like the same things as you or not. You've got to take risks.'

'It all depends on how much confidence you've got in yourself. To talk to a stranger you don't know, you need a certain amount of trust.'

'My friend comes to my room and listens to my music. I make her a cup of tea.'

'You can still be friends with some people you may not like and help them if they need it.'

'Sometimes your friends don't always agree with you and it can cause problems.'

'He said that I was 'bloody mad' and I said: 'That makes the two of us!', and we've been the best of friends since. I tell him what I think of him, and he tells me what he thinks of me. He's bossy and so am I, and I can give him as good as I get.'

'You have to know me as I am.'

'Sometimes my friend seemed to be more trouble than she was worth. People expect you to look after them, and you get the blame. You can't make a long-term relationship. After someone dies, you can always remember the nice things. You've still got the memories.'

'When my friend died I stayed quiet for three weeks.'

'Speaking for Ourselves' class: City Lit, London
(Transcribed extracts from discussion)

Mrs Day

Mrs Day is always my friend. I always go next door to talk to her.

She was talking to me about her husband dying last year at Christmas. She was crying. She was very sad. Now she lives on her own. He died of pneumonia.

I went to see her yesterday and she kept me talking for a long time. I will go again tonight before it gets dark. She is a nice friend.

Stephanie Ceres: Kirkdale Centre, London
(Handwritten)

In your company 'Julia'

Why is your friendship so dear; and a precious
thing to me
I think, because, when I'm in your company,
my better self comes uppermost in all
I say and do,
Through your eyes I see things from a
different point of view.

My weaknesses you overlook - and failings
you ignore,
You draw out all the best in me,
and bring it to the fore.

In the radiance of your mind a very different
world I see,
I become something more than just myself,
all the time I'm in your company.

Jeannie Miller: Tower Hamlets Institute, London
(Self-typewritten)

(ii) Boyfriends, girlfriends, and partnerships

Boyfriends

'I want to be with my boyfriend because I love him very much. My mum and dad don't want me to be like that, but my life is more important. I'm different to my mum and dad. My relationship with my boyfriend is important to me.'

'My boyfriend always calls me "sexy" because he loves me too much.'

'Boyfriends are important to me. My boyfriend has got lovely blue eyes and nice black hair. He is very tall and handsome, with a lovely personality. I love him a lot. I hope we will be together for the rest of my life. My boyfriend is special to me. He is the best boyfriend in the world and I want the world to know it.'

'Boyfriends look after you. If you've got a cold they tell you to take something for it. They carry your bag if it's heavy. I like working with my boyfriend, like doing the washing up together, because he does not nag me like other people do. I enjoy being with him. It's good to have a boyfriend to love, and to know that he loves me. I think he is nice looking.'

'Boyfriends should be kind and talk to you nice. Because they have got feelings for you they say things like: "I missed you today, where were you?" I go for good looks and modern style of clothes and talent all combined. A boyfriend gives you the eye when you're walking down the street, or his eyes will gaze across the ballroom floor, then he will walk over and guide you.'

Carol, Helen, Sue, Linda and Rose: William Brinson Centre, London
(Some self-written, some dictated and transcribed)

'I bought her tea yesterday...'

Sandy: *I bought her tea yesterday and she'll treat me at Butlins – I like having a girlfriend, it's OK.*

Jean: *We work well together; I buy him for his birthday and he buys me. I met Sandy at the old centre, 1969 – I've been going with Sandy for 18 years, he asked me. We never fall out. He phones me to go to his house and he comes to my house for tea. I sometimes stay for the weekend.*

Jean: *We went to the Crow's Nest for dinner. Sandy copied me to find out what cutlery to use because he hadn't been before.*

We've thought of getting married, we might do it through time.

I think it's true love. Sandy helps me put my coat on every night. Love makes you happy.

I would get married to stop people from talking.

Sandy and Jean: St Clair ATC, Kirkcaldy
(Transcript of discussion)

Sandy and Jean.

'Having a relationship is being friends...'

Elspeth: *Having a relationship is being friends, going out and about with each other. We're not bairns, we're adults. We don't need someone to hold our hands.*

Peter: *Elspeth and I get on fine.*

Elspeth: *We have our ups and downs. It's company having a boyfriend. It's no fun going about on your own. It's better having a boyfriend than just all girls. I make us both coffee at lunchtime.*

Peter has a bad habit of hitting me. It gets on my nerves but I've got to live with it – I hit him back sometimes.

I'd like to get married but Peter tells me I'm an old granny.

It's not true love but it's love. If it was true love we'd go out every day but we don't.

Peter: *She's too old for us to be married, she's 43.*

Elspeth: *I don't think it matters if you're handicapped. We can manage just like others. A lot of handicapped people can get on. I don't think it's a good idea to live together without being married. People would talk.*

Elspeth and Peter: St Clair ATC, Kirkcaldy
(Transcript of discussion)

'Having a relationship is OK'

Michelle: *Having a relationship is OK. I went with a few boys before I went with Craig, before he started at the centre. I asked Craig out first of all and he said yes.*

Craig: *We have arguments and fall out often.*

Michelle: *We're planning to get engaged at Butlins.*

Craig: *I didn't say that!*

Michelle: *Mum says it's OK to get engaged.*

Craig: *I was pleased she asked me out. We don't go out after the centre at night.*

Michelle: *We'd like to go out as a couple. My mum lets us but Craig's mum has stopped it for some reason and I don't think it's fair. Craig's mum doesn't approve of our relationship and I don't know why – she must have something against me.*

Craig: *It's difficult.*

Michelle: *You need a boyfriend to have a physical relationship and have a family.*

Craig has a habit of lifting his leg and kicking me. He did it when I was only playing with him and we fell out. He bites his nails, I don't like that.

Craig said he had saved up money for my engagement ring. I asked his mum why she wasn't letting us get engaged. She didn't give me a reason. I think she doesn't want us married and having a family. She doesn't want her son to be away from her.

I don't think it's up to families if we get engaged. We're grown up, not kids, and should get to do what we want. It shouldn't have anything to do with anyone else.

I would like to get my own house and settle down and just visit mum. I think it's love and was hurt when we couldn't get engaged.

Sometimes it makes me sad if we've had a fight. It doesn't matter if you're handicapped – you can still have a relationship. You have to get married, not live together. If people had children without being married, the children would be called bastards.

Michelle and Craig: St Clair ATC, Kirkcaldy
(Transcript of discussion)

Robert and Ros's story

How it began

Robert: *We met at A school, and became boyfriend and girlfriend. And we've been going six years...I met her before I became 16. And I fell in love when I met her...We make love. And I got her a Valentine card...and we went to the club together.*

Ros: *I like him. He's very kind. He give me a Valentine card...He plays jokes on us. Everytime he tickle my feet...and I don't like it...and I tickle him. I told him off. 'Don't you dare ever tickle me again.' He starts to laugh. (They both start to laugh.)...A long time ago...Oh, you...you were talking with other girls. I didn't know. It makes me upset. Sometimes he shouts. He says, 'I hate you'. He's shouting at me, before my face. He says, 'It's you. It's your own fault'. Then he starts crying. The person who told me, a girl, A. I told her, 'What are you coming to me for?' You sit there crying for me. I want you to stop being selfish.*

Robert: *I was crying for you.*

Ros: *I saw him kissing her...make me upset.*

Some good times

Robert: *We went out when we went to Keilder.*

Ros: *We went walking and I had a blister on my foot.*

Robert: *And Ros had a blister on her foot. And we went horse-riding, canoeing and rock-climbing. Came back and Ros and I had something to eat. And I made love to her.*

Robert: *We went to North Shields together. Rosalind and me, and Wendy and Gordon. We had wine, steak and Yorkshire pudding. (They laugh together. This is a shared fantasy. They did go out one dinner-time – to a fish and chip cafe.)*

Ros: *Gordon bought four bottles of coke, right.*

Robert: *And we got drunk. (Again, laughter.)*

A problem with Gordon (whilst on a trip to France with the college)

Ros: *And Gordon upset us.*

Robert: *Gordon upset us. He was worried about me and Ros.*

Ros: *He started to cry.*

Robert: *Started to...started to cry.*

Ros: *He leaned over the back of the seat and gonna try and kiss me, and I said, 'Get off. Leave me alone'.*

Robert: *Aye he did.*

Ros: *That's why he tried – he would make Robert jealous. Kissing me to make Robert jealous.*

Robert: *Uh-huh.*

Ros: *So I told him.*

Robert: *He's got Wendy.*

Ros: *He still tried to kiss me.*

Robert: *To make me jealous. To make me vexed.*

Ros: *To make Robert jealous. And then he started to cry.*

Robert: *Gordon cried in his bed. He cried at night, in his bed. I was going to sleep and he started to cry. He said he was worried abut Wendy and me and Ros.*

Ros: *Not letting him near me any more. Wendy told him. She told him but he still kept on crying.*

Robert: *You told him what to do.*

Ros: *I told him what to do but he didn't.*

Things they would like to do

Ros: *Shopping.*

Robert: *Shopping...Make love with her.*

Ros: *Walk by the sea-front.*

Robert: *Sea-front.*

Ros: *Throw stones in the sea.*

Robert: *Get stones for the sea.*

Ros: *Then get some fish to eat.*

Robert: *Then get some fish to eat and come back to my house.*

A time apart

(Ros left school to go to the college one year before Robert. They did not see each other at all during that time)

Ros: *Well, sometimes we had to be apart. Edward, he started after me. He made me upset...wouldn't let go of my arm.*

Robert: *And I was crying for you.*

Ros: *'Cos he said I was daft, didn't he.*

Robert *Well, he's a fool.*

Ros: *I don't like him any more 'cos he starts after me. The last time was the Christmas disco. He came over to me and starts pulling my arm. I hate him. I told him to leave me alone.*

Parents

Ros: *My mam, well my mam knows about Robert. She looks at me 'cos I knew my mam knows I can't...Well, you know my mam! Says, 'You'll make your dad jealous'. (Ros laughs.) Sometimes my mam knows. Sometimes my mam knows about him. My dad knows about Robert sometimes. But I'm embarrassed. She'll say 'What! Is that your boyfriend!?' Eee...like.*

Robert: *I've got a sister called Sarah and Rosalind knows my sister. They met in A School. Sports night in A and...and Ros was there and they became friends. And when it's my birthday it's Sarah's birthday as well. I think Ros's coming to the party. I've invited Rosalind. (Sarah, Robert's twin sister is training to be a teacher. In the event Ros did not go to the party.)*

Visions of the future

Robert: *Not allowed to get married. Too young.*

Ros: *I can't get married. I'm not old enough yet.*

Robert: *We'd go to church. Give rings. Get engaged. Get a house. Get a car.*

Ros: *I can't drive. My mam won't let me 'cos I'm not that old to learn to drive properly...Working with horses. I want to get a job but my mam'll help me 'cos I can get one. And I'll feed the horse. Clean the horse. Come back and get my tea. Then go home.*

(Where would they live?)

Ros: *Well, there's my mam's like. But she won't let me move away myself. But 'cept we all have to die, then I have to look after myself. I like to do cooking myself...make coffee...do shopping as well and washing.*

Robert: *I'd like to sweep up the stables with Rosalind.*

Robert and Rosalind: Newcastle
(Tape transcript)

Chapter Four
Transitions

The contributors to this chapter have, between them, encapsulated the complex and multi-dimensional nature of transition and change. Inevitably there is some overlap with other chapters. Many of these 'transitions stories' are based on remembered events and their impact. Some of the sought after and welcomed changes involve developing close relationships and getting married. But there is a single unifying theme. People describe the changes in their lives and their *feelings* about those changes. Therein also lies the richness and diversity of the accounts.

Loss is a major theme, and losses were often experienced at an early age. Sarah Hunt's father, for example, died when she was a 'newborn baby'. Others recount the loss in childhood of the people who mattered: parents and grandparents; a favourite aunt and uncle. There was the sense of loss through removal from home and being placed as a child in a long-stay hospital. Loss is experienced in later years too. Mary Matthews lost her mother through death and her father to an old people's home. And, in later life, Bill Challis rues the closure of his hospital and describes the sense of anticipatory loss he now feels.

To strike a balance, there are many contributors for whom transitions – into student and other more adult roles – are actively welcomed. 'Growing up' and becoming 'more independent' are celebrated. Achieving adult status brings rewards, and often opens other doors such as the opportunity to get married.

Often change entails a move. The accounts in this chapter include moves into and out of hospital; and into (and sometimes out of) hostels, group homes and flats. Some changes are sought: Doretta wanted to leave the family home and move into a flat. But George Mustard, when first asked about leaving hospital, was not keen: 'At first I said I didn't want to go'. Change, even when sought, can be difficult to cope with and support is important. Some contributors describe the people who have supported them through times of transition and change.

The personal changes are set against a backcloth of social and institutional change. Vera Stone remembers 'the panel', and Alex McLean 'the parish'. There are descriptions of family life in Bristol and Glasgow. And there are accounts of changes in long-stay hospitals from the perspective of those living there. One hospital which was 'like Durham jail' was regarded, 38 years later, as a 'loved' home.

The chapter starts with some accounts of life transitions. There are contributions on 'growing up', adopting adult roles and becoming 'more independent'.

The focus shifts then to people making changes in their lives. This is a varied selection. It includes 'Shared Action Planning', setting up home independently and getting married. The authors each record their personal satisfaction with the outcome of the change in their lives.

Not all change is sought or welcomed. There are involuntary transitions in people's lives. Sometimes it's the loss of someone who matters, and the grief that follows. Sometimes it's loss of home. It can be the loss of a way of life.

Finally, there are longer stories where authors adopt the perspective of a lifetime to look back and reflect on the changes therein. This longer time perspective allows a depth of experience and accumulated wisdom to emerge. There are major life themes covered here: abandonment and rejection in childhood; admission to and life within the long-stay hospital; death in the family; courtship and marriage; the caring role of women; growing older and retirement.

Contents

Transitions through life

Growing up

When I was a child I used to get up to more tricks than I do now. I've grown up to be mature and I do sensible things.

My life used to be one of complete happiness as a child. I had wonderful parents who treated me in a sensible way.

Now that I'm grown up, I am interested in pop music and have written the words for songs. I like make-up and having a more outdoor life, seeing different places.

I would like to be a journalist and write about historical times.

Linda Collins: William Brinson Centre, London
(Handwritten)

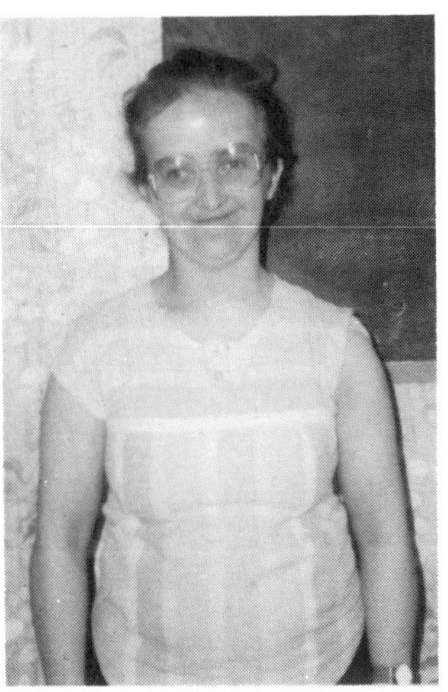

Helen Massey.

Growingrowing up

When I was a child I started school when I was only five years of age, and I had to leave when I was 15. Now I work in the William Brinson Centre in Arnold Road.

When I was little I used to have a doll. Now I have got two teddy bears: their names are Allen and Graham.

I started smoking when I was only 18. I still smoke now, and I am 32.

I used to have boyfriends when I was a child, and now I am an adult I still have boyfriends. I have got one now and his name is Graham. We are engaged to be married and we will be very happy then when that happens.

Helen Massey: William Brinson Centre, London
(Handwritten)

My life

The biggest change for me was the teachers in school, they spoke to you in a bad tempered way, they ordered you around, ~~but~~ but you can cope there but it was awkward because if you didn't come to school one day, they wanted a phone call, they hassled

The biggest change for me was the teachers. In school, they spoke to you in a bad-tempered way and they ordered you around. It was awkward because if you didn't come to school one day, they wanted a phone call, they hassled you. At college they know how to speak to you, how to treat you – more like an older student not a five year old kid, they talk to you calmly, they let you think.

In school I felt we were forced to leave, they were quick to make you take the next step. I wanted to stay there another year to have time to think about what I was going to do next. Maybe you want to do college but maybe I didn't.

But now I'm here, I am glad I came. I've done new things, different to school. There's lots of students here and they speak to you. In school I was bullied, sometimes called names like 'Pakki', but not in college.

In a way I think I'm treated differently because I've a learning difficulty. I am not a good reader, I can read easy words but not hard ones. Teachers in school made me feel like a twit; they would embarrass you in front of others if you couldn't do something. At college anyone can, if you've got a problem, ask for help, and then if they're busy they'll say, 'Can you wait a minute?' or 'Have you anything else to do?', and when they've finished they'll come and talk to you and then they help you. They don't do it for you, you do it yourself.

Teachers in school used to be serious, they never made a joke – but college is different; you have to work hard, you can sit and have a joke – I'm happy to come to college.

Shameem: Hammersmith and West London College
(Handwritten)

My life

I started when I first left junior school and went to secondary school. I made some friends. I found some of the maths and reading a bit hard but it did get better. It is better but it can get a bit hard still, especially my maths.

When I got elected I didn't know what to do. The students' union president organises all the meetings. I met some people who I never saw before so I got shy the first few times. Then I got to know most of them.

Rebecca: Hammersmith and West London College
(Handwritten)

How things have changed since we became adults

'My mum treats me like a grown up now.'

'When I was small, I'd play up if I wanted something. Now I've stopped, my mum has started to listen to me.'

'I go shopping on my own.'

'I travel on my own. I go to Dublin from London on my own now.'

'It feels nice to be grown up, but I miss being a child sometimes.'

'I used to do handstands on my bed, but I'm scared to do it now.'

'Since I've grown up, I've learnt a lot of new things.'

'I talk different, use different words. They don't boss you about so much.'

'When I was little, I took more interest in myself and had more confidence in myself. When you were a child you could have learnt more; now I'm older, I find it more difficult to learn things.'

'When you get older you get more wiser; you seem to know more things.'

'I can go out more on me own, and I can go and have pint of lager in clubs.'

'I used to go to church when I was a child. Now I don't.'

'A Chance to Speak' class: City Lit, London
(Transcribed extracts from discussion)

Living more independently

'If I move out of the hostel, I'm going to learn how to cook.'

'We did social training in the flat downstairs at the hostel before we moved out, and there we learned how to cook.'

'I had to start doing all those things after my dad died.'

'When we first went to visit the hostel, they didn't even ask me and my mum to look around.'

'I'd like to buy a flat if I had the money. Living on your own would be too quiet. But living with some friends, you don't know if you're independent as you'd have to share things.'

'It's all right if you know your money.'

'I liked living in the group home so I was disappointed at having to go back to the hostel when I lost my balance and had problems going out shopping.'

'I go to the hostel for a week's short-term care. It's slow but it's more easier. I've never lived away from home before so I'm still not sure, and I still get homesick.'

'It's harder for an older person to move away.'

'If you don't like where you are living, pack your bags and go!'

'Speaking for Ourselves' class: City Lit, London
(Transcribed extracts from discussion)

Making changes

My name is Lorraine Versey

My name is Lorraine Versey. I am 32 years old and am also blind. I was invited to go on a three-day course with two other friends and three members of staff. We spent the time talking about our lives and the sort of things that we would like to do in them. What was nice was that the staff were given the time to listen to and understand us. We drew up a plan for each of us, with five goals written for each. We told the staff what goals we wanted and they helped clarify them with us.

When we all got back to the centre, we were asked to say who we wanted to attend our planning meetings. I chose a friend of mine who lives in her own home, as well as two members of staff who went on the course and who would understand what I was saying. We meet in my friend's house. At the meetings we talk about the things that I would like to do, and sort out who are the best people to help me achieve them. We also decide who is coming to the next meeting and when we are going to hold it.

The meetings are better because there are only the people there that I want, they are held in a quiet place and they are looking forwards, *not* reviewing the past. Changes have happened much more quickly than when we used to have reviews. I have been invited to my friend's meeting to help her say what she wants.

As a result of my meetings I get out of the centre more, and meet people who are interesting. I also have started going to the theatre, amongst other things. These changes would not have taken place if the centre had carried on planning my life rather than listening to what I want to do.

Trainees' Committee

This started as a result of a request by me at one of my reviews. As staff had meetings I thought we should too. I got all the trainees together and asked them who should be on their committee, and we voted for them. We have Dave, a member of staff, to record our meetings and help clarify some issues that come up. I chair the meetings. We decide how to spend the money that is made from our Christmas play. We use it to buy everyday things such as a new stackable stereo and some LPs that are in the 'pop' charts. We also discuss things that affect our everyday life at the centre, such as getting the broken locks on the toilet doors repaired. We have found that the things we ask about do get done. We need to make staff aware of things.

Lorraine Versey: Rushmere ATC, Ipswich
(Dictated)

I have been living in a flat

I have been living in a flat with three other people at the hostel for nearly a year. Before that I lived at home with my mum. I used to worry about her a lot and I still do a lot. My mum lives in sheltered housing now very near me.

Since moving to the hostel I have learned to do my own washing and cooking. At first it seemed very strange living on my own but the staff helped me. My mum and I see each other a lot still. I like going to the cinema and to the coast.

I like the people I live with. I have made new friends. I travel on the buses on my own.

I would like to start looking for a job soon.

Les: A Social Education Centre in London
(Dictated)

My name is Doretta

My name is Doretta and I am 25 years old. Last year I decided that I wanted to have a home of my own so that I could have more freedom. My mother was quite ill when I made my decision so we could not really discuss what I wanted to do. Even now I am not sure how she feels about it.

I told my keyworker David that I wanted to leave home. He and my specialist social worker approached a Housing Association who were building new flats near me. We all had a meeting to see if they would allocate a flat to me. After a month I got a letter from them saying that they had accepted my application.

While I was waiting to move, I had support from a homemaker who helped me go and buy all the furniture and fittings for my new home. My keyworker and social worker also helped me buy various things for the flat.

I moved in on my birthday, with help from lots of friends. I was very excited, and nervous, to be in my own home at last. David came and put up my curtains and Jane, another friend, came to help straighten the place out. I then invited all my friends round for a good flat-warming party.

I now do all my own shopping. There is a good parade of shops near my home and I have got to know the shopkeepers well. I can also go out if I want to, we have a nice pub nearby where I can take friends for a meal and a drink. It is really nice cooking my own meals and looking after my own house, although cleaning is not too much fun!

I am very glad I decided to get my own flat. I control my own life and no one makes decisions for me. I am much happier now in my own home.

Doretta Adolphine: Wellington Centre, Ipswich
(Interpreted from signs and sounds)

My marriage to Margaret Denman

My marrige To margaret [illegible] Denman
I have Been married to margaret for about 7 mouths
I am very happy with my wife Becuse she is very kind
wife Becuse I love margaret I Got married
on the 19th september at Biggleswade at Reg. Offico
and it was a nice day there was a lot
of pepole came to the wedding Douglas was the
Best man we Got married at 11 oclock Debbie
Game and Jeff the sun was shineing when we came
out side margaret looked very nice on the day.

I have been married to Margaret for about seven months. I am very happy with my wife because she is a very kind wife. And because I love Margaret.

I got married on 19 September at Biggleswade Registry Office and it was a nice day. There was a lot of people came to the wedding. Douglas was the best man. We got married at 11 o'clock. Debbie came, and Jeff. The sun was shining when we came outside.

Margaret looked very nice on the day. When we went into the marriage rooms to be married I was very nervous... When I was putting the ring on Margaret's finger I was very nervous and shaking like mad.

Margaret had a nice white dress and white shoes. Her hair was very nice and cut. Margaret had flowers in her hair. Her dad brought her to the Registry Office in a nice red car. He had to give her away. Then Margaret had to put the ring on my finger. She was very nervous.

I was glad when it was all over, but when we got outside we had photos taken of us together under the tree. And then with my mum, my brother Dennis and my sister Lynn. Uncle John took them then we went to Nikki's Wine Bar for a wedding reception. We had a very nice dinner and then a disco. We then had a drink of wine. June took some photos of me and my wife outside. My friends came from the group home, they did enjoy themselves.

My father-in-law is a very nice man. He paid for the Wine Bar in Sandy. It is our first wedding anniversary on September 19th. We are going to have a party at Nikki's Wine Bar. We are going to do a list of people coming to our party.

David Marsh: Bedfordshire Special Adult Learning Programme, Biggleswade
(Handwritten)

Helping people who are moving out of hospital to find out what they want to do

'When I came out of hospital, there was nothing like City Lit. You need to get your confidence and nerve back. It's no good shouting at people, it makes them more nervous. Give them a lot of kindness, talking to them and making them feel they are wanted. Doing it without words for some people can be hard sometimes.'

'You need to get used to it and get to know people's names.'

'Moving back to London is very frightening at first – learning to get around by bus on your own.'

'Your brain is trying to think things out before you know what you want to say.'

'If you're not used to making choices, don't give too many choices all together. Take it slowly.'

'Ask the person what they do, what they need and what they would like to do.'

'Help them with drawing their money out of the bank.'

'Help people to keep in contact with people from the past, who they've known in the hospital.'

'If you've been in hospital for many years, you can't help some of the ways you are.'

'Speaking for Ourselves' class: City Lit, London
(Transcribed extracts from discussion)

Involuntary transitions

About my life

Mary Matthews.

I used to live with my parents in Westbury Park, Bristol. My dad used to work in the bank and my mum did the housework and cooking. I used to go to the Bush Training Centre.

My mum died, and my father sold the house and went into an old people's home at...I moved into 9, Priory Road, Clifton, another elderly people's home. I've been there eight years now.

I share a bedroom with a friend. We've got two beds, two lockers, two wardrobes and some chests of drawers. I do the drying up and putting away, and also lay the table.

In my spare time I do knitting, watch TV and go to a club on Monday nights. I like going out, sometimes just for a walk on my own. I come back and have my bath.

Mary Matthews: Lanercost Centre, Bristol
(Dictated as part of a reminiscence group project)

Helen Stewart's story

I was brought up from the age of five by my grandmother. She became ill and went into hospital. I was told by my family that I was going out for the night. I was brought to the hostel where I now live. I didn't know where I was going.

I went up to the hospital to see my grandmother, who was dying, by myself. My sister was very angry and told me I had no right to be there. I told her that it was my gran and that I wanted to see her. She had a drip and was very ill. I loved my gran. I think my family were trying to stop me from being upset.

I am happy in the hostel now and have friends there. I often visit my mother at weekends.

Helen Stewart: Thomas Fortune Work Centre, Glasgow
(Dictated)

When the building is finished

When the building is finished I'm going to live in the convent. That'll be two years. Sister's going to find me a bed and a wardrobe to put my luggage in.

I'm very pleased about it. I don't think I'll miss my mum and dad. I'll come back for weekends. I'll give it a try. I'll miss my little Yorkie. It's what mum and dad want. It's up to Sister, she's the head.

If I don't like it, I don't know what will happen. I don't want to stay at home – I sometimes get bored.

Carolyn Woods: Putney and Wandsworth AEI, London
(Dictated)

My brother has left

My brother has left home now. There is just me and my mum at home. I miss him. The house is quiet now.

Dawn: A Social Education Centre in London
(Dictated)

I live with my nanny

I live with my nanny. She has looked after me all my life. My parents died when I was small. I love her very much. Last year I was very worried because she had a bad leg.

I have been coming to the centre for a long time. There have been a lot of staff changes and new people.

I go for short stays at a hostel near the centre and I like them.

I think this book is a good idea because staff need to be trained.

Sally: A Social Education Centre in London
(Dictated)

Changes in my life

I went into St Lawrence's Hospital when I was small. It was horrible in there. Horrible grub and tatty clothes.

Viv got me out of there and I went into a group home. It was horrible. I didn't like it at all because there were too many rows.

I am in a flat on my own but I do not like it all that much. It is sheltered accommodation. I do not like it because Joan has arguments about me.

I would like to move to Chetwynd Road where my boyfriend is. My key workers are going to get together to see if they can find me a flat of my own. I am staying with Bill at Chetwynd Road tonight. My boyfriend is not well so I am going to make him a card.

Carol: Camden Institute, London
(Dictated)

Sadness

When my grandmother and grandfather died I was upset, and when my mum and dad died, I felt awful.

When my mum died she fell off the bed. I was in the bedroom with her; I thought she was gone then but she died on the Friday. I felt awful. I started to cry. I sat down and cried. The neighbours got her back into bed – I just sat down and cried. She fell off the bed on Thursday and she died Friday afternoon.

Mum had her hair net over her head as always and her white night-dress. My father took me downstairs – I was still upset. I was much too upset to do anything. My sister came and my brother-in-law, I think.

When night came I was laying in bed, I couldn't sleep. A neighbour was with mother but she was by herself when she died. I felt very awful. My mother was very good to me. I had good parents – mum and dad were very good.

Eleanor Mary Hearn: Portway Centre, Bristol
(Dictated)

Sad

My aunty is dead and my uncle too
They are buried
A long way away
In Wales.
I'm sad
I miss them
I've never been to the grave
I'd like to go
I would cry
I cry in bed
I miss them.

Pearl Chilcott: Portway Centre, Bristol
(Dictated)

Knocking down our home

May I, as a patient with many years spent in mental hospitals, express with absolute horror the very thought of being put into what is termed 'a community home'? What is going to happen when we suddenly find that the people we have gone to when we have problems and difficulties will not be around to advise and comfort us, and give us solace...?

Believe me, I have been on both sides of the fence when it comes to nursing. I have spent 35 years experiencing 'brutality at its worst' in Rampton, never knowing if I would ever be transferred...to a place where you would find a complete reversal. Here is a hospital of care and dedication. Just look around and you will see the nurses with a party of young people out for a stroll round the grounds of the hospital. Some will be confined to wheelchairs for the duration of their lives...

I am well known all over the hospital, and I meet and talk with everybody I can in the course of the day. With a joke or two with the higher hierarchy, even they are human. But I am more happier talking and entertaining the nurses and their patients when they come over to the 'Friendly Leaves Club', where I play the electric organ all day. I feel over the moon when they sing and dance to my music. I feel elated; I feel that I am making them happy and it makes me happy, believe me.

I was born during the First World War in 1916 when the Zeppelins bombed London. I was born during one of those raids and I contracted meningitis, which in turn gave me chorea or commonly known then as St Vitus Dance. I am pleased to say it seemed to leave me when I got older, in my late teens.

Having reached the age of nearly 70, I am well settled here. I am of informal status, which means I am able to discharge myself if I so wish. But I want to remain where I am. I have friends all around me. What more can you want in life?...

The world outside does not bother me any more. I have been indoctrinated through a system which destroys all freedom of thinking. I have spent most of my life incarcerated behind bars, high walls and locked doors for so long, that I do not feel secure if I am not behind them. I do not want too much freedom, just enough to let me know that I can come and go if I desire...

Bill Challis: Leavesden Hospital, Hertfordshire
(Extracts from self-typewritten account)

Lifetimes of change

Vera Stone.

When I was young

When I was 12 I used to live in Heber Street, next door to Mrs White. When she used to come to her door she was always scrunching sweets. She used to say: 'You can't have any – that's the last one I've got'.

I used to work at the Redlights factory at Dove Lane in Redfield. I used to dip the sparklers in some white stuff. After that we did Red Lights, which was something that went on the end of the sparklers. I did not like doing them. It was because I saw a man getting burnt in the Red Light room. His hair and his face were all burnt and blistered. I didn't feel very well after that and decided to leave the job. I told them, 'I'm not coming back no more', and I walked out. I went to the doctor and she put me on the 'panel' for shock – unfit for work.

They asked me to go back to the factory but I said, 'No way – I'm never going back'. So then I helped our mother with the cleaning at home. Dad couldn't do it because he had a heart attack and he was in bed. I was only 14 at the time.

I used to go to Whitehall School and left when I was 14. We used to have to stay in for school dinners. They were rotten – the meat was fatty. I used to take the food home in a bag and give it to the cat – she was in the coal house having the kittens. I was caught by the cook and she took me to the headmistress. She said: 'You ought to eat that yourself – you haven't got enough fat on you as it is'...

When my dad was bad in bed I looked after him – I took his food upstairs and gave him his medicine. When he needed to get up to go to the toilet I had to ask Graham, the next door neighbour, to help me get him out of bed. He was only 64 but he was very weak.

He used to go to Frenchay Hospital for heart tests until he fell out of bed. I tried to pick him up but I couldn't. I said to him, 'Why didn't you call out?' He said, 'I couldn't'. The doctor kept coming every day. When he fell down blood was coming out of his mouth. My mum told me I was not to mop it up, the nurse was to do it.

One day mum said, 'Go and see how dad's getting on'. There was a noise like a train in his throat, a rattling noise. Mum said, 'You better go and fetch Graham next door'. (This was in Whiteway Road.) Graham said, 'Get on the phone to Ray (my brother) – he's just passed away'. I went upstairs and saw him lying there dead and I was really shocked – I couldn't believe it.

Graham asked me to leave the room as they were going to lay him out and wash him. Then, later on, Ray said come and have a look at him, he's only asleep. I went and had a look. It was the first time I'd seen a dead person. I was only 12 at the time – still at school...

The funeral was at 11 o'clock at Arnos Vale. Only men went, no women, so I didn't go. I wanted to go, but they said there wasn't enough room. I was upset about that.

My mum had ulcers on her legs. So she went to Southmead Hospital. I went with her. The doctor said he would remove them off one leg, but that he would have to amputate the other one. But she died before they could operate. She died suddenly of thrombosis – she was in hospital and she fell off the trolley. The nurse picked her up. The nurse phoned and said, 'Your mother has just passed away'. I felt terrible. I thought she was going to get better – it was another shock.

I went to the funeral at Greenbank Cemetery. I was about 15 at the time. My brother Ray said he would look after me, but that if he couldn't I would have to go into a home. So I went to live with my brother up at Whiteway.

First of all we lived at Turner's Gardens, then the house got too much for me to look after, so then we moved up to Whiteway (my dad died there) and we stayed there ever since.

My brother got married at Easter four years ago. The wedding was at Lockleaze Church – I remember it was raining. Me, Joan and Marion (my two sisters) were bridesmaids. We wore mauve silk dresses, long ones and we had bouquets. We had the reception in a big hall up at Lockleaze. I enjoyed the day – it went off very nicely. We drank champagne.

Vera Stone: Lanercost Centre, Bristol
(Dictated as part of a reminiscence group project)

My father died

I like me classes at
adult education. I go a
"Speak for myself. "Cooking:
and "Lifestyles
We were waiting for a
bus and to walk a long .
way to peckham. I go
shopping by myself on Saturday
and do housework.

My father died when I was a new-born baby. And I went to Maudsley when I was 16. Then I went to Darenth Park. Then I came home to my mum until she died in an old people's home.

Now I'm in a nice flat. I do everything myself. I'll be on holiday soon with my sister Mary and Bill. I've got a lot of friends where I work at Crispin House. It's a day centre. We don't know what will happen to it but it's somewhere to go.

I like my classes at adult education and go to Speak for Myself, Cooking and Lifestyles.

I go shopping by myself on Saturday and do housework. In the evening I watch telly. I knit blankets. It doesn't take me very long. I knit quickly and then I look for someone to sew the pieces together. I can sew but I find it boring. I do not have a sewing machine and I would be frightened of using one.

Yesterday I went to see my friend Edward in an old people's home; Ada Salter in Crystal Palace. Edward went to Southend today. George is my friend. He sees me now and again.

Sarah Hunt: Southwark Adult Education Institute, London (Handwritten)

I was at a school for bad eyes

Rachel and Alex McLean.

Alex: *I was at a school for bad eyes. I left when I was 14 and then I got a job. I was there till I was 23. It wasn't much of a job so then I went on the Parish. It was the Parish in those days. Then I went to South Burgh Street until I came here. I don't know how many years ago that was.*

My dad was a tram driver. He was 27 years in it. My mother used to work when she was a girl at Rockhall. She was a spinner. I was born in 1925 and she didn't work after that. My father only died in 1983. I nursed him for six months. I've got two sisters though! My twin sister used to work in the shipyard, her man's a twin too. My older sister is down in England.

Rachel and I married in '83. David was there, he took the photos. Then we went to Wales for our honeymoon. We went twice! It was very good. I wouldn't go back to single now. She does all the work. I do some tidying, a wee bit.

Rachel: *My dad was a storeman. He was a small man, ever so nice. My mom used to work in a hosiery place. My sister's in East Kilbride. I've got a brother too. He was in the spastics at Hillington, he was a toilet cleaner.*

Alex: *I remember the war, when we were staying in the Drive and going in and out of the shelter all the time. The school got burnt. It got a land mine straight through the roof, people were killed. Do you remember the ration books? I used to go and get the messages for my mother. I would clean the house from one end to the other. It was linoleum in those days, not carpet. I wasn't in the Home Guard, I was grade 4 medical. It was bad eyes that did it. I had 14 operations on one eye and 16 on the other. That was the way I was affected as a twin. I wasn't getting properly fed, you see. I was 10 and a half years when I got it...*

Rachel: *My wedding was quite nice. It was a good day, a nice day. It was a scorching day! It was too warm. I was married in church. I had a green dress and a jacket and a pink hat. I've still got it.*

Alex: *A nice wee church...*

Rachel: *We had six come to the reception at Esquire House and we had a do here too.*

Alex: *I'm retiring in two years. When we retire we are going to go touring, touring Britain on a bus and sometimes a train. We'll go to Helensbugh! We are in a multi-storey, 17 up. The lift broke down on our first night. They break down a lot. Sometimes one is on. We like it there, we've got a view, lovely.*

Rachel and Alex McLean: Whiteinch Centre, Glasgow (Dictated)

George Mustard's story

I was born down Heddon in 1929 and when the war broke out, that was when I was 13, I shifted up to East Cross Street, that was up the town. I left school when I was 14. I started to work in the shipyard, and when I was working I had a fall and it made me take epileptic fits. After that, when I was 19, I went into Prudhoe Hospital and I was only supposed to be in there two weeks. I came out in 1985. I was in there 38 years.

At first, when I went in all the doors and everything was locked. I only used to get two pence ha'penny in pocket-money a week and could only spend it at the canteen, and if you didn't spend it the money went into the office...

The first job I got I was working in the gardens. I worked in the gardens 14 years. And later on I worked in the stores. If the stores had still been there I wouldn't have come out of Prudhoe. I loved working in the stores.

When I first went in, there were 89 lads in the home where I was. We used to go to bed at seven o'clock at night and we used to get up at six o'clock in the morning, and everybody used to have to bring their clothes down and put them on the seat where you used to sit. It wasn't ordinary tables where you sit now. It used to be like these work benches with forms round and everything. Couldn't pick and choose your own seat – you had to sit where you sat and were put. You had to sit there, and you had to eat what was put down to you, 'cos if you didn't you'd have to do without.

We used to get ready for to go out of the back. Everyone used to go out of the back door. Staff used to be there and they used to make sure you'd been shaved, hair combed, clean clothes and everything before you were let out.

When I first went in, it was like Durham jail. There was 25 lads in each dormitory and there were some beds on the landing and some downstairs. Used to sleep as though they were in rows. You got your clothes from hospital. You had one suit for Sunday and one for week days. The shoes wasn't like the shoes what you wear now. They were like these boots..like boot-shoes. You had boots, four of them...

(How did staff treat you?)

When I first went in, some of them used to be bad. If you were alright with them then they'd be alright with you, like. But if you were cheeky to them or the likes of that they wouldn't stand anything. They'd clip you as soon as look at you, when I first went in.

Lots of us used to always run away. Used to be blocks on the window 'cos the window just used to open small like. And many a time when we went up to bed on a night – there used to be two nightmen – some of the lads used to watch out while other lads used to be screwing the blocks off the window...Used to take the window frame right out, climb down out of the window and over to the tailor's shop, get a pair of trousers and a coat and run away. We haven't gotten very far some of us – some of us used to always get caught before we got to the top of the drive. We used to get put to bed for a fortnight – that was far better than getting up and going to work at six o'clock in them days...

Some of the lads, if they ever wanted a smoke, and if anyone was there giving you a smoke, you used to get wrong. You'd be put on punishment.

But later on there used to be dances at night. There used to be pictures of a Friday night, dances of a Tuesday night. We used to go dancing and the pictures. When we used to go to the dance, lads'd sit at one side, lasses at other side. Lads had to get up and take a partner. The lasses couldn't mix with the lads or anything like that. When they said take your partners for an old-fashioned waltz, or anything like that, the lads went up. Might have been another lad's girlfriend and he'd say, 'Canna have a dance?', and she'd say, 'Why, I'm waiting for someone else'....

Every first Saturday in the month was visiting day, that was when your people used to come to see you. Between July and August that was sports day. Used to have the sports on the field, racing and high jumps and all that stuff. And I used to always go on the high jump, and I used to always win. Just used to get a prize – there wasn't cups or anything like that in those days like what they do now.

Then I was shifted up to the Drive house. You had to look after yourself. Used to be the staff house at one time, but staff shifted out and it was made into houses for the patients what could look after their selves... There were five lads. We all used to put money: so much for the phone, so much for the rent. We had to cook our own food. We had our own washer and everything, and drier, TV and everything. The house where I was in had a video. I used to love the video...

When I first came on to the scheme, I worked at Bleechmere for 12 weeks, and used to go by bus. And after the three months was up they said, 'Would you like to go back or what would you rather do?' I said, 'I'm getting to know the staff' and I says I'd be upset if I was to go back, for all I liked to work in the stores. So Miss Miller, the social worker, she got us a full-time bus pass which I could use to travel and I just used to travel from Prudhoe every day, five days a week. I used to get to Newcastle for about quarter to eight and I used to go to get a bus from the park to Bleechmere. I had to do the same coming back. Sometimes it used to be nearly seven o'clock when I was getting into the house, and I had to start and make my tea...

After a time they said: 'What would you rather do? Would you rather wait to get a house or would you rather let us?' So I said I'd just keep travelling to Bleechmere. Then they got us put in here, Leechfield Hostel. I been in here 'cos the only time I used to see my people was on a visiting day, the first Saturday in the month. My father used to come and twice a year, Christmas and summer, I used to get a fortnight's holiday and used to come home and see them. I used to always go down my sister's down Halifax, Christmas and summer. I used to always come to Sunderland first to see my father and sisters. I got eight sisters and a brother. My father died when he was 81; I'd just come out of Prudhoe, two years gone January. My mother died in 1971. I was in Prudhoe. When they came and told us my mother had died it nearly broke my heart. My brother came and took us home to the funeral.

That's mostly why I came out. I see more of my sisters now... There's one of my sisters what lives in Pennywell. I go there on a Saturday for my tea and see her daughters and that. On a Sunday my sister what lives up Redhouse, I go there for my dinner and my tea.

(What did you feel like when you moved out of the hospital?)

Why at first I said I didn't want to go. I says I didn't know where to go 'cos I loved the hospital, I loved the house and everything...

Before I'd left Prudhoe I'd never took an epileptic fit for about three years. When I was to come out the doctor she says, 'When you go out we might as well put your tablets down'. But she did the wrong thing I think. When I came out I started taking fits again. When I was in Prudhoe I used to get my monthly supply myself. I used to take my bottle to the pharmacy and get the monthly supply, and when that was finished I just used to go and get a monthly supply again. When I came here I had a monthly supply and they said that I wasn't taking them, which was something I would never do. I know better than to refuse to take them. It was the doctor what changed them...

Last week or fortnight since, they sent for us 'cos they said they know I'd like to live out (*of the hostel*) and everything. She's put my name forward. It'll be about the end of August or beginning of September. There's another two lads and two lasses coming. They live in Prudhoe. They used to live in the private house. I know them very well. They're going to live in the same house. I said I wouldn't care whereabouts I went so long as I was out like. They're shifting me next two streets to where my sister lives, Pennywell...

(What do you think now about being in the hospital? How do you feel about it?)

Why, if it hadn't been for that I might have been married now...I've never got the chance to get what you call a nice girl, what's out there, 'cos there wasn't very many good ones in Prudhoe. There just used to be one or two, you know. I just used to go about by myself...It was the best place of the lot, living on the Drive.

George Mustard, Newcastle
(Extracts from tape transcript)

I was born 41 years ago

From time to time I meet or vist my sisters Jean and Agnes and my brother John. My Foster parents are getting old now and I still go to see them. They were

I was born 41 years ago in Hawkhead Hospital in Paisley.

There was nine children in my family. I have a twin brother and I also had twin sisters, but they died when they were babies.

When I was wee my parents didn't keep well and they couldn't look after my sister Jean and me. We were put into Chaple House nursery, then to bigger homes, and then we were fostered by Mr and Mrs Forbes.

Wilma Rhodes.

I went to school with Jean, in Paisley. After we left school Jean went to work in a factory. I went into Broadfield Hospital. When I lived there I used to help the nurses to look after the handicapped children in the nursery, and I also helped look after old people.

About three years ago I was discharged from hospital to live in a hostel. At first I found it difficult to settle because I missed my friends and helping the nurses.

Since last October I have been coming to Outreach. I learn how to do things for myself. I do voluntary work with a playgroup and in sheltered housing for old people. I also go to swimming and I have learned to play badminton.

From time to time I meet or visit my sisters, Jean and Agnes, and my brother John. My foster parents are getting old now and I still go to see them. They were good to my sister and me when we were children and they used to visit me in hospital. I don't have any contact with my other brothers or sisters.

In August I am going to spend a short holiday with my sister Jean. Jean lives in her own flat and she worked in an old people's home. If I had a job I would like to work with children. Although I like where I live just now I would like to live in a flat of my own, perhaps with someone to share it with me.

Wilma Rhodes: Strathclyde Outreach Project
(Handwritten)

Jackie's story

Life in the new flat

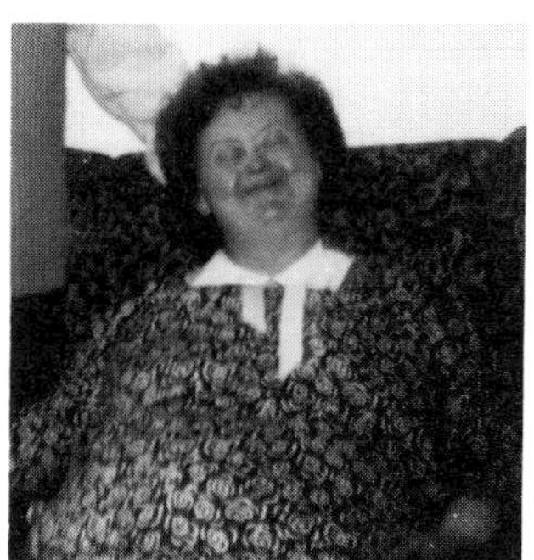

Jackie Heyworth.

Hello, I'm Jackalin Margaret Heyworth. I live with my own husband, Mr Heyworth Armstrong. I like to do stories of myself and my husband. I copy it up in books. I'm learning how to read and write at Longbenton High School College.

I like to do my housework. Sometimes Billy helps. I cook in my own slow cooker. I got it as a wedding present from the staff at the hospital...Cook mince and chicken. Do shopping on Thursday mornings...Go down the hypermarket, sometimes go down North Shields. I go in the car. Brenda takes us. She's a care worker. She just comes round to find out and tell you what to do. She helps me tidy up when she comes. She does all the money. I have a pension book. I pay all my stamps: my light stamps, my gas stamps, my rent and my TV stamps, telephone stamps...Then I have my recreation money. That's my pocket money. Pays for the centre. I got to give one pound fifty to the Cleveland Centre in North Shields.

Sometimes they fight in the centre. One person was playing war with me the other day when I came out earlier, when I came out about three o'clock. I was getting the bus to come here, and Eileen R came over to us. I'm a quiet person. I was annoyed.

Mrs D and Mr M are in charge at the centre. We do hospital jobs. You put needles into the tube, just bang them in. They put them in hospital, keep them alive. I get paid every Friday. I like my work.

Memories of earlier times

I was eight when I came here. I was born in 1947. I was born in Australia, over the sea, and I came here with my parents from Australia...with our John and our Harry and my nephews...and Peter and my sister-in-law.

I got a mam but she's abandoned me. Put me in the courts. My dad and mam split up. I was eight when they split up. It's all in my record book. My story's in my record book in the hospital. That's my story. It affected my speaking. When I get excited I'm stuttering too much. When I get excited I've got to cool down. Elsa M helps me with my Makaton and that's helped me.

The hospital was dreadful. My mam's got me in there. First I was in Ryton Hospital near Prudhoe. That's for the handicapped. I was nervous when I first been.

Billy was on E Villa and I was on B Villa. That's in Prudhoe in the hospital. I didn't like it. There was fighting everywhere, them patients. They'd be doing arguing. A person would tell them off. I used to have to go outside, until I calmed. I'd be sent outside. I'd have to calm myself. I got told off.

I went to my aunt's sometimes. I'd go for holidays and went back in again. My aunt's dead...when I was in Prudhoe. I was in a bad state. She was cremated. My dad told me. They asked us if I wanted to go but I said no. I didn't want to see everyone cry.

Sometimes I worked. It's like the centre. We'd do the Christmas tags, stringing them up.

Billy and a new life

When I met Billy I used to go for walks with him. I used to go down to see Billy. He was my boyfriend. I had him about 10 years. I helped him. He had trouble washing his clothes. We went down Prudhoe shopping together.

He asked us to marry him. He went down on his knees and he asked us, and I said yes. I was in the paper.

Jackie Heyworth: Newcastle
(Tape transcript)

Chapter Five
Creativity, imagination and fantasy

This chapter contains a collection of creative works from people with learning difficulties – stories, poems, drawings, paintings, a play, pottery, photographs – as well as people talking about their work. It also provides a bridge between the first four chapters which have been about aspects of personal identity, and the last four chapters which are about aspects of social identity.

People use their creative powers in different ways and for different reasons. For some it is an important, sometimes unavoidable, vehicle for self-expression, for the articulation of hopes, fears, fantasies, or an attempt to give order to an anarchic world. For others it is the expression of technical competence. Some people manage to combine both these aspects, and find the creative process agonising but worthwhile. Others, by contrast, simply find drawing, painting or pottery a relaxing and absorbing thing to do. If it turns out well, that is a bonus. These contributions reflect all these aspects: they have not been selected as necessarily the 'best' of their kind, nor in terms of the effort required to produce them, although some contributions are especially pleasing to the eye or ear, and some require additional information about the contributor to create the full impact of the achievement. It is clear that, for example, Sandy Marshall's poems (which also appear in other parts of the book) are an essential part of his expression of his inner feelings. When he read them out to the people he spends his days with at the centre, they were surprised that this man who kept himself to himself could produce such articulate ideas and feelings. It is clear also that Christopher Harman's drawings show a technical competence and an expert eye for shape and form. Howard Oldfield's pictures are unique and striking. When they were exhibited they were bought for the Calderdale permanent collection, much to the surprise of the workers in the hospital where he lives who admitted that his paintings were usually thrown in the dustbin. It is also clear from the account by the students at the Downlands Day Centre that working with clay and colours is just enjoyable in itself.

What these contributions also represent, perhaps more so than in other chapters, are the very positive and enabling interventions of their tutors. Several art/crafts/design tutors spoke or wrote to us about the important challenge that working with people with learning difficulties has given them. Not a challenge in the sense of achieving the unachievable, but in terms of rethinking what art and creativity are about, what constitutes 'good' art, and what makes for creative work. One tutor, Hilary Dyter, said she liked to think of creativity in its widest possible context, not only in terms of creating paintings and poetry. She described it in different ways: as an attempt to 'capture some of the world's beauty'; and as a way of 'people finding their way back to themselves'. In so far as the following contributions represent examples of self-expression then they echo some of the observations made in Chapter One on self and identity. They are a testimony to the human spirit's will to survive.

Although many of us may have our imagination and our capacity to fantasise influenced or dulled by the routines and pressures of formal schooling and paid work, nevertheless these are areas of the mind which are our own and, relatively speaking, beyond the total control of the outside world.

Hilary Dyter sees this capacity of the human spirit to survive in the work of one of her students, Alan Williamson (see colour plates): 'He is a person whose enthusiasm for life is all-consuming and yet he's had no contact with his family from an early age, has been in one of the institutions...in the north of England for most of his life. Also his refusal to give in and give up has nothing to do with having worked out a *raison d'etre*. He can't read or hear or discuss. When he approaches a blank canvas, he approaches it naked, as it were. No preconceptions, nothing'.

Similarly, another contributor, Andrew Hoyle from Devon, conveys in his wonderful picture of *Geese* a capacity to observe and enjoy the world around him, even though in his everyday life he will only speak to a very, very small, selected number of people.

Another tutor, Gail O'Farrell, who teaches at Camden Adult Education Institute, wrote to us: 'Another reason we find creative work particularly valuable for our students is that there is no "right" way to do it, and therefore it does not set up the same range of anxieties about "getting it right" that more formal work does. For someone who is accustomed to failing, this can be a great relief. And again this release can then allow for more substantial activity and learning to follow'.

Two poems are from a small booklet of poetry written by students at the Lanercost Centre in Bristol. The centre describes its aims as helping 'people with learning difficulties to learn the day-to-day skills necessary to live in our world. High among these skills is the ability to express ideas and feelings. We established a Poetry Workshop to help people to do that'.

These skills are not skills in the ordinary sense of the word, but, to quote Hilary Dyter again, 'a question of allowing the inner confidence to develop by not making value judgements'. Such a view is contentious, for it challenges the notion that there is 'good' art, except in so far as it has the capacity to move us. She continues: 'I've worked with all sorts of people, mainly art and creative writing and have never yet failed to find a response. I was very excited when I first realised that this was also true of people labelled mentally handicapped. There was Susan in one of my early classes. Completely self-contained, she was a manic knitter and crocheter. One day she showed me some remarkable work she'd done. It was a piece of crochet. Seemingly, at first glance, formless. There was no way it was going to be a garment. But in fact it was a series of intricate triangles. I got her to do some drawing and what she produced was strongly like South American Indian work. Double outlines around all the figures. An art therapist would probably make something else of it, but I was overcome by the way she'd spanned centuries and continents without any conscious knowledge of what she was doing. This is why I can't take art movements seriously'.

Lack of space prevents us from presenting any more than one-half of the pieces we could have included in this chapter.

Contents

Tile Mural Garden *(June Williams, David Flanders, Keith Porter, Peter Millins, Janet Strutt, Shirley Doolan, William Brinson Centre).*

Pottery Plaque *(Janet Strutt, William Brinson Centre).*

Coiled Vase *(Christopher Harman, Tower Hamlets AEI).*

Castle *(Christopher Harman, Tower Hamlets AEI).*

Plate Design *(Christopher Harman, Tower Hamlets AEI).*

Geese *(Andrew Hoyle).*

'INSIDE OUTSIDE'

An Exhibition of work by local artists, many of whom are seen by others as outsiders but who do not see themselves in this light.

"I don't see myself as being on the outside of anything, more like in the centre of things really."
FRAZER BARTLETT

PIECE HALL ART GALLERY, HALIFAX
30th JULY – 28th AUGUST 1988

Open daily 10.00 am – 6.00 pm
Admission Free

The following pictures were taken at an exhibition called 'Inside Outside', held at Piece Hall Art Gallery, Halifax, August 1988.

Objects *(Felt tip. Howard Oldfield, Stansfield View Hospital, Todmorden, Yorkshire).*

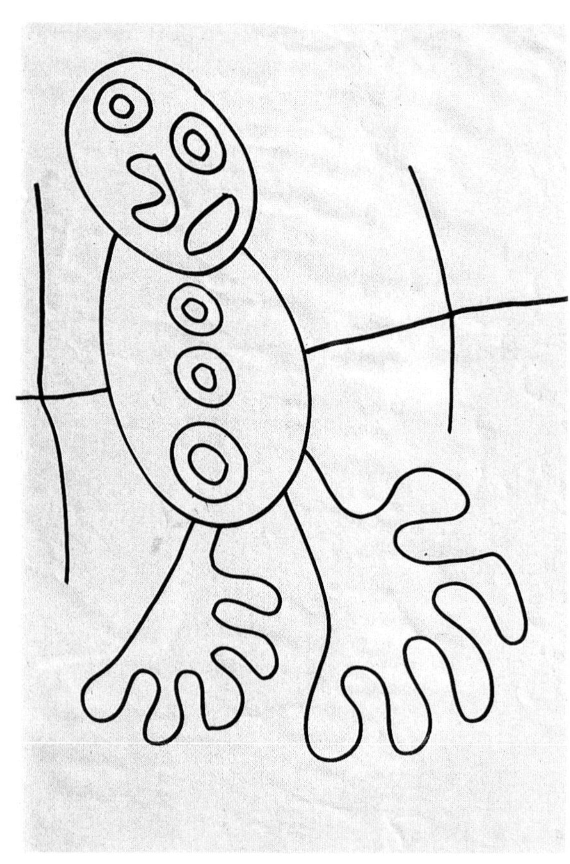

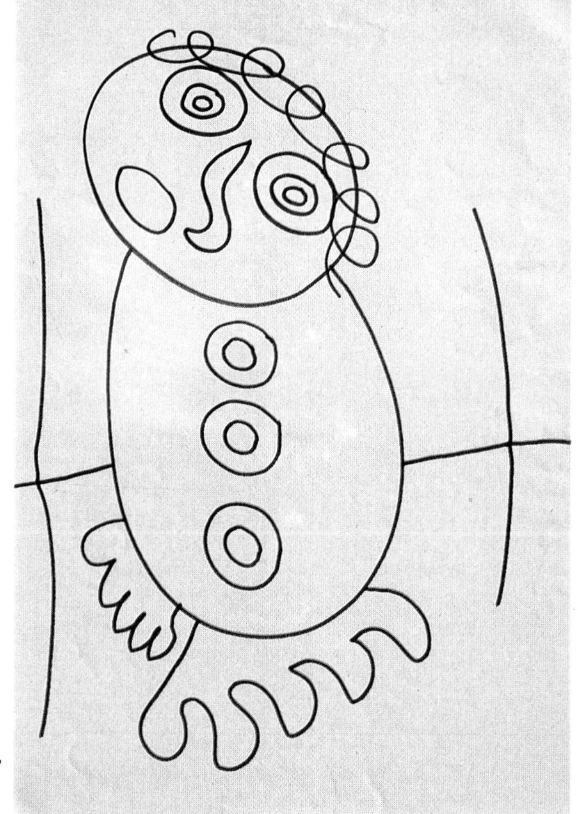

Person 1 *and* Person 2 *(Felt tip. Howard Oldfield, Stansfield View Hospital, Todmorden, Yorkshire).*

Coal Mining *(Oil paint. Brian Suthers, Hebden Bridge ATC).*
'I have been doing drawing and painting for a long time. This is my first exhibition. I like art. My drawings are on the Worth Valley Railway and others are on mining of coal into the trucks, and a picture of Windermere in the Lake District.' (Brian Suthers)

Shapes 1 *and* Shapes 2 *(Screen print. Sylvia Calvert, Queen's Road Centre, Halifax).*
'I like painting. Art is colours. I do colouring at home'. (Sylvia Calvert)

razer Bartlett (Queen's Road Centre, Halifax) standing by his Picture of Duncan *(Poster paint).*

Still Life *(Poster paint. Duncan Wadsworth, Queen's Road Centre, Halifax).*
'I've done paintings of scenes, flowers, patterns and of a bowl of fruit in it. It's alright working with oil paint. I like it the best. I like experimenting with paint like when I squeezed the paint on to paper and made a pattern. Then I flattened it down onto the canvas lots of times. Then I filled it in with pink background paint.' (Duncan Wadsworth)

Chris Herring Looking through a Sculpture *(Poster paint. Frazer Bartlett, Queen's Road Centre, Halifax).*

(Top) King Kong *(Felt tip).*
(Bottom) Hop-a-long Cassidy *(Felt tip).*
(Ronnie Gaukrodger, Queen's Road Centre, Halifax.)

'I'm not angry' *(Oil on canvas. Frazer Bartlett, Queen's Road Centre, Halifax). 'I've always liked painting. My paintings are either what catches my imagination or what it could be about.' (Frazer Bartlett)*

(Top) Tree
(Bottom) Abstract *(Acrylic on canvas).*
(Roy Brett, Stansfield View Hospital, Todmorden.)

Duncan Wadsworth (Queen's Road Centre, Halifax) standing by, from left to right: Abstract *(Oil paint. Duncan Wadsworth); (top)* Visit to a Sculpture Exhibition *(Oil paint. Duncan Wadsworth); (bottom)* Amaryllis *(Oil paint. Duncan Wadsworth);* Print *(Kevin Poppleton, Calder College, Todmorden);* Collage *(Print, collage and melton crayon. Betty Ambler, Queen's Road Centre, Halifax).*

Self-portrait *(Oil paint. Alan Williamson, Queen's Road Centre, Halifax).*

Haworth Station *(Oil paint, Brian Suthers. Hebden Bridge ATC).*

Still Life with Fruit
(Oil on canvas. Duncan Wadsworth, Queen's Road Centre, Halifax).

My dream

My story is about my dream.

There were people talking. It's when I was a boy. I was 28 – a man then. I was thinking in my bedroom. My eyes were looking around and seeing the pictures and colours on the walls – grey, blue. The mat was blue and orange. The colour of the door – blue. Green curtains, green TV. I dreamt about myself...getting out of bed. My gran's in it. I got up, went downstairs to get a drink. I went back and went to the toilet. Then back to bed. I went to my mum who was asleep – I woke her up to say 'hello'.

My gran's walking with her stick. She's got a bad leg. She said: 'What are you doing up and in the toilet – get back to bed'.

I could see my gran in the moon. 'I can see you in the moon.' I pray to her. Me and my mum take flowers to her grave.

A lot of stars come out at night from my room.

It's the TV that makes me frightened. It wakes me up.

I remember going shopping with my gran. She liked going in cake shops and paper shops. We went down the cafe. I had sausage, egg and beans, with coke to drink. She had chips and beans, with a cup of tea. The cafe was in Broadmead. She liked knitting shops. They are full of different colours. She knitted tops, jumpers.

Brian Holley: Lanercost Centre, Bristol
(Dictated)

Nature is wonderful

Nature is wonderful in providing pleasures
For girls and boys to enjoy;
And which some may look upon as treasures -
Since they may not get the chance
To get out often - even to dance.

When you are in the countryside
You can sometimes see the clear blue sky
Reflected in the rivers and lochs;
Like looking through a looking-glass.

Sandy Marshall: Thomas Fortune Centre, Glasgow
(Self-typed)

Trees *(Christopher Harman)*

Murder, mystery and suspense

SCENE: 44 LEWISHAM ROAD, LONDON SE13

CAST: Narrator
The wife: Pam
The husband: Patrick
The policeman: David
The robber: Andrew
Friend: Jane

INTRODUCTION

NARRATOR: It's 5 p.m. outside Pam and Patrick's flat.

ENTER PATRICK AND PAM (CARRYING SHOPPING BAGS)

THERE IS A LOUD NOISE AS
THE FRONT DOOR IS KICKeD in
PAM: HeLP! iF You don't get
out, I'll Phone the POLice.
THE MURDERER STABs PAM with
A KNIFE AND KiLLs her

PATRICK *TO PAM:* 'I've lost my key.'

PAM: 'How've you lost your key? It could be in your bedroom somewhere. Lucky I've got a spare key.'

PAM UNLOCKS THE DOOR AND THEY GO INSIDE. THEY PUT THE FOOD AWAY IN THE CUPBOARD. THEN THERE IS A RING AT THE DOOR? IT IS JANE

PAM: 'Come in, do you want a cup of tea?'

JANE: 'Yes, please.'

THEY HAVE TEA AND THE DOORBELL RINGS

PATRICK: 'Someone's at the door!'

PAM GOES TO ANSWER THE DOOR

THERE IS A LOUD NOISE AS THE FRONT DOOR IS KICKED IN

PAM: 'Help! If you don't get out, I'll phone the police.'

THE MURDERER STABS PAM WITH A KNIFE AND KILLS HER. JANE GRABS HIS WRIST HARD. JANE STRUGGLES WITH THE MURDERER AND GETS THE KNIFE OFF HIM. HE FIGHTS BACK AND GETS THE KNIFE AGAIN. THE STRUGGLE CONTINUES. PATRICK RUNS TO THE TELEPHONE AND DIALS 999.

PATRICK: 'Police! Hurry! Come to 44 Lewisham Road straight away. My wife's been killed. The killer is still here and trying to kill everyone else too. I can't stop him.'

THE POLICE ARRIVE ALMOST IMMEDIATELY

ENTER POLICEMAN

DAVID: *(Grabs murderer by the arm.)* 'I arrest you in the name of the law. You're charged with murder and attempted murder.'

(TAKES THE MURDERER AWAY, STILL STRUGGLING)

Andrew Mackintosh and David Peters: Ravensbourne Adult Education Institute, ILEA
(Self-written)

Our holiday

One day we decided to go on a trip to the sun. Bernadette suggested that we go to Barbados. Lily thought Jamaica or Spain would be a good idea. Africa is what appealed to Valerie. Mary suggested Italy.

Though all of these places sounded nice, we decided that Africa would be the most exciting. We went to a travel agent in Camden Town to book our tickets. We met John, the travel agent, and he explained everything to us about the trip. Then of course we had to pay our money. But fortunately we had a lot of this because Bernadette had found a sack of gold during a treasure hunt.

Everyone went home to pack their things. Bernadette packed a sun hat and sun glasses, and she also remembered to bring a bedtime story. Lily sorted out her summer dresses and shorts. Valerie packed a bikini and her drawing materials, her pencils, paints, and a drawing pad. Mary remembered at the last minute to bring the sun tan lotion so that her skin wouldn't burn.

We all met at Heathrow Airport an hour before the plane left. Just as we were about to board the plane, Martin came running up to us, clothes flying out of his suitcase. He'd just been to Ireland with his parents and rushed back to Heathrow so that he wouldn't miss the trip with us. We were all glad to see him. We showed the stewardess our tickets and got on the plane. Now we were all set to go.

Soon after our departure we heard some banging on the top of the plane. When we looked out the windows we discovered that there were some apes trying to get into the plane. They looked more frightened of us than we were of them. We quickly let them into the plane, and they told us their story.

They were originally from Africa but had been captured and brought to England. They had been put into Regent's Park zoo. They didn't really like the zoo at all and missed the sunshine and the jungle. When they heard about our plane they decided to try to hitch a lift home. Once inside the plane, they had a good scratch and settled down to sleep.

Finally, we landed in Africa. The monkeys celebrated their homecoming with a tea-break. Except instead of tea, which they never liked anyway (it was an English drink), they had coconut wine and banana milkshakes. Then they hitchhiked back to their real home, the jungle, happy to be there at last.

We all decided to go and stay in a hotel in the city. The name of the hotel was the Shakers Hotel, and we are going to get really shaken up there.

We met in the cocktail bar and ordered some drinks. Bernadette ordered a pineapple daiquari; Lily had an orange fizz; Martin had an ape's brew, and Valerie had a pineapple and orange Bacardi.

Now we were really relaxed and we sat back to watch our first African sunset. However, Martin enjoyed himself so much with his monkey's brew that in the end we had to carry him back to his hotel room where he fell quickly asleep on his bed.

Martin Brennan.

The following morning we went to Martin's room to see how he was feeling. Only, Martin wasn't there! His bed was empty, but then on his pillow we see a note. It says (and I quote):

> 'Beware of monkeys. Beware of apes.
> Don't get any closer to Martin.
> We've taken him to be our leader.'

They had taken Martin up to the roof. We could tell because they'd dropped his clothes along the way. Then down the fire escape, and off to the jungle. But what they didn't know was that Martin had dropped banana skins along the path so that we could tell where he was going.

We followed the skins through the jungle. When we got nearer to Martin, we heard the monkeys chattering, and we could hear one unusual monkey chattering as well. As we got closer, we could see that it was Martin. It turned out that the monkeys had cut his brain, and now he felt just like a monkey too. He told us that he wanted to stay in the jungle with his new friends. Even so, they have put him in a cage to make sure that he stays.

We decided that we must make a plan to rescue Martin. Lily suggested that we dress up like monkeys in order to get to the cage and take Martin out. We found some monkey costumes and put them on. Then we mingle with the other monkeys, but they don't notice us. When we get to the cage, we find that the key is in the lock and we let Martin out.

We found the place where the monkeys had put Martin's brain and we sew it back into his head.

Now we want to go back to the hotel, but how can we find the way? Bernadette says that we can follow the banana skins back. It's getting dark and we hear strange noises. We can hear water rushing by. We know that we are near a waterfall. Then we hear hyenas howling at the moon, and not far away a wolf is howling too. We've been carrying Martin for quite a while and he's getting very heavy. We decide to put him in the water to wake him up. It does the trick!

'Ow!', says Martin, scratching his head. Lily has just thrown a bucket of water over him. He looks around – he's in his hotel room. The whole thing has just been a nightmare. He hasn't been to the jungle at all. Martin swears he'll never drink ape's brew again!

Martin Brennan, Valerie Cookson, Lily Husson, Bernadette Browne:
Camden Adult Education Institute
'The students write when they feel at home and trusted to be themselves. Basically we allow the writing to happen with the assistance of art, fairytales, pictures, and lots of jokes.'

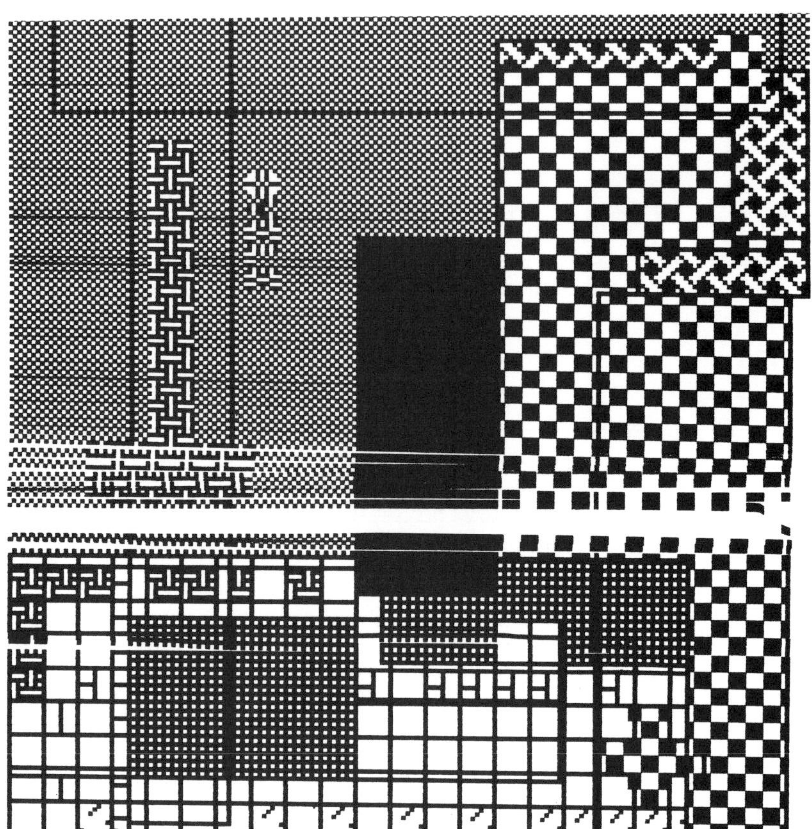

Pattern *(Dele Fakoya, Seltec, Lewisham. Drawn on a computer).*

House *(Terry Hobbs, Seltec, Lewisham. Drawn on a computer).*

In the countryside

When we take a walk in the countryside,
We are seeing things
Which are our National Pride,
Like birds flying in the sky -
And trees which lift their heads
Till they seem to touch the clouds
With brooks running by
On their way to rivers or the sea
Where children camp
And also a garden where a clump of roses
Grow, along with woodland flowers
And where you might see children enjoying tea.

And when we go to the sea,
There are some children paddling in the water
Looking for shells to take back
For their collection;
While other children might be eating.

Sandy Marshall: Thomas Fortune Centre, Glasgow
(Self-typed)

A Panmure St. Secondary School girl

A Panmure St. Secondary School girl waved
When we were parked
In Dundee at the shops -
And she staved
Off the hunger I felt going without Mary
Till I got home again.

Sandy Marshall: Thomas Fortune Centre, Glasgow
(Self-typed)

Africa

Buses blown to pieces
By bombs, cannons.
People dressed up
As soldiers
The people be dead
No food
No water
Too hot
Hot wind
Horrible
The sun
The moon
Clothes, jelabir
Cool you down
WATER.

Elephants
Cows, oxen, goats, donkeys
Market – shops,
Open-air markets
Fruit, water-melons
Big green.
Sheet-coats
Brown, beige, dirty
Orange, pink saris
Purple, jelabir.
Some people carrying
Baskets on top of
Their heads;
Full of food.
Donkeys carried
Two sacks of food,
They were going to market:
Water melons,
Dead cow, dead camel.

Christmas

Starving people, they've got no food,
No clothes, you can't make beds,
Sleep on the floor.
They've got no food, starving,
No plates or bowls.

'I'm going out to a disco tonight,'
You're lucky, Mary.

Don't use knives and forks,
Use fingers to eat.
Have turbans, carry baskets
On top of their heads.

Houses look like straw,
We have water.
Christmas, they don't have Christmas.
Some black here, some black there,
Some white everywhere.

We have presents
Be disappointed if they didn't come:
They be more than disappointed
When rain doesn't come.

Christmas cake,
Cut it in slices,
Take it all round:
Share it.

Old pots, a lot of money
And clothes.
Send them to the people:
Oxfam, Barnardo's.
Charities.

Group poems: Poetry Workshop, Lanercost Centre
'We first work as one group, talking about our experiences and ideas. We use a variety of materials to stimulate our minds: pictures, sounds, role-play, other people's poems. Then we move into small teams to think and talk in more detail and, we hope, to write down some of our thoughts.'

Hurricane

Howling wind
Up in the air
Rainstorm and lightning
Rattling the doors
It was frightening
Candles alight
At night
No electricity
Everywhere trees cra
s
h
i
n
g
by everyone.

Tuesday Reading and Writing class: Tower Hamlets Gateway Club.
(Group composition, dictated)

Lanercost Centre Camera Club: Three black-and-white photographs.

Kathleen O'Grady.

Lost someone

Lost someone
Sad and crying
Upset
Feeling horrible
Lonely
Shock
Mind wanders
Mourning
Take the hurt away
Have a cuddle, it helps

Irene Arbon, Kathleen O'Grady, Barbara Peters, Carlos Tunberg: Putney and Wandsworth AEI. (Impressions of a photograph were written down and then the group put some of these together to make the poem)

He's not telling his name

This is a Story a bout Someone
Life ahead of him

he is not telling his NAME The Story
Start with there were a boy He
was very Sad He was miss someone
He love very much He wished He was
marred He would be very happy then

This is a story about someone with life ahead of him, he is not telling his name. The story start with, there were a boy. He was very sad. He was missing someone he love very much. He wished he was married. He would be very happy then.

He could not do things we can do, like he cannot wash his clothes and clean his self. He can do other things. He can cook and wash dishes. He likes going places and this is the end of this story. That's all he wants to say.

Yourfully

?

PS This boy would buy a car to work but he need to go for the driver test. It would not work.

Sandy Gibson: Thomas Fortune Centre, Glasgow
(Self-written)

'I made pots...

'My name is Alison. Hairdresser lady, curlers in her hair. Did like it. Pictures, draw pictures.'

Alison.

Mark Siddle.

'My name's Mark. We built a garage, we've built a Post Office, all different things we've built, and the car wash, fire station. We made it in pottery originally, at Challney. We thought of the ideas, we did. We were doing a village and we were also putting on displays at Luton Central Library.'

I made pots and I made loads more pots, small pots and more pots and more pots and more pots and more pots. Loads of pots I made, for my mum, my sister. Made some pots for my Aunt and my other sister, that's all I made.' ***Alan Tyrell.***

Alison Cope, Mark Siddle and Alan Tyrell: Downlands Day Centre, Luton
(Their words were transcribed at Challney Community College where they attend an art/craft session to make pottery and talk about themselves. The students at the session have exhibited at Luton Central Library)

Cemeteries

Some people may think cemeteries are gruesome
Places to go - with their head-stones -
But I think some of the inscriptions
Are nice, and have a bit of spice
About them

Sandy Marshall: Thomas Fortune Centre, Glasgow
(Self-typed)

Chapter Six
My daily life

The first four chapters of this book focused on aspects of self and personal identity. The following four chapters shift that focus away from the personal towards issues of *social* identity and the social lives of people with learning difficulties.

This chapter has been divided into four sections: my life, my day; home; work; and leisure. As a whole, the chapter contains comments and descriptions of the ordinary day – getting up, going shopping, doing housework, going to the centre, going to work, going out in the evening or at weekends. The first section – *my life, my day* – underlines some of these ordinary, undramatic and mundane experiences. At the same time, the ordinariness of some of the contents of the shorter contributions possibly hides the effort that went into producing them. 'I go shopping', for example, was originally written on to a word-processor by Christine Purton, a young woman with Down's Syndrome who is just learning to write.

The second section focuses on *home*. Many of the descriptions here reiterate the themes of transition from home to hospital, to children's home, hostel, or to independent living which were explored in Chapter Four. Other accounts tell of the strains of hostel-living, when residents 'poke their noses into your business' (Fiona Baird). Some contributors are able to look forward to, or rejoice in, their independent living, whilst others feel such a move is beyond them.

The third section in on *work*. To distinguish between home and work in this section and the previous one is, in some ways, misleading, for it underestimates the amount of domestic work that is carried out in the home. What struck us time and again in reading these contributions was the extent to which women with learning difficulties, whilst on the one hand, explicitly or implicitly, denied the expectations of having and rearing their own children, are nevertheless expected to do the housework and generally care for family members. It is interesting to compare Ronnie's life story in Chapter Nine where he is looked after by his sister, and Vera Stone's story in Chapter Four where she goes to live with her brother on the basis of looking after the house. (The confinement of women to the private sphere of the home is something which is challenged by women in Chapter Eight.)

Historically, in the 'mental deficiency colonies' – hospitals, homes and other residential institutions – the domestic work of the women residents was actually essential to the maintenance of the institution, and it is not surprising to find these institutions were reluctant to let the more able women residents move back into the outside world, or into work outside the institution. Often, too, as the excerpts which begin this section show, this was *unpaid* labour (see also the oral history by Potts and Fido, 1990).

What also emerges from this section is the contradictory experiences of work. On the one hand, boring, repetitive and badly exploitative, reinforcing the levels of poverty at which many people with learning difficulties already live on state benefits. Sometimes, it would seem that the contributors are not simply learning to follow 'ordinary lives' but learning to survive. In a series of discussions on life that are not included in this chapter, one person with learning difficulties commented: 'If you've been on the dole for six months, you learn how to survive'. On the other hand, many people take pride in their work and their skills, see them as an important route to psychological if not financial independence, and feel themselves capable of undertaking more skills and more responsible work.

The last section – *leisure* – contains vignettes of relaxation and fun: an amusing incident on holiday, a wedding, a play, an obsession for football, a visit to the library, having coffee out. But it also contains feelings of resentment at the threatening nature of pubs and clubs and going out after dark. This is an aspect of life reinforced later in the book (in Chapter Eight) by a group of women with learning difficulties.

Contents

My life, my day

A day in the life of Donald Lack

Donald Lack.

A DAY in my LIFe. DONALD LACK
I Get up at 6.30. I dont have breakFAST.
Make my bed. BRUSH my teeth I comb my
hair, put my aftershave on – IF I have
time Left-I sit on bed and DO my
cROSSWORD till 7.30 when-I go up to the
Bus STOP–I take two buses to get to
work-I come to the centre and same OF
my PALS come to speak to me until –
its timie to get marked in - I do gardening
up till dinnertime and play pool in the
dinner how and then I sat a waited FOR
Next CLASS to come in Its better to be
here it the centre-than on the streets
When I get home sometimes-I have a
SLeep if Im tired. I wake up put-
My SLIPPERS on and-I go though to the
KITChen to make my Tea and I eat it-
in the kitchen, I have onion Rings, —
potato-cROQuettes and 4 pork Turkey
sausages and 2 Rolls That I put in the
oven I had my IRON BRU, After tea
-I Left my dishes to soak + and did them
Later. I went to WATCH the TV - I

I get up at 6.30. I don't have breakfast. Make my bed. Brush my teeth, I comb my hair, put my aftershave on – if I have time left I sit on the bed and do my crossword till 7.30 when I go up to the bus stop. I take two buses to get to work.

I come to the centre and some of my pals come to speak to me until it's time to get marked in. I do gardening up till dinner-time and play pool in the dinner hour, and then I sit and wait for next class to come in. It's better to be here at the centre than on the streets.

When I get home, sometimes I have a sleep if I'm tired. I wake up, put my slippers on and I go through to the kitchen to make my tea and I eat it in the kitchen. I have onion rings, potato croquettes, and four pork turkey sausages and two rolls that I put in the oven. I have my 'iron brew'. After tea I leave my dishes to soak and do them later. I go to watch the TV. I watch *Celebrity Golf, I Take the High Road, Auf Wiedersehen Pet* and then *Brush Strokes.* After that I go to my bed. Finish my juice. I put the light out and go to sleep; five days a week I eat, sleep and work. It's not bad.

Donald Lack: St Clair Centre, Kirkcaldy
(Self-written)

Sarah McGreevy,
Portway Centre, Bristol.

Sarah McGreey's day.

WEDNESDAY 20th APRIL 1988

We watched breakfast time on television and I went to sit down on the settee.

This is the fire – we didn't put it on but I was cold.

This is the sitting room

This is the wardrobe

This is the bathroom.

This is the record player

This is my bedroom.

My dad woke me up this morning with a cup of tea. He said its time to get up for breakfast and he kissed me. I got dressed in my bedroom. I put my jeans on.

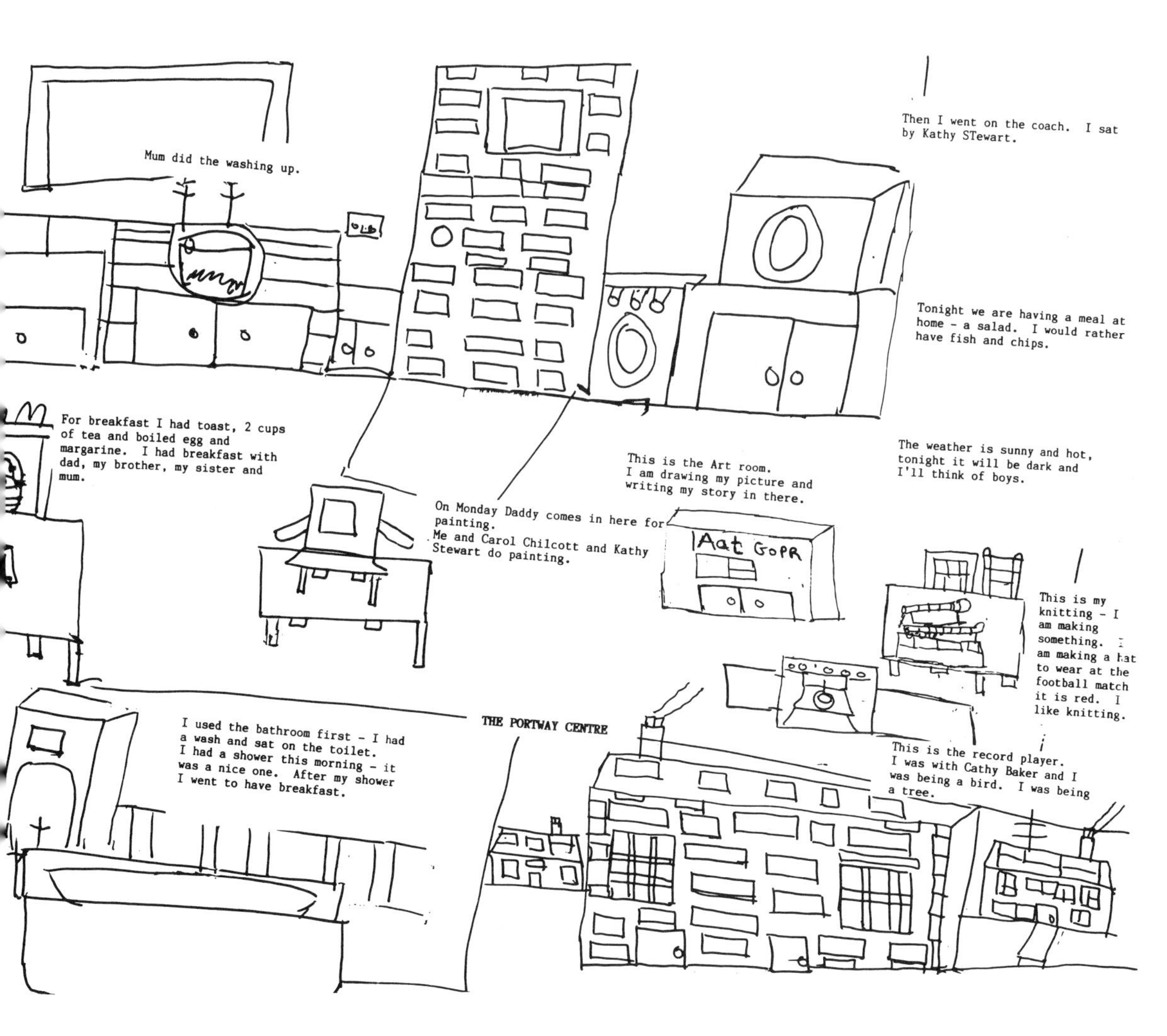
Mum did the washing up.
Then I went on the coach. I sat by Kathy STewart.
Tonight we are having a meal at home - a salad. I would rather have fish and chips.
For breakfast I had toast, 2 cups of tea and boiled egg and margarine. I had breakfast with dad, my brother, my sister and mum.
This is the Art room. I am drawing my picture and writing my story in there.
The weather is sunny and hot, tonight it will be dark and I'll think of boys.
On Monday Daddy comes in here for painting. Me and Carol Chilcott and Kathy Stewart do painting.
Aat GoPR
This is my knitting - I am making something. I am making a hat to wear at the football match it is red. I like knitting.
I used the bathroom first - I had a wash and sat on the toilet. I had a shower this morning - it was a nice one. After my shower I went to have breakfast.
THE PORTWAY CENTRE
This is the record player. I was with Cathy Baker and I was being a bird. I was being a tree.

Our lives

I will be 28 on the 4th May. It is a Wednesday this year. I live with my auntie and my uncle. My grandma lives on the ground floor. My auntie is on sixth floor.

My uncle goes to the hospital today about his leg. He has a pain in his leg. It is my auntie's birthday on Saturday. She is going to be 54. My mother died in February 1984. Her birthday was on 2nd October. She died on 15th February. I went to the funeral on February 27th. Then I went to live with my auntie and uncle.

I am going to Applejacks tomorrow. I go two days a week now. Tuesdays and Thursday. I get tips on Tuesday. I do cooking first. I cook tomato soup and things on the menu. The customers pay for meals there. Customers leave tips on the table and I collect them up. I put it in the tray next to the till. On Thursday I get wages. I get 80p a week.

On Fridays I go to Godwin Court. I had a birthday party there.

Cyril Bell: Camden Institute
(Dictated)

Robert Drysdale.

A day in my life

I get up at 6.30. I have my breakfast at 7.00 – cereal, fried egg on toast and make a pot of tea. I take it in the kitchen. I wash my dishes at dinner-time. I watch Good Morning Britain on TV to ken what's happening. After breakfast I shave and brush my teeth. I go to the shop to buy a paper. I see what's on TV. After my tutorial at work I do some contract work. It's a bit boring – it's too easy for me. I'd like to do more variety of things that suit me, like cooking. I like going out.

I go in at 3.30 to my house and put on my telly. At 4.30 I get prepared for my tea: hamburger and chips. After that I have a cup of tea and a chocolate biscuit. At 7.30 I go out for a walk on my own to the supermarket to get some things. When I came back I watch TV. I watch the late film and when it's finished I go to bed.

Robert Drysdale: St Clair Centre, Kirkcaldy
(Spoken and transcribed with assistance)

I go shopping

I GO SHOPPING EVERY NIGHT AND EVERY MORNING.
I BOUGHT A SHOPPING BAG TO PUT THE FOOD IN.
I GO SHOPPING WIH ALAYN AND THE STAFF ON SATURDAYS.
WE GO SHOPPING ON SATURDAY AFTERNOONS.

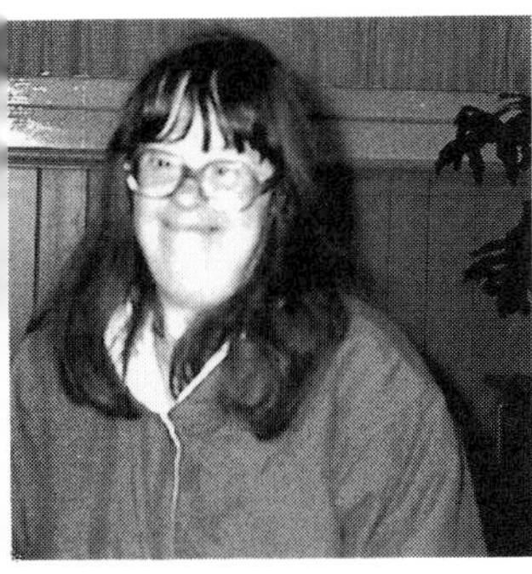

Christine Purton.

I go shopping every night and every morning. I bought a shopping bag to put the food in. I go shopping with Alayn and the staff on Saturdays. We go shopping on Saturday afternoons.

I went to a music night on Friday at the Neighbourhood and my boyfriend Alayn Austin come up. We had a ladies' night out and a men's night out. We had tea and afters in boxes.

Christine Purton: Kirkdale Centre, Syndenham
(First word-processing)

Now and in the future

I go to typing, basket-weaving, reading and writing classes. I'd like to go to cookery classes with Diane like I used to, but her mum doesn't want her to come into Lewisham. I'd like to go to drama too like I did at Mulberry. I've written a play so that me and my friends can do drama.

What I really need to do over the next few years is get a job. I need practice at interviews. Donna might help me. I want to go on the course called 'Thinking about Work'. I need a job where I can get good money so I can support Diane when we get married. Right now I'd like a Saturday job. £1.70 isn't enough for me. I have to save for holidays and to get married to Diane in a few years' time.

Andrew: Leemore Day Centre, Lewisham
(Taped and transcribed)

My name is Steven Field

My name is Steven Field and I like coming to college, because it is good and you learn better. I like all the staff, including Liza, who is one of the helpers at the Project.

The Project is good. We work hard laying slabs and bricks and that. I like it there. There are about 19 of us. I can't remember how long I have been there, but it must be a long time. I will probably be working doing gardening after this.

I watch telly most of the time at home. I watch *EastEnders, Coronation Street, Emmerdale Farm, Neighbours.* All of them are best. I take my dog out for a walk. He is called Trixie. He eats dog food. He is white and two years old. I can't remember what kind of dog he is.

My mum lives at home with me. She works in a flower shop and she likes it. Sometimes she brings flowers home.

Steven Field: South Lewisham Institute
(Dictated)

Home

My life

I live with my mummy and daddy. Daddy owns a shop and nanny helps him there. Mummy and I and my sisters do the cooking and help in the house. It is important that we keep our legs covered so I wear trousers all the time.

I enjoy horse riding and shopping – I do both of those from the centre.

At home I do not go out – only to the local shops. My sister does not go out either.

Jesoda: A Social Education Centre in London
(Interpreted from signs)

Our lives

I am 33. I have just moved into a group home. It is a very nice place. I get on with the people quite well. I put a lock on my kitchen door because people were coming into the kitchen and pinching stuff. It was a good idea to move away from my foster parents. I am more independent now. I cook for myself. I cook cabbage, potatoes, peas, sometimes faggots. Sometimes I have sprouts and that and toad in the hole. I can do my own washing and that as well. I put it in the washing machine in the laundry room, and when it's finished I put in the drier.

I had some friends up Saturday. I had a nice party with Tina, Muriel and David and Billy, who lives in my place. Simon and Shelley came and Cathy and Timmy, and Keith. We had drinks and that. The staff helped me clear up afterwards. Two people played the guitar and we sang. David played his drums. Billy plays the guitar.

Eugene Lynch: Camden Institute
(Dictated)

Six stories from the Thomas Fortune Work Centre

'I live in a hostel. My mum lives in Islay and I visit her for holidays. Sometimes she comes to see me. I am happy in the hostel. The staff are nice. Sometimes, however, some of the other residents are annoying. They say annoying things and poke their noses into your business. They like telling tales.

I work at the Thomas Fortune Centre. I like it. We have fun there. The rooms could be made nicer though.

I go to the Curran House Club, which I enjoy. There is dancing, table tennis, records and snooker. One thing at the club is unfair. The girls are not allowed in the snooker room. I don't know why.'

Fiona Baird

'I was brought up in children's homes and now live in Balshagray Hostel. There are lots of rules there but they don't bother me much.

I would like some day to move to another place – perhaps Key Housing.

I like going to the Curran House club where I enjoy dancing and meeting people but the ginger and crisps are rubbish.'

Sarah McGinley

'I live in a hostel. It is okay but I don't want to stay there always. They treat you like children. I don't save my own money. When I go out I have to tell where I am going.'

Marilyn Goodson

'I live in Balshagray Hostel. I like it there. I feel I need to be there as I am a diabetic. I can manage my own injections but I like to have someone there to check everything. If I wasn't a diabetic I wouldn't need to be in a hostel. I work at Thomas Fortune Centre. I like my work but would like more variety in the work. I don't like it when there is no work. I like going to clubs.'

Ian Haughey

'I share a flat with a friend I met when I was in the hostel. We get on well. We keep it nice and clean. We have to take our turn to clean the stairs. A card comes in the letter box when it is our turn. Sometimes the woman next door doesn't clean them right.

I work at Thomas Fortune Centre. It is good there but boring. I like darts, snooker, pool and playing football. I used to go swimming. The centre used to go to Strathclyde Sports but they don't now. I miss it.'

Peter Blake

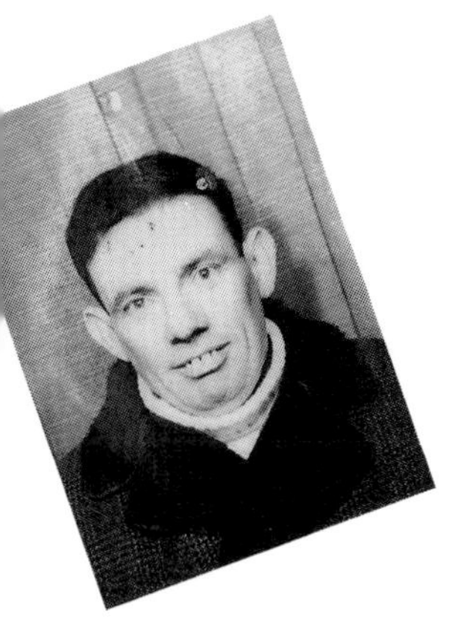

John Clark.

'I live with my brother. There used to be two brothers and me, but one brother stays with his girlfriend now. I miss my mother very much. I would like a flat of my own. I could manage. I can cook and keep a house clean. I put my name in Clydebank because my sister is there and she will help me, but it takes a long time. I will need furniture and carpets but I think my social worker will help me get some of it.

I used to go to Curran House Club but I don't bother now. I got angry at the carry on some folk have there. They get away with it too. Sometimes they are told to stay away for a few weeks but they get back. I think they should be thrown out.

I might go to another club in Drumchapel.'

John Clark

All from the Thomas Fortune Work Centre, Glasgow
(Dictated)

I used to live on Frenchay Ward

I used to live on Frenchay Ward at Hortham Hospital. The hospital will be closing down and so will the ITU (Industrial Therapy Unit). So I've moved to the other side of Filton to a place called the Red House. About 12 other people live with me; I do the polishing on Saturdays and cooking on Fridays. Mary Webb helps me with the cooking. I go to my sister's house in Bath some weekends from Friday night to Sunday. My sister, Ruth, cooks meals for me – she has two children and a husband. My other sister is Jean and she lives at Newport; she has six children and a husband.

I liked the staff at Hortham Hospital and I am sorry to see it closed down. I'd like to go and see Terry, the boss of the Industrial Therapy Unit at Brentry Hospital.

I like doing the gardening at the Red House but not Lanercost Centre, where I go in the day. I don't like it very much at Lanercost but I do like George Hill, the previous manager.

Robert Tooze: Lanercost Centre
(Dictated)

Letty and I live together in a group home

Letty and I live together in a group home in Sandy. We have a cat called 'Fluffy' and a budgie called 'Joey'. Fluffy spends the night in my room. He sometimes sleeps on my bed. When I come home from work, there is a warm hole on the bed where he's been asleep.

Letty and I live alone but we have a lady called Jill comes to see us every day except at the weekends. Jill comes to see us to make sure that we are alright and washes our hair for us, and makes sure that we have a bath properly. She also writes out our grocery order on a Friday evening and we go out on Saturday to buy everything. Letty and I always have our lunch out on Saturday at the cafe in Sandy. On Wednesday, Jill is taking me to Bedford to buy some new summer clothes for my holiday. I need a new coat. Letty went last week and bought new shoes and a new coat.

Every Tuesday a lady comes to help us with the housework and cooking. Letty and I take it in turns to stay at home when she comes. She comes at 11.00 and we clean out the budgie's cage. Then we clean one room really well. Each week we do a different room. She leaves at 12.30 and I have my lunch which is a sandwich. Then I sometimes do my washing. The lady comes back at 3.00 and helps me get the evening meal ready. I like cooking, it is my favourite job. I enjoy doing salads and making cakes. I don't really like ironing.

Every day during the week, except Tuesday, we have a cooked meal at work at lunch-time. In the evening we make some sandwiches. On Sundays I cook something like pork chops or toad in the hole. After tea we wash up and then we watch television, or I sometimes do some ironing. I go to bed quite late, sometimes not until 1.00. On Monday evening I go to evening class in Biggleswade. On Thursday evening I go to Gateway Club in Biggleswade.

June Cave: Special Adult Learning Programme, Biggleswade
(Transcribed after discussion)

Work

Work memories from the 'colony'

'We'd only uniform all the same. White aprons and hats all the same, and black stockings and boots. Sometimes shoes and no underclothes like we have now. We had striped knickers and buttons at each side. An old-fashioned skirt all week and then at the weekend these old dresses, dark green dresses. We'd only one for the weekend, dark green with white aprons. We hadn't anything else.'

Doris

'In t'olden days I worked on a villa. Scrubbing on your hands and knees. I worked at night till 7.00 at night. Bathing them and putting them to bed, them being short-staffed. That's how they think I got me bad leg from, when I used to do a lot of scrubbing every morning and every night. They didn't have vacuums or things like that, like they have now. It was all kneeling, mucky, dirty side-rooms to do.'

Irene

'We didn't get any money then. We'd not any money, we had to work for nothing. Work for nothing in them days. Then when it changed, you know the change-over, they started giving them money and he said, "You can buy some clothes now of your own!"'

Doris

All from a hospital in the north of England
(Taped and transcribed)

My life

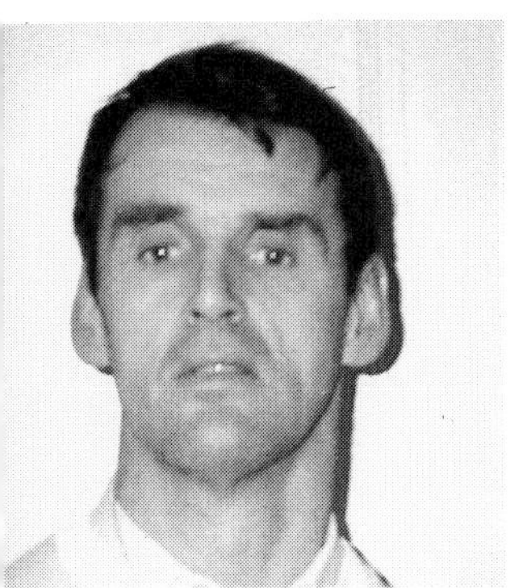

Jeffrey Reynolds.

I work in the gardens. I sweep up and water the plants. I take orders down. I cut the edges of the grass and help to take the plants to the car. My favourite plants are geraniums and fuschias. I like working in the gardens. I get paid – the money goes in the book on the ward – about £3. I buy sweets, Coke. I buy drinks in the club. I save money to buy clothes. I bought an English book, a dictionary. I am doing English, Maths, Computer Work, at Adult Education.

I help my sister in the garden, and my mother and Barbara and I help to feed the guinea-pigs. They belong to my niece – Kate. We go shopping on the market. I help Barbara with the groceries and shopping – the heavy shopping. My mother is old. My father is kind to me. He has done me a tape. I play Scrabble with my family. We play seven at cards.

Robert, my nephew, is referee for football. My niece goes to High School at Sheringham. She works at night-time for a fish shop. She has a boyfriend but I haven't seen him yet. Robert plays cricket with his friends; I got one of his friends out for duck.

My other sister is Pam. She is now working in an office at Side Strand. She sometimes comes to visit me here at Little Plumstead.

I play darts in the club on Thursdays. I win – usually! I play snooker as well. I have my own snooker cue. I also play volleyball, netball-passing and bowls. I am not very good at bowls or passing.

I watch judo on the television, karate, kung-fu plus wrestling. I like sport.

I've got a girlfriend - Janet Mayhew. I see her at weekends. She's been my girlfriend for nine years. I buy her things. I am going to see her this weekend. She has tea with me.

I went to the car boot sale. Last Sunday I went to Horse Trials at Little Plumstead. Took a photo of the horses. I used to go horse-riding.

I like football. I used to play football. I've retired now from football. I am 45 now.

Jeffrey Reynolds: Little Plumstead Hospital
(Tape transcript)

I am going to start a new job

I will be working in Thamesmead. I'll get a
uniform. I'll be working days, nights and
weekends.
it will give me experience and good money.

I am going to start a new job and work with people and get good pay. I will be working in Thamesmead. I'll get a uniform. I'll be working days, nights and weekends.

It will give me experience and good money.

Ronald Kearns: Thameside AEI
(Handwritten)

My life

I chop up the veg I sometes
I cut my finger on a knife I worked down
stairs whth RosMery last week
Iam working in the kichen this week.
I be working whth Robert Robert made my
Birthday cake whith chery in iT
I went to ST Stevens hospial in fulham
on wenday the afternoon at 2 oclock.
So IT cold not come to class that day.
So I had a day off. I told the

I work at Applejacks. I am in the cafe this week. I put the cups up and lay the table. We open at 10.00 in the morning. We have a break at 11.00 until half past 11, and next week I will be in the kitchen. Rosemary will be in. I might be working with her.

I chop up the veg. I sometimes cut my finger on a knife. I worked downstairs with Rosemary last week. I am working in the kitchen this week. I will be working with Robert. Robert made my birthday cake with cherries in it. I went to St Steven's Hospital in Fulham on Wednesday afternoon at 2.00 so I could not come to class that day. So I had a day off. I told the teacher I would not be in the class. Applejacks is trying to get me a full-time job with pay; I've been at Applejacks a year and a half.

Noreen Breen: Camden Institute
(Handwritten)

Money

Tuesday Reading and Writing Class, William Brinson Centre, London.

'We get paid on Thursday. I get £3.00. I buy sweets. I keep saving for my holiday. We're going to Great Yarmouth in June. We're going down to Blackpool in August. I'd like to get more money.'

Rose

'The reason why I get a low wage is because I get a pension every Monday night. I'm also entitled to a Christmas bonus and I don't get that. It's just not fair. I wish I could have a bank book to get money out of. It would be nice if my wages could go up. I'm not complaining about it. I just expect it. I wouldn't be as wicked as that (to complain) but some of them would.

I also spend money on cakes to fetch up to the centre to give them a feast. Sometimes I buy a record.'

Linda

'I want to get more money. I'd like to get £8.

I get £3.50 for work in the mornings in the centre.

Before she left, Mrs James said we'd get more money, but we have not had it yet.

Sometimes I get money at the hostel for helping out with the cleaning.

My aunt buys my clothes. I use my money to buy the *Radio* and *TV Times.*

I save £2, and spend it at the club on a Saturday night.'
Carol

'I get £2.75, and when I get paid I go round to the kiosk and sometimes I buy myself a magazine to read, and some cigarettes and matches if I have not got any. Other times I buy a deodorant.'

Helen

'I get a book to get my money out of the Post Office. I put it in the building society and I get interest.

If I had enough money I'd like to visit my cousins in America.

I get £3.50 in the centre but I'd like to see my money go up.

I like to work for my money. I like buying clothes and jewellery with it.

When it's something special, like a birthday or Mother's Day or Father's Day or an anniversary, I get something for my mum and dad.

I like to get some flowers for my brother. My mother goes there (to the crematorium) but I don't go there because it upsets me. And I get some flowers for my nan, she's in there too.'

Susan

All members of the Tuesday Reading and Writing Class, William Brinson Centre, London E3
(Some self-written, others transcribed)

Work at Ludun

It took them two-and-a-half years to get me a job at Ludun Workshop. It is good to have a job and to earn money as well. I started on 30 March 1987 and I have been on the payroll for a year now.

I am very happy to have a job there and the people are very nice to speak to. We make wooden toys for the shops. I rub them down while Jim and Peter spray them. The other people put them together. We make wheel-barrows, cots for dolls, push horses and lorries for the children to ride on. Plus we make trikes.

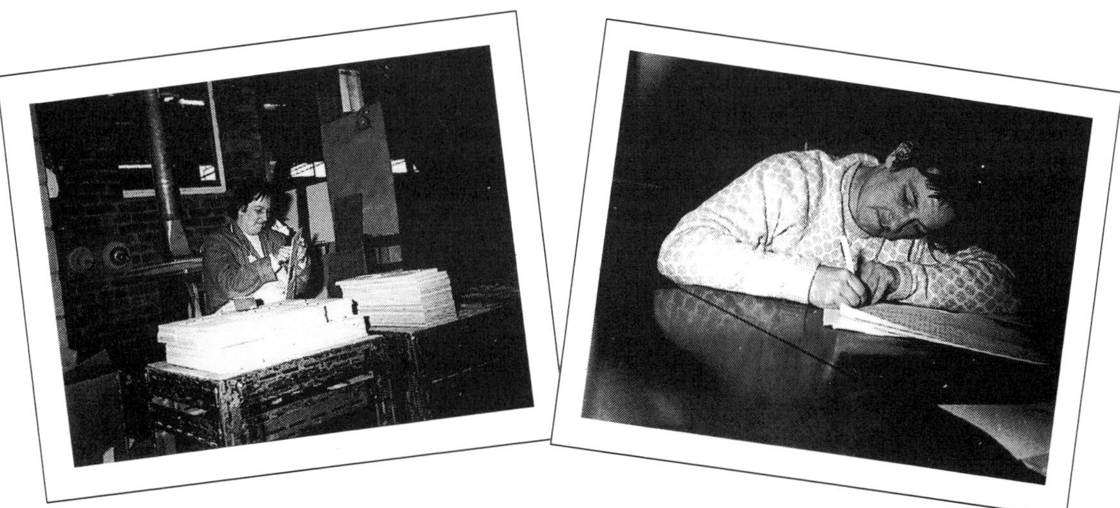

Marion Martin.

We have got a nice cloakroom where we can put our coats. We eat in a canteen. We start at 8.30 in the morning and work until a quarter past five. Fridays we leave at five past four.

I am glad I got a job and earn £75 a week. If we work Saturday morning we earn extra. I can buy things for myself now, and also buy my nieces and nephews things as well. It has changed my life because I can afford things which I never could afford before.

Marion Martin: Bedfordshire Special Adult Learning Programme, Luton
(Handwritten)

I went for a job

I went for a job to work at Prestos; I have had no reply. I am going to apply for a park-keeper's job to look after the children and keep the park clean. I'll have to make sure there are no bottles smashed on the floor so the children don't cut theirselves. I'll have to keep the toilets clean and make sure there is no mess on the floor. I will have to make sure nobody falls in the lake; if they do fall in I'll have to jump in and save them. I can swim.

Colin Livermore: Thameside AEI
(Handwritten)

Ian going to apply.for a Park keepers
job to look after the children and keep the
Park clean I'll have to make sure there are on
bottles smashed on the floor so the children
don.t cut theirselves

Work

'Work can be a bit hard sometimes. Some of the students do packing. We all work very hard here in the William Brinson Centre.'

Helen

'I didn't like doing the rucksacks. They make your hands dirty. I like doing the lavender balls.'

Rose

'I like to help out on the military pins. Somebody counts the pins and puts them in the bags. I staple the bags to the cardboard. Tommy Prince packs them into little boxes. Doreen Cocklin puts them into big boxes and puts them into the stock room.

I used to go on those big electric machines when we used to do gadgets to put in bedside lamps. I used to tie my hair back in case it got in the machine.'

Linda

'I like lavender balls, when we put lavender inside the balls of flowers and we pack them.

I liked the army shirts that we used to do – we used to iron them.

The best job I liked doing was skipping ropes, screwing the handles on and folding them.

I think they do more work in the woodwork shop than we do. They used to make cots and ironing boards and picture frames.

Work is important to us and I hope we can get more money here.'

Susan

'I love doing stapling. I do it in the morning. I staple the plastic bags of drawing pins to the cardboard.

My boyfriend used to count out record sleeves and put them in a big box.'

Carol

All from William Brinson Centre, London E3
(Some self-written, some transcribed)

Leisure

The lady in the 'Singing Kettle'

I saw the lady who was wanting the Cavalry
Charging, in the 'Singing Kettle' today
She was the lady who served Fiona and I last year,
and she was talking
About how I must spend
A lot of my time in restaurants.

Sandy Marshall: Thomas Fortune Centre, Glasgow
(Self-typewritten)

Holiday

Dad, mum and I were going on holiday, and took the caravan with us; we stayed in a field away from everyone. One evening dad asked us, would you like to go out in the evening? We said yes, we would like to go out; he saw us both washing our hair which was wet, we had to dry it, we went to find a place to dry it. But we could not find anywhere so we decided to go back and put a wig on instead. Then we went out with him with our wet hair underneath our dry wigs.

Pamela Reynolds, Portway Centre, Bristol
(Self-typewritten)

The happiest time

We went on holiday, mum, dad and me, same place in Cornwall in a caravan near the pubs. I packed my case, put all my clean things ready, and got ready to go out on the booze. After we went to that place we got pie and chips. I was happy because me, mum, dad and my sister and her husband Alan, my brother-in-law, went out to buy me a ring. After we came back, we went out on a boat trip, fishing. There were lots of shops in the town everywhere, which made me happy. I got a date with some girls on holiday and that made me happy. I feel happy when I go to see my girlfriend Eileen. I play tapes when I'm happy. I have a can of beer with my dad. I like football. I like Bristol City. I stay at home and help my mum and dad vacuum-cleaning; I feel happy, I feel like singing.

Alan Marshall: Portway Centre, Bristol
(Dictated)

I like competitions

I like competitions in the club but I do not like people arguing and fighting. Some fight over girls and others are bad losers at games. I have a girlfriend, but my brother thinks I can't get married. He doesn't think I could cope. I do not like drunk people in pubs and being pestered for money by some drunks.

Sandy Gibson: Thomas Fortune Centre
(Dictated)

At discos

At Discos I dance and get chatted up by boys. 'What's your name?', they say. I tell them. 'Where do you live?', they ask. I tell them I've got a boyfriend already. So they ask, 'What's his name?' 'Terry is his name', I tell them.

Kim C. Moss: Coborn Street SEC, Bow
(Dictated)

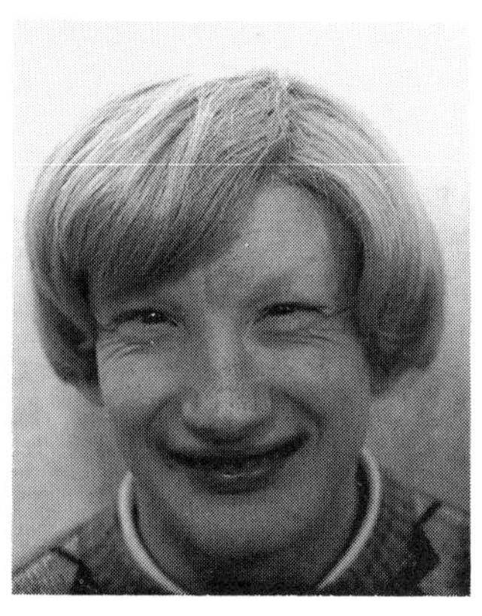

John Fordyce.

I've been to a wedding

I've been to a wedding. When my big brother got married. After that we went to the section. Some went home and some came to get a meal, and we were sitting at the top table and some were sitting at the side, and some came at night. We had a band and a disco, and one of the men played guitar and drums. We didn't have any records. That was on till 11 o'clock, and drinking from three o'clock in the afternoon. I went to a silver wedding. Then they went for their honeymoon. My brother and my sister-in-law, and after they came back they took money to buy a dog. Then went to Blackpool for their honeymoon. The dog's called Trixie. They've been five years married now. Then they got a wee girl called Maria. She's coming up for four years this year. She's three just now. She's four in August. That's all I can think of just now.

John Fordyce: Whiteinch Centre, Glasgow
(Dictated)

My sister is getting married

My sister is getting married on September 3rd. It is a Saturday and she is called Teresa. She is getting married to Dave in a church, the lot with a video in it as well. This bloke that's a photographer is taking the photographs that we know from darts. Her mate Lorraine's dad is going to do the video for it. My sister Joanne is going to be a bridesmaid, so is Tracey, Dave's sister, Nicola (that's my cousin's daughter), and there's going to be a page boy too (my cousin's son). After the wedding there is the reception in the club. The top table are going to have champagne and we are going to have a cold buffet to eat. There will be tea and coffee and sherry there as well.

There will be quite a lot of people there; there might be about 180 because she has asked her mates as well and they will probably come.

My uncles are coming from Ireland, they are Brendan, Peter, Paul and Ita.

My sister and her new husband are going on honeymoon to Malta. My brother is going there as well, but in August, so he can tell them what it is like before they go.

I don't wish it was me getting married, there's plenty of time to enjoy your life first.

Collette Battle: South Lewisham Institute
(Dictated)

Football matches

Last season I wrote the numbers of the matches I went to. They were: 1. number of matches in one season, 2. number of teams seen twice in one season, 3. number of away games in one season, 4. first time the against column has been higher than the for column. I have also equalled the number of new teams seen in one season. The highest win and defeat is the same, 5-1. Remarkably, we have won by that score five times against Southampton, Oxford, Newcastle, Sheffield Wednesday and S.V. Hamburg. Remarkably, we have lost by that score only once to Watford. I have seen Spurs score five times on another couple of occasions against Southampton, again, and Barnsley. Both matches ended in 5-3 wins for Spurs. I have seen three foreign teams, all from different countries: Italy, Inter-Milan; West Germany, S.V. Hamburg; France, A.S. Monaco. I have seen six testimonials: five for Spurs' players and one for an opposing player. I have seen 32 different teams. The record so far is played 75, won 38, drawn 14, lost 23, and the goals column is: for 142, against 102.

Kevin Tye: South Lewisham Institute
(Method unknown)

I go to Biggleswade Library

After work on Monday at 4.30 I go to Biggleswade Library; I take two books out. I like to read love stories. I like to read before I go to bed, and when I get into bed before I go to sleep.

Femmy is my social worker. She takes me in her car. I look first, then choose a book to take home. The library is very quiet, with people reading and choosing their books.

Before going home I like to look through the record section.

Sometimes Femmy and I walk back to the centre, just in time for tea.

John Barfield: Bedfordshire Special Adult Learning Programme, Biggleswade
(Dictated)

Chapter Seven
Experiences of oppression

This chapter focuses on the painful and oppressive aspects of the lives of people with learning difficulties. This is not a new subject. Many of the 'revelations' of ill-treatment in institutions from the 1960s up to Frank Thomas's account of institutional life, first published in 1981 (in Ryan and Thomas, 1987), have thoroughly exposed aspects of this side of life. In the accounts which follow, many more sources of oppression are indicated – sexual harassment, violence and harassment from neighbours, harassment at work and in the street – in addition to the forms of control and punishment exerted by those in positions of authority as carers: family members and welfare workers. Not surprisingly, this external oppression also surfaces as inner frustration and despair.

This chapter is divided into three sections which deal with these sets of experiences: harassment; frustration and despair; and control and punishment.

We discuss further, in the 'Conclusion', the dilemma we faced of extracting from people the expression, in written or verbal form, of experiences which are painful, and which require time and emotional support in order to come to terms with them. Too often, people with learning difficulties have been expected to deny or repress difficult feelings and bad experiences. This difficulty is shown very clearly in the taped interview in the first section (on harassment) between a keyworker and one of her clients who had been raped. In the end, the event and the contributor's reactions to the trauma are articulated by the interviewer herself with affirmations from her interviewee. Perhaps the experience was too close to be remembered. We have, however, decided to include this because it is clear that sexual harassment is not an uncommon experience (see also the women's group experiences in Chapter Eight). Other forms of harassment are related in this section: a couple whose house was set on fire and who needed police protection to feel safe in their independent living; and harassment from children and teenagers and colleagues. It is apparent from the group contributions in this section that people with learning difficulties gain greater assertiveness and strength to deal with these forms of harassment when they are discussed collectively, when the onus of the experience shifts from an experience of individual assault to one of experience of *oppression as a group.*

It is also clear that people with learning difficulties – as an oppressed group – suffer from similar forms of oppression, but oppression expressed in different terms from other oppressed groups in society – women, black people, older people, for example. Aspects of stereotyping or labelling, of denial of opportunities, expressions of power, violence, or sexualised violence, or where attempts at resistance or assertiveness are seen as threatening and deserving of punishment – 'keeping them in their place' – all of these feature in this chapter.

The second section contains articulations of despair and frustration. Frustration at a body which will not control itself, which has fits, at a brain which sees no logic in the organisation of letters in words, at words which 'don't come easy', at uncontrollable anger, despair or loneliness, and at helplessness during a family argument.

The final section – *control and punishment* – relates experiences of institutionalised control and enforced dependence. The first few contributions are from the elderly residents of a hospital looking back at their lives in a 'colony'. From these contributors we begin to get a sense of the past from their point of view – an aspect often lacking in the written histories of mental handicap (see Potts and Fido, 1990).

Following this, Beryl Allen's story reflects upon the constraints her family placed upon her life, whilst Anita Binns relates the difficulties of others' assumptions about her. First, there is her local Social Services Department who see her as a dependent, passive and ungrateful client; second, her stepmother who treated her as 'daft'; and third, the abusive attitudes of some of her neighbours.

The final contribution in this section is an interview where both the interviewer and interviewee have been long-stay residents in a mental handicap hospital. Winnie relates her experience of being sent away to a secure unit in a psychiatric hospital. The note on which this interview ends is an important one, and points the way to the next chapter on struggle and self-determination, as David explains:

> 'Well, what you do is, at the hospital if you don't like something, see what they like about the food and sort out problems with them. Then make arrangements to have a meeting and then sort everything out, and then make a meeting with the staff of each ward and get one of the residents on each ward to find out what they sort out. That's how you get the problem sorted out really...Normal people will have to get used to seeing handicapped people outside, used to seeing them shopping and doing their work like a normal person does...'

David and Winnie

Contents

Harassment

Tell them the truth

There goes the mongol up the street
Getting on the looneybus
The schoolbairns call
Making funny faces at us
Calling us names
Headcase, spassy, wally
Nutter, Dylan, Twit!

There goes the dumb-bell into the nuthoose!
The schoolbairns are all daft themselves
They should see a psychiatrist
About their brains
It makes you mad, it boils up your blood
Their wooden heads are full of nonsense.

They've got nothing else to do
Except make fun of us
We are human beings
And should be treated as equals
Treated as adults
Tell them the truth.

Donald Lack, Robert Drysdale, Margaret Williamson, Derek Mustard, J. R. Grubb, Joan Cargill, Robert McMahon: St. Clair Centre, Kirkcaldy
(Group poem, dictated)

Contributors to the group poem 'Tell them the truth'.

People sometimes tease me

People sometimes tease me. Call me names and run away. I used to live with my mum. She was ill and in hospital and I moved to a hostel. Then mum died. I miss her. The children near the hostel make me very angry. I have thrown a brick because they made me so angry by calling me names. They make me cry. It's not my fault. It makes me very angry.

Malcolm, A Social Education Centre in London
(Dictated)

When people take the mickey

When people take the mickey I feel very sad but not sad because they take the mickey out of me, sad because they are taking the mickey out of themselves.

You want to know why I say that? Because if they've got something better to do, they wouldn't take the mickey out of handicapped people. But they don't have nothing to do all day but go round taking the mickey out of handicapped people.

The teenagers are the worst because if they did what I do like go swimming, come to college, go to work, or spend your time doing something better, they would have no need to take the mickey.

Sean Rooney, Putney and Wandsworth AEI
(Dictated)

My mum left me at my sister's

(Interview extracts)

Susan: My mum left me at my sister's. We were staying at my sister's.

Interviewer: Where was your mum going?

Susan: She was going out, and she left me up my sister's and he come in.

Interviewer: Who's that that came in?

Susan: Neil...boyfriend

Interviewer: So that's your sister's boyfriend?

Susan: Yes, and he was watching me and I don't like that...and um he kept watching me what I was doing and put his hand round me and keep touching me up I told him I didn't like that to go away and he didn't go away and um he followed me he still followed me.

He kept trying to get my clothes off and I said no I don't want to take my clothes off he tried to make me and I said no I kept fighting him off but he kept bothering me.

Interviewer: So he raped you?

Susan: Yes.

Interviewer:	*What happened after that? Did you tell your mum straight away?*
Susan:	My mum found out 'cos I didn't start me period...
Interviewer:	*So what happened during that time? Did your mum have a go at your sister's boyfriend?*
Susan:	Yes.
Interviewer:	*Did your mum tell your sister?*
Susan:	No.
Interviewer:	*So your sister didn't know at first? Did she find out?*
Susan:	No.
Interviewer:	*So you became pregnant and you had a baby?*
Susan:	Yes.
Interviewer:	*Did you keep him?*
Susan:	My mum tried to adopt him, put him in a home. I said I want to keep him. He is my son.
Interviewer:	*So you had a little boy and what's his name?*
Susan:	John.
Interviewer:	*How old is John now?*
Susan:	Five...
Interviewer:	*Do you remember the time? How did you feel when after it happened, after he raped you?*
Susan:	Terrible.
Interviewer:	*And I understand from talking to you in the past that you've had a lot of nightmares and trouble over it?*
Susan:	Yes.
Interviewer:	*You still have nightmares about what happened?*
Susan:	Yes, I do
Interviewer:	*It makes you feel quite frightened, doesn't it?*
Susan:	Yes...
Interviewer:	*What about your sister, do you get on with your sister?*
Susan:	No, I don't talk to her
Interviewer:	*Why is that?*
Susan:	She's with him.
Interviewer:	*She's still with him?*
Susan:	Yes, I don't speak to her.
Interviewer:	*Yes, and does she know that John's father is her boyfriend?*
Susan:	No, she don't know.
Interviewer:	*Was the police informed, did your mum phone the police when he raped you?*
Susan:	Yes, yes.
Interviewer:	*And what did they say?*
Susan:	Just said didn't do nothing...
Interviewer:	*Does he still try to bother you?*

Susan: Yes, he still comes round.

Interviewer: How does that make you feel?

Susan: Just frightened.

Interviewer: Do a lot of people in the centre know what happened to you or is there only a few?

Susan: A few people know.

Interviewer: Would you like to tell me who the first people you told about it?

Susan: I told, told um that lady.

Interviewer: The one from Rape Crisis?

Susan: Yes.

'Susan': Albion Road Social Education Centre, Hackney
(Tape transcript)

Terrible

This is about the Place and about John Dracula. He said to me, 'Do you want to go on the heat-sealer machine?' I said, 'No, because my eyes are too bad'. I just got out from hospital and I couldn't even see the holes to feed into the machine. He said, 'Even a two-year-old can see the holes in this machine'. He used to be a prison officer before in Horfield. 'If you don't do it properly, I'll have to go and see the boss to have your money put down.' I went red with anger, I was fuming. He took me in the office; I met the boss. I felt terrible, I felt like slamming someone. I came out. I went in the toilets and he was following me. He accused me of putting a white jumper down the toilet. I said, 'I did not'. But he told me I did. I was fuming, and I took the plug out of the heat sealer and I had it in my hand and said, 'Do you want this across your head?' He didn't say anything. I didn't do it. I was worried inside me, it wasn't worth the effort, so I just walked out of the building, had a quick fag, came back in and got on with my work. I was suspended that night for a week. It was a horrible time and I don't think anything of him any more, John Dracula. I don't go to the Place anymore.

John Symes, Portway Centre, Bristol
(Dictated)

We were sitting down watching telly...

(Interview extracts)

Maria: You have been married for quite a long time now?

Jenny: Yes, six years...

Maria: And your husband, he goes to a different centre every day?

Jenny: Yes, he don't want to, if we see him, you know, we get fed up with him, if we see him all the time.

Maria: Exactly, you have got to be apart for a while to enjoy each other's company when you get back home, yes.

Jenny: When we get to...he sees me, he waits for me at the bus stop.

Maria: *Every day?*

Jenny: Not every day, only Thursday.

Maria: *Right.*

Jenny: Sometimes we go, I know he's learning a bit difficult.

Maria: *Right, he has got learning difficulties too a bit like you. Well the important thing is, what I wanted to talk about with you just now was all the problems you had when you moved to a flat with your husband, with Terry...so you live with your husband in an independent flat yes?*

Jenny: Yes.

Maria: *Now I want you to tell people about, you remember, you had a couple of fires in your home.*

Jenny: In our flat, yes.

Maria: *Right, how did the fire start?*

Jenny: We didn't know, we were sitting down watching telly and there was a film on. We made ourselves a pot of tea and then I went in the front room and when we went back we saw all the net curtain burnt.

Maria: *Yes, that was very bad. How did the fire start, do you know?*

Jenny: Someone put something through the letter box you know, yes, someone put it in.

Maria: *Do you know why they did it, or who did it?*

Jenny: No.

Maria: *So don't you have any idea why people do such horrible things?*

Jenny: I don't know who did it, that's why we have a policeman every night now... we've got to keep shutting the door and we get so hot in there.

Maria: *Well you have to have a window open sometimes – do you live on the ground floor?*

Jenny: Yes.

Maria: *So it is easy for people to throw things.*

Jenny: Yes, that's why we've got to be moved away from here...'cos we don't do anything, we went to a house...we went for a meeting right and I know Terry's got a temper. We can't do it because we don't want to get in trouble.

Jenny Langton: Albion Road Social Education Centre, Hackney
(Tape transcript)

Experiences of handicap

(Group discussion)

'When I was younger, I started taking turns and that. I used to attend the church regular till about 14 or 15 and then the priest stopped me – tellt me not to go back in case I frightened the old folk and injured myself on the benches. Up at the old centre Graham kennt my temper.'

'Aye, the boss put her out the door one day.'

What's it like working in here?

'Terrible.'

How is it terrible?

'If I had a job – they're cutting back on jobs – where do I go if this place is shut down.'

'There's plenty jobs we could do. In a cafe – in the market serving tea and coffee. I'm quite sure we could do that.'

'There's plenty things we could use but we don't get the chance. The only one thing that is stopping us really is we're working in here and we're labelled and that's what 'cos I hate being here. If you're in here you get labelled as handicapped. I don't think we're all handicapped, because I hate being labelled. It's dreadful the way we get treated like dirt.'

'Treated like muck.'

What do you think yourself?

'I think it's not right. I don't like being labelled.'

'The kids on the bus, the language they use. I detest it.'

'The school bairns call you names.'

'When we go for a job, the employers treat us like common muck.'

'They say, "Come back another day and we'll think about it". And then they say "no" because you're handicapped.'

'Some employers will not employ handicapped folk, and they should because we should get a chance as well as everybody else.'

'I'm sure we could do a good job as everybody else.'

'In fact we probably could do it better than some other folk.'

'They say, "Oh, you cannae go on the bus yourself – you're handicapped! " I tell them one day. One of staff said, "Are you going on the bus yourself?" I say "Aye". One of the staff was wondering what I did in my spare time – "Are you allowed out on your own", he said. "Do you go anywhere at weekends?" I said, "I do go away places. I go away on the bus down the High Street. I meet Derek and we go and have a cup of coffee and a bit of blether – we enjoy that!"'

'You've got to get together sometimes and have a chin wag with somebody.'

'The way the folks outside treat you like handicapped you're no exactly. You're just the same as normal people, in fact you're better than most folk outside, 'cos if they knew really what was going on in the centre, they would think twice about calling you handicapped. They dinnae realise what's going on in a centre.'

'No – because they've never been in a centre.'

'These people should swop places with us!'

Francis Logan, Derek Mustard, Elspeth Brannan, Graham Bisset: St Clair Centre, Kirkcaldy
(Transcribed)

Frustration and despair

Crying

I went to a pub with our dad. My uncle made my dad drunk, and I got upset about it. Uncle upset my brother because he'd stolen a car, and after we went out to the pub and dad had a drink and a game of darts. Where dad goes I go. When dad was drunk I felt bad inside. My nephew came back to the pub, and broke Aunty Jill's glasses. There was a real fight. I was frightened, there was nothing I could do. Brother Ian took his ex-girlfriend out. Cecil started it all. The old man who lives on our old street in Avonmouth.

My tummy's going funny. I get angry. I go for a walk in the park. Mum said, 'Don't be long'. Cecil said to me, 'Piss off'. I feel very bad about Cecil, he beat his wife up. I still felt bad when I came back. I said nothing to Cecil. Cecil drinks too much.

Alan Marshall: Portway Centre, Bristol
(Dictated)

At my lowest ebb

The reasons why I say I'm at my lowest ebb for a long time, is because I don't get speaking or singing, and also because I have to bottle up my ideas. The folk in the room sometimes - more often than not - don't let me be happy, and so I can't let my ideas - whatever they are - emerge freely. Also trying to find inspiration is sometimes difficult. I like to get out in the clear air, away from the smokiness there is around inside the centre - to think of ideas. Such a row goes on in the room, sometimes I just can't think right and I want to be happy, and some people just don't want me to be that way. Though even when I'm in the countryside - sometimes I don't get inspiration.

I feel I can let my thoughts run away better on paper, rather than speaking them. 'Words don't come easy to me' when I speak sometimes, though sometimes the opposite is the case - can't think of words to type out, but a profusion comes from my pen sometimes.

Sandy Marshall

Sandy Marshall, Thomas Fortune Centre, Glasgow
(Self type-written)

The epileptic

How can you be fit
In an epileptic fit,
When your mind is in a turmoil
And everything you do,
Whether familiar, or new,
In unconsciousness you spoil.

You really get caught
Whenever you get an attack
Until you rebuild
Your memory, that's stilled
To remind you of things away back.

And till you are free
From that spasm and spree
You are very hard to convince;
And the acts you perform
Just like hail, thunder and storm.
Your body and mind in spins.

Ettie Cohen: Tower Hamlets AEI
(Handwritten)

I don't like my life

I don't like my life because of my epilepsy. It lets me down a lot.

It doesn't let me do what I like. It feels awful. I get double vision and I see something that isn't there like a TV or a person. It is frightening. I know when it is going to happen because I get dizzy and I crash on the floor.

Dele Fakoya, South Lewisham Institute
(Method unknown)

Could do better

Last Monday the other members of my English class sat heads bent working quietly. I was sitting at the front of the classroom next to my English lecturer who was marking one of my essays. 'How do you spell meant?', he asked me, and wrote my version of the spelling at the top of the page. 'Is it M-E-N-T?', I volunteered, by now I was sweating, my mind racing. I could not see the letters, there was a big hole in my mind, no letters appeared. My lecturer wrote two more spellings of meant, and told me which was the correct one. I could not see that it was right, and suddenly I am eight years old again. The teacher had marked my list of spellings – one right, my average mark.

At ten years of age in junior school I am told to go away and write out the spelling of 'wonder' a hundred times. I can still see the van I saw with the advertisement for Wonderloaf on its side, not the words just the van.

I handed in my completed spelling list. 'Well, Kathleen, how do you spell "wonder"', asked the teacher. I got it wrong!

My school report informed, that with spelling I could do better. The same old story. I did try with the spellings, but they were like a plate of jelly. Just as I thought I had it right, the letters would slip down the hole in my mind, like jelly falling from a plate.

The next teacher gave me some advice:'Read, dear, it will help your spelling'. I did start to read, it was my last term at school. I went to the school library and took a book down from the shelf, it was about a Collie dog. I went on reading. My love affair with books had begun.

At 16, my brother asked what I was reading.*Anna Karenina*, I told him. 'My god, you're reading *Anna Karenina*, yet you can't spell it', he said.

From Collie dog to *Anna Karenina*. Had I in two years cracked this spelling thing? No! At work I started as a cadet nurse working in the out-patients department. 'How do you spell Upmoor, Kathleen?', sniggered the out-patients clerk. At 36 I could not spell Birmingham place names.

Last Saturday night a patient's daughter told me, as I was filling in an admission form, 'Nurse, you have spelt Frances the female way, it's with an "i" for a man'. I wanted to wipe the smile off her face; instead I crossed out the 'e' and wrote 'i' in her father's name.

What has caused this hole in my mind; what caused letters to turn to jelly?

Dyslexia, Aston University told me, and gave me a definition.

> 'Dyslexia. This term is used to describe a consitutional development pattern of learning that does not favour an easy acquisition of fluency in symbolic material.'

Fancy words for the hole in my head, but it does not show what dyslexia means.

Dyslexia is pain when my eight-year-old daughter says, 'Mum, how do you spell...?', and I pretend I am deaf because the hole in my head is letting the letters fall through again.

Dyslexia is murder. When you feel like murdering the bright student in class, whose work has just been read out, and you are told, 'That is what your work should be like'. 'Bet you have not spent a week writing that essay, you have no hole in your head', I want to scream at her.

Dyslexia is next time. Next time I will do better. I'll get that A grade for my essay, not another C. If the letters don't become jelly again I may even learn to live with the hole in my head.

Is 'may' spelled MEY or MIY? Oh no, here we go again, letters being jelly in my head.

Kathleen Oakley (SRN), Birmingham
(Hand-written)

I went to a school for special needs

I went to a school for special needs...for people who didn't get on with other people. I didn't know why I went there, it was never explained to me. I don't know how my mum felt about it, I never asked her. I never asked anybody except one teacher who said it was because I didn't get on with anybody, which is not true. I don't know what the truth is. It was terrible at the school, I kept getting bullied by kids, because of my temper tantrums. I used to hit the bloody roof, throw chairs, the whole lot...people winding me up made me angry. I don't know why people wound me up...it made me feel angry. Now I walk off. College is different because I can get on with more people, I am older and more mature, and that's it. Everybody has helped me to get more mature – staff and other students. I sometimes find it easier to get on with women than men. I enjoy being in college. I would have liked to have gone to Holland Park as my brother went there. I felt miserable going to special school even though my other brother went to a special school. He can read but he can't write. I tended to protect him even though he was older than me. I can read but I can't write. I now feel I can read and write better, and feel a bit more confident about it.

Colin: Hammersmith and West London College
(Tape transcript)

Control and punishment

Memories of the colony

Certification and admission

'I were at home with me mother and sister and brother. I must have been 15 or summat like that when [I came in]. I left special school when I were 14 years old to work in t'mill. I did spinning and weaving. I only got 10 shillings a week but to me it were worth it.

I've no idea at all [why I came into the colony]. I can never find out. Anyhow, I'm not bothered. It could be, as they say, I were 'black sheep o'family'. They've all died now, that's why I can't get to know anything.

A man took me to the park. It wasn't me mother. Me mother was looking for me. Brown (Executive Officer) – 'Oh, blow that bloomin' thing'. I used to go running to me mother. Mind you they used to come down that street and make you come out to door. Ooh, I hated him! He weren't only after me. He were clever; he got hold of nice girls in there. They were just like me.

It's not true what was written down. They just did it to keep us locked up, so that people would think we're mental. [When admitted] I cried a lot. I didn't like it but you couldn't do nothing else!'
Grace
(Transcribed)

Grace was sent to a 'colony' in 1933 at the age of 17. She was said to be in need of 'moral protection'. She was discharged in the 1970's to independent living.

'My grandfather didn't say where I was going. He told me I was going somewhere but he didn't say where. That's what got me, he didn't say where! If he'd've said where I were going, I expect I didn't want to come!

Fetched me straight up here to the mansion. I were frightened when I come. What is this place? I saw Matron, then I got took over to 'Laurels'. We talked across with one o'nurses. I was wondering what that place was. It was all woods, thick woods. Woods on that drive coming down.

A good few lived down there. Every day it was just...well boring there in 'Laurels. Couldn't go outside at night. I felt awful. I'd rather have been outside than back in a place like this. I wanted to go back out! Then I got fetched over here [main site]. They were closing the Laurels down. It's flats now, it could've been left for us to go into!'
Frank
(Transcribed)

Frank was sent to the colony in 1932 at the age of 15, being in need of 'care and control'. Only now is discharge being considered.

Institutional routines

(Going to the weekly picture show in the Recreation Hall)

'Patients were lined up outside their villas. Those that wanted to go were checked in number so that they knew when it was time for them to come back after the show that the same number that went down were returned. All the male patients used to sit on one side of the hall and the female patients on the opposite side.'

Ernest

Bath-times

'You never got bathed on your own, you'd get staff with us and you had to wait in queues. You weren't allowed to touch the baths yourself. Taps were took off 'cos they were like taps you had to screw on and when you'd had your bath they took 'em away; or else some people would kill themselves, drown themselves.'

Grace

Punishments

'Patients had to be careful how they behaved in their work and on the villa or wherever they were 'cos there was strict staff in those days and any offence, they used to be up before one of the senior doctors. In the case of first offences, they were warned of the serious nature of the offence and what would happen if that or anything like it was repeated. Then they were placed before the doctor and they lost all their privileges for a certain length of time. As far as privileges were concerned, used to be going to films and concerts and in the hospital grounds, Recreation Hall and money included.'

Ernest

'Punishments [villa] 17 it were when they used big punishments. They were scrubbing floors and carrying sand, bags of sand, and if they dropped them there is somebody behind them to tell them to pick them up and keep carrying them. And when they scrubbed the floors, they had to scrub it again, keep doing it all the time, that's why they got tired! They used to be in pyjamas and they used to have a dressing gown on.'

David
(All from a hospital in the north of England.)

I lived at Newbridge Road

Beryl Allen.

I lived at Newbridge Road, St Anne's Park.

I used to go to Redfield to see my auntie every Friday afternoon – to tea – I was 18.

My dad used to work at St Anne's, Broadmills – the paper works – he used to operate machinery there. My mother died quite a long time ago from cancer. She had a hysterectomy and then went back to doing housework. Then she died quite suddenly of a heart attack – she was 70. After that my dad looked after me. We were still living at St Anne's Park and we had two cats. I used to want to help at home but my mum wouldn't let me do anything. I used to get frustrated because I wanted to help but I couldn't. So I used to just sit around idle and I got bored. I'm quite capable of doing the things I wasn't allowed to do. Now I go down to the training kitchen once a week to learn cooking. At Mortimer House I do dusting, make my own bed and sometimes do my ironing.

My father died five years after my mother and he looked after me up until then. He wouldn't let me do anything at home either.

I'm 59 now and this happened quite a long time ago.

After my parents died, I couldn't get in anywhere to live so I ended up at Glenside (a psychiatric hospital) for a while. It was quite frightening to be there, but I don't remember much about it. After that I went to Hillside – it was horrible. It was noisy with all the young ones. I did cooking, washing, ironing, made my own bed. I used to go out with my friend Daphne on our own. We went down the shops in Whiteladies Road and used to go to a cafe – we used to buy cream cakes.

Beryl Allen: Lanercost Centre
(Dictated)

Anita's story (Part 1)

Anita Binns.

I've lived in this flat for 11 years; in just the last couple of years I've had to have the assistance of a home help. But when I first got a home help I could do a little bit, but now I can't even dust or hoover because of me asthma, and I've had me home help taken off us. And now I haven't had one for quite some time so I wrote to the Director of Social Services, and a couple of people I know who worked in Social Services, and I wish I hadn't because the person that I wrote to him about was sent a copy of the letter and when she came to see me she told me off for complaining...

When she first started she came, and she was really abrupt with me, and then she stopped me home help for 14 weeks, and in 14 weeks the place had gone from clean to dirty, and the manager of the ATC that I used to go to phoned the Vice-Chairperson of Social Services, and he got on the phone straight away and I had a home help by Monday. She obviously thought I was wrong in complaining; I mean I had every right to say what I felt...

And I mean I was getting the service free at the time, but now I'm having to pay £1 a week for that home help's service which I'm not getting.

I didn't get on at home with me step-mother, and she made life really difficult for us. Sometimes I had to go to bed at six just because me father was going out.

I would have to go to bed or she would set about us. In fact, one night I came in from work and she'd called the police and said I was causing a disturbance, when I hadn't even been in the house and me dad was working away at the time. And every time I took me wages in she took them off us, and I only got about £8 a week, and she gave us £1 back for me lunches and me transport up, and it was 50p a day there in those days. I mean sometimes I only went home with £5, so I mean I never got a hand on me money until after I got paid off, and I got wise to meself and I just used to give her me board and then look after me own money...

I mean she treated me as if I was daft, as if I couldn't look after me money, and she didn't care about it...

So I went back home till I was nearly twenty, and I went into the hostel...When I moved over to Gateshead the attitude was, I came across all kinds of things, you know like people calling us and that and really being horrible to us. In fact at one stage I was a bag of nerves, but I find now on the whole if like a teenager talks now I just learnt to ignore them, and if they get too bad I call the police.

In fact, the last occasion I called them out the policeman who came out said we're going to have to try and get you some peace, so they patrolled the street for a few weeks, and if they saw anybody floating about asked them what they were doing there, and although I've lived here 11 years, there's still some people in the street who won't like even talk to us. In fact, it seems like the ones who got children are the ones who talk to me...

I feel terrible, I feel as if I've got two heads, which is far from the truth, I mean I've come across some attitudes and I felt really upset and angry, I mean it's the same in the hostel, they think that we're all mental.

Anita Binns: Newcastle
(Tape transcript)

David Sykes interviews Winnie Fairclough

Winnie Fairclough. *David Sykes.*

(David is a former resident of a mental handicap hospital; Winnie was, at the time of interview, a resident.)

David: *Tell me summat about being in a children's home.*

Winnie: Well, I took poorly there.

David: *Was anything happened what were good in your life?*

Winnie: No, not really, She kept hitting me, so I had to defend myself. I just took a piece out of her arm. Put a fist in her face. It was an accident. So I got sent away for that.

David: *So, anything else besides?*

Winnie: I had polio in the children's home.

David: *So what happened there then, Winnie?*

Winnie: I got up and I was feeling alright. I was eating my breakfast and felt alright. And then I was dressing and I fell on the floor and didn't know any more. When I came round I was in hospital, but there were no sugar lumps or needles then.

David: *So what happened after that?*

Winnie: I didn't used to go out much there so I don't know how I got it.

David: *It must have been very difficult for you there.*

Winnie: Well they gave me an operation. I nearly died with it. Then they saved me life and then I had a lumbar puncture to keep me alive. Then I was on a special machine.

David:	*Well, let's get back on to you Winnie and to schooldays.*
Winnie:	I never went to school.
David:	*How did you cope, then? If you didn't go to school?*
Winnie:	I think I had a little bit of schooling before I had polio, but not much.
David:	*So how did you cope with getting on your shoes and getting dressed? Did you have help?*
Winnie:	I had help.
David:	*How come you came to up at the hospital?*
Winnie:	Irene P got me here. Came to see me. I had 17 years at Rampton. I think that was too much. It wasn't my fault really. It was an accident. She shouldn't have kept hitting me. I got her hand in the way. I thought you weren't allowed to hit anyone.
David:	*Yes, you can get them for that.*
Winnie:	This was in a children's home you know.
David:	*Yes, but they're not allowed to hit you unless you been naughty and summat like that. Discipline's how you've been brought up and how you've got yourself into places like that, if you've done summat wrong. Now you're landing yourself up after you've been so far, do you like being at the hospital where you are now?*
Winnie:	S'alright.
David:	*How long have you been there?*
Winnie:	Getting on for four years now I went up there. About Christmas it were.
David:	*So are you really enjoying being up there and doing what you're doing?*
Winnie:	I like it on Cherry Ward. I help on Cherry Ward, looking after the kiddies.
David:	*So does that keep you occupied?*
Winnie:	Yes.
David:	So would you like to work with other handicappeds?
Winnie:	I asked Dr Burroughs if I can look after some babies after I left this place, after I go up to Bradford living nearer me mother. He said yes. That's what I want to do.
David:	*Would you be happier being nearer your mum.*
Winnie:	Yes.
David:	*'Stead of having your mum toiling from Bradford and trailing all the way up that hill and then trailing all the way back down again and back to Bradford.* *So you never went to school in Bradford?*
Winnie:	No.
David:	*Would you like to come to college more than one day?*

Winnie: No, 'cos I like working. I get a bit fed up sitting down.

David: I agree with you there. I do get a bit fed up with sitting down sometimes. Mainly when I'm at home, and I get bored stiff with not being up at the hospital and I have to do housework and keep myself occupied, or if I don't I'm going to crack up. So mainly when you moved out of a place like that you want to be grateful for what the staff have done for you. I've seen both sides of the story of the hospital. I've seen some death. I've seen some work. I've seen some breaking stuff and some fighting.

Winnie: I was there when that man died in the quiet room. He used to call me Minnie.

David: Who were that? Can you remember his name?

Winnie: John, weren't it?

David: Was it John Sweeney?

Winnie: Can't remember his second name. But he kept getting better.

David: He died, didn't he?

Winnie: Yes he died in the quiet room. But it were a bit quiet for him. He died in peace and quiet.

David: So do you think it's very nice for people to die like that in hospital like that when we're alive. To tell you the truth, Winnie, we all got to go through it some time.

Winnie: I know.

David: We can die any minute. While you're still alive, millions of people are dying every minute of every day. So what do you think of life, Winnie. Do you think you're enjoying yourself? Do you sometimes have bad friends or do you have good friends?

Winnie: I don't really bother with them to tell the truth. 'Cept Mary. Mary mostly. She's my friend. I knew her a long time. I knew her at Westwood.

David: How did you get to know her at Westwood?

Winnie: Can't remember.

David: So you can't remember owt about Westwood?

Winnie: No.

David: Can you remember a lot about the hospital where you are now?

Winnie: Yes.

David: Can you tell us about it?

Winnie: Not really. Just don't like the food there.

David: Yes, what's up with the food?

Winnie: What's up with it! Everything!

David: Can you remember what's up with the food? It could be anything.

Winnie: No.

David: *Is it the same meals all the time? Same meals...Well, you know what to do, get a meeting going and discuss it with all the rest.*

Winnie: I've seen Dr Burroughs about it but...

David: *Yes, but see you've got to sort it out and discuss it with the same people what lives up there...with the other people...Then one of you had to go to the staff and speak to the staff. Make arrangements for a meeting. Find out. See what the rest of them think. Don't you? So you don't know what to do?*

Winnie: No.

David: *Well, what you do is, at the hospital if you don't like something, see what they like about the food and sort out problems with them. Then make arrangements to have a meeting and then sort everything out, and then make a meeting with the staff of each ward and get one of the residents on each ward to find out what they sort out. That's how you get the problem sorted out really. It's very interesting helping yourself and other people. And helping them get out from there into the community. Normal people will have to get used to seeing handicapped people outside, used to seeing them shopping and doing their work like a normal person does. 'Cos you see, normal people, some of them think that the handicapped would be better in a place like that. It's really interesting to see people that are handicapped work outside. Working in a small place and doing shopping with normal people. So you'll be doing the same, won't you?*

Winnie: *Well, I can go home if I want to...any time I want. It's up to me, Dr Burroughs says. Me mum's got a room for me now.*

David: *Yes, but could you cope with looking after yourself if your mum died?*

Winnie: *Well, I think I can.*

David: *You've got to think that you need help to look after yourself, you've got to run a house. You got to go shopping and get your food. You've got to pay the rent. You've got to pay the electric when electricity bills come in. All that mainly is what you've got to do.*

David Sykes and Winnie Fairclough: Calder College, Todmorden (Tape transcript)

Chapter Eight
Struggle and self-determination

This chapter is about overcoming adversity. It carries a strong message of hope. People *can* overcome. Life *can* change. This collection of stories bears witness to the strength of human will.

Four main themes emerge:

- the human drive to communicate with others
- the will to move on and achieve independence
- the capacity to rebuild shattered lives
- the power of self-advocacy.

Communication starts with finding words, and this can mean more than 'finding a voice'. Sometimes it's the written word which counts. In a sense this whole book is about the power of the written word. But the written word is important at an individual level too, as our examples from Doreen and Dele show. It is a form of self-expression and one that lasts. It is, for that reason, very special, and particularly so for people who traditionally have little access to the power of the written word.

With access to the written word people can begin to tell their stories to others and to make sense of their lives and experiences. Modern technology has begun to give that access and has enabled many contributors to recount their stories for inclusion within the pages of this book. We include two examples here: by Tommy McManus and Susan Campbell. Both authors have severe physical handicaps. 'Writing' their stories was, for them, not only a struggle to make sense of their lives but also a sign of their determination to communicate with others.

Communication also entails being listened to. We include some contributions from members of a Women's Group who speak and are listened to. They have contributed some extracts from their discussions with the hope that their thoughts and ideas would find a wider audience of people willing to listen. As one woman says: 'It is important people listen to us'. Issues important to all women emerge: relationships, parenthood, jobs, personal safety and, interestingly, women's role as carers.

People find self-expression in many ways, including through dance, song and poetry. We include an example of each. One is Wanda's individual story of her struggle to continue to dance, even following serious illness and confinement to a wheelchair. The New Era Minstrels have contributed a joint account of their choir and a series of individual statements of what the choir means to some of its singing members. Poetry is a means of self-expression and a communication with others. The poem by Sandy Marshall expresses his personal struggle to find a niche in life.

A second major theme of this chapter is people's determination to move on and achieve more autonomy in their lives. Usually moving on means acquiring a new home, as George Alexander and Tommy Goard were able to do. Sometimes it's not that easy and other, influential, people have to be persuaded. The struggle for Jenny and Margaret, in setting up home together, and for Chris and Sue, in getting married, was convincing people that it was possible. Their determination saw them through.

Another major theme of this chapter is people's capacity to rebuild their lives. Four people describe their personal struggles to overcome adversity. The extract from Huw Redwood's much longer story describes his fight against his escalating weight and the indignities, and the depression, he suffered on the way. Two poems (by Stefan Dubery and Jeannie Miller) continue the theme of rebuilding lives. And in her story, Doreen Young describes her loss of home and child, and her long years in hospital. But she did not accept her fate. She was determined to leave and did so on many occasions by running away. Eventually her determination paid off when she and George left to get married.

Self-advocacy is also about struggle and self-determination, both at an individual and at a collective level. Three of our contributors have found a voice through belonging to self-advocacy groups. Their struggle was personal, but it was also shared with other people in their respective groups.

Self-advocacy has helped change the lives of Ronald, Peter and Anita. No doubt it will change the lives of others. It is a movement of the present and, undoubtedly, a force for the future.

Contents

Communicating with others

(i) Finding words

Doreen Cocklin.

This is the first time

This is the first time anything I have said has been written down.

I don't know what to say.

But I like what I see. It's good how it comes out. Nice!

I like that, that's all right.

Doreen Cocklin: Tuesday Reading and Writing Class, Tower Hamlets Gateway Club, London
(Dictated, then transferred to word-processor by tutor)

Dear mum

Dear mum,

I am using a word-processor. What is most important in my life is in the future that I understand what is going on around me.

From Dele.

Dele Fakoya: South Lewisham Institute, London
(Produced on a word-processor)

(ii) Telling one's story

Tommy McManus.

This is Tommy's long life

WHEN I WAS 3 YEARS OLD MY FATHER TOOK ME TO LOURDES. ME AND MY DAD STAYED THERE FOR ONE WEEK. I ENJOYED THE HOLIDAY AND IT MADE ME FEEL BETTER.
ALSO WHEN I WAS 3 I WENT INTO THE CHILDRENS ANNEXE FOR AN OPERATION WHICH DID NOT WORK.
I DID NOT LIKE THE SIGHT OF THE HOSPITAL AND I WAS VERY PLEASED WHEN I LEFT THE PLACE.
WHEN I WAS FIVE YEARS OLD I WENT TO ST.

I was born in Ireland on the 27 May 1954 in County Longfoirt to Irish parents. I was born spastic. We came to England when I was two years old because my father needed work.

He was a builder. We came to live in Luton in Morden Close. It was a three-bedroomed house.

When I was three years old my father took me to Lourdes. Me and my dad stayed there for one week. I enjoyed the holiday and it made me feel better.

Also, when I was three, I went into the Children's Annexe for an operation which did not work.

I did not like the sight of the hospital and I was very pleased when I left the place.

When I was five years old I went to St Matthew's infant school. I had sticks to help me walk but I also used them to hit people. Then I had to go to the office for a good telling off.

While I was at St Matthew's School we moved to a town house in Pomfret Avenue. It was a nice house but it was not very suitable for me because there were too many stairs. I met a friend as soon as I moved there. He was very nice and played with me. I am still friends with him...

When it was half-term holiday, I was at home and I fell down the stairs. I was 12 years old then. I hurt myself very badly and had my arm in plaster for 10 weeks. After the 10 weeks, I had to go for a check-up and then I had an X-ray. Then the doctor said I had to keep it on for another week! When the week was up, I had the plaster off and my arm felt very heavy for a few days...

In September of the same year I started at Richmond Hill School, still getting around on my sticks. There were no other children who had difficulty getting around or needing sticks at all.

In my first year there, they had a competition from Brooke Bond tea and I was one of the second prize winners. We had to write a story. I cannot remember what I wrote about. The Mayoress of Luton presented us with our prizes. The prize was a story book. The teacher in this class was very nice. When she left to have a baby I was sad.

Then I moved into my second year and had a man teacher. When you were naughty he pulled your hair. I got my hair pulled more than once. We had very hard work to do. I enjoyed maths best and I was good at it. We had cookery every Tuesday which I also enjoyed very much, and on Thursday it was woodwork but I was not allowed to join in. They thought it was too dangerous for me. I thought they were very mean not letting me join in. I thought they would at least allow me to do something.

I was very pleased when I left the second year because I was moved into the fourth year and the teacher's name was Mr Hamilton. He was very nice but he was very strict with some of the boys. Most of the boys were very helpful to me if I got stuck on the stairs. I was very sad when I left Richmond Hill School because I had enjoyed being there.

Then, as soon as I left school, I went to the children's clinic in Dallow Road for a test to see if I was fit for work. I wanted to be a telephone operator. I was very disappointed when they decided I was unfit for work.

Then I was sent to a centre and I went there every day. At the centre we made toys and cocktail sticks. I hated making the cocktail sticks. We did hair rollers and rubber ducks. I enjoyed them for they made a noise. We made trains out of plastic which also made a noise, but I liked the rubber ducks best. We all had a good laugh while we made the toys.

I was at the factory working for three years. At Christmas time we all had a special job to do. One time we did have a party at Christmas when we all got together, also we had a present given to each of us. The boss was very nice, his name was Mr Fountain.

At this time I was still living at home with mum and dad. Because my father was ill and my mum could not manage both of us, I had to go somewhere else to live. On the 30th November 1979 I went to the Oaks to live. It is a modern equipped home with all the modern conveniences. Going to the Oaks was not an awful experience, it was a very nice experience and the people and staff were friendly, especially Marion and Margaret. They helped me to feel welcome. The boss, as I called him, who was John Higgins, was the first person to manage the Oaks and also the Acorns which is for young mentally handicapped children.

I am very sorry to say that my dad died soon after I went to the Oaks.

I have a single room which is a bed-sit. I have my own TV and a video, also I have a stereo system. On the shelves are lots of photos of family and friends...

I had to go to the Luton and Dunstable hospital for an operation to have my big toes done on both feet

- to straighten them. The nurses and doctors had a job to revive me with the anaesthetic. I had to have oxygen - to bring me round. Going back after a few weeks for a check-up, I was told that the first operation was not successful and that I would have to go back for a major operation on my feet, which I did have, and had to stay in hospital for three weeks. Also, I had to go to have my wisdom teeth out, but I was not in very long for this...

I keep myself busy by going out in the week. Tuesday I see Corinne at Challney Community College where I get tuition, also I attend Charles Street on Thursdays where I meet lots of other people. I hope this will go on for a long time yet because I like to get out and about.

This is my life story so far. I hope you enjoy reading it as I have enjoyed writing it.

Tommy McManus: Challney Community College, Luton
(Tommy and his tutor talked about his life and discussed what exactly he would like to say. Then he put it on the word-processor)

My story

My name is Susan Campbell. I was born in Watford in 1941. I have two brothers, John and Ted...My mother and father have been very good to me, but I only have my father now as I lost my mother in 1967.

When I was a baby, I went to a Sunshine Home for blind babies and young children. I went to a boarding school, in Sunningdale, when I was nine years old until the age of 14. This was a special school run by the Catholic Church for the partially sighted, where great emphasis was put on religious knowledge. Normal education was very limited which is why I am attending literacy classes. After that I went back to Watford. I spent a lot of time in and out of hospital, from 1959 when I went for the first tests until 1978 when I had the last operation in Great Portland Street, most of the time I was in Watford but I also spent a year at Stanmore.

I had five operations on my hips. I was not able to walk very well at first and at one time was in plaster for over a year. My mother had a chance to see me walking after the first three operations, but for the last two operations there was only my father to help me.

I then spent two more years in Watford Hospital before coming to Hitchin to a home for the disabled. I have been here now for six years and have had to learn a whole new way of living. Learning from scratch how to mix with people and make friends, being in control of my own life at last. It is very nice here and I have made some friends. After years in hospital it is lovely to live in a place that is a home as well as a Home. I can now go out with friends when I want to, and I can choose for myself when I get up or go to bed. This is something that I had never done before...

The staff are very kind and helpful. I don't go out a lot, as I can't walk very far. I am not very interested in television because my eyesight is still very poor, so I listen to the radio and play tapes a lot. When I do go out, I have to use a walking stick to help me and have to walk slowly or go by car because of the difficulty in using public transport...

I have literacy classes every Monday and Wednesday mornings from 10.00 a.m. to 12 noon which I enjoy very much... When I was young I missed so much school that I am now working to fill in the gaps...

We have a computer room for the residents, which is open from 11.30 in the morning to 7.30 in the evening. There are four BBC Microcomputers for the residents to use, with a large selection of games and word-processing programs available. Most afternoons all of the computers are in use. I prefer the mornings when there are usually only one or two other residents in there and it is quieter. I like going in as I feel I am doing something. I wrote an article for the magazine with the help of the assistants. I have now moved on and decided to write my autobiography. The others write letters and play games. This is the only way for the residents to write to people. Some of the residents can use the keyboard, but a lot of them have to use either rocker switches or the touch switches...

I can honestly say that the last six years at the Cheshire Home have been the best and happiest I have known. Moving here has given me a new lease of life, and a chance to learn at last how to mix with new people and live a life as near normal as possible...

Susan Campbell: Cheshire Home, Hitchin
(Dictated)

(iii) Being listened to

It is important people listen to us

In January we started a Women's Group at our centre. The group is only for women at the centre. We can use it to talk about things that are important to women.

We agreed at the start of the group to meet upstairs in the sitting room. We meet for an hour and each member of the group takes it in turn to make coffee and to wash up.

To start with we spent time getting to know more about each other. We brought in photographs of when we were younger and told each other about things in the photos. Our social worker told us about herself and where she lives. We take it in turns to listen to each other.

We start each week by saying what has happened since we last met. We try to help each other if problems come up. When somebody's been in hospital we talk about it.

The group is private. We all agreed at the start not to talk about what is said in the group when we are in the SEC. Some things are personal.

When we had been meeting for two months we made a list of things we would like to discuss in the group. People had different ideas. All of the things are important for women. This is the list we wrote:

1 *People going out after dark.*

2 *People asking us for money.*

3 *How to stand up for yourself and say what you want.*

4 *Feeling safe.*

5 *Women's jobs.*

6 *Relationships: families, friends, boyfriends.*

7 *Sex and AIDS.*

8 *The way we look: clothes, going to buy clothes.*

We have begun to talk about some of these things.

As the group is private we do not want to give our names, but we would like to be included in the Open University anthology. We think it is good for women in centres to meet together. It would be good for groups of women to meet up.

There are things you need help with that you can't talk about with boys, like periods.

We decided to write down some of our ideas on the subjects we have talked about. It is important people listen to us. We are not children.

When I told my mum I was in a women's group she said I was a girl. I said I was a woman. Now she knows I was right.

Women going out after dark or on their own during the day-time

'My mum and dad don't let me go out unless I am on the centre transport or the Gateway bus.'

'I go out after dark but my parents go with me. Never on my own. People get mugged.'

'You need to know where you are going, get yourself lifts arranged, carry your address in case you get lost. It is best to go where it is more crowded. Barnet High Street is more safe than the road by the Leys. That has no lights.'

'It is hard for ordinary women to go out, but they have husbands or boyfriends. Women with a handicap can't really go out.'

'Parents need to decide if you can go out because you can't do it.'

'I make my own decisions but my mum doesn't like me to go out. So if I go out I worry about her because she worries about me. It is boring being in every evening though.'

'Women get raped. I heard it on the news. That's why my mum likes me to go to clubs with transport.'

'Clubs are boring though. They finish too early and you just see people from work again!'

'If you have a boyfriend you can go anywhere. You are safe with a boyfriend.'

'Sometimes men get hit or mugged.'

'My mum would let me go more places if I had a boyfriend. My sister has a boyfriend and she goes out every night in his car.'

'Members of staff have boyfriends.'

'So do people in the centre. I know two people who used to go to centres who got married.'

'You find it hard to meet boys. Some try to take advantage. You can't tell by looking at me that there is anything wrong. My father says that people can take advantage.'

'They could try and touch you.'

'That can happen in the day as well as after dark.'

'A man tried to touch me on a bus once. I moved where I was sitting and he stopped. It was horrible.'

'If someone does that you should tell them to take their hands away.'

'I would be frightened.'

'You have to be very clear if you really don't want someone to touch you, and say so very firmly.'

'And then tell your parents.'

'Or the police.'

'What if there wasn't a member of staff? If you were on the 221 to the centre?'

'I'd tell the driver. Or another woman.'

'You can carry alarms. I would set an alarm off.'

'At night you can go out with another friend. It's safer. It doesn't always have to be a boy or a man.'

How we would like to see ourselves in the future

'I'd like to be richer than I am now, £4 a week.'

'I'd like to have a house and a boyfriend.'

'Or a husband?'

'I would like to have a husband and children and a house like my sister.'

'I would like a proper job, to go to work properly and save up for a house.'

'I might not be able to get married. I'm getting too old to have children now. My periods might stop soon.'

'You need a husband to have children. It's hard to look after children on your own.'

'Staff can have children. People like us need help.'

'You would need a husband or boyfriend to help you. You would need a boyfriend for a long time first.'

'Babies are a lot of hard work. People like us might not be able to look after one. Babies wake up at night and cry.'

'People like us don't have babies. No one in the centre does apart from staff. Some people have their stomachs taken out.'

'I'd like to choose my dates and have a house to take people to.'

'I'd like a boyfriend or a best friend to go out with at weekends.'

Families – women as people who do lots of caring

'All except one of us still lives at home with either a mum or dad.'

'Some of us have lost a mum or dad.'

'My mum died when I was small so now I look after my dad. I can't leave home because he needs me.'

'Yes, my dad died. I cheer up my mum. She would be lost without me. I take her breakfast in bed.'

'My sister moved away when she got married.'

'So did my brother.'

'And my sister.'

'My sister is getting married soon. Then she will go away. She is my best friend. I will miss her.'

'I missed my sister when she got married. I used to go out with her.'

'I've always been at home with my mum and dad.'

'So have I.'

'So have I. Apart from short stays and centre holidays.'

'My mum and dad need me. They wouldn't want me to leave.'

'You worry about your parents when they get on.'

'I worry about my mum. She has blood pressure. I worry about where I will live if she dies – I've tried a few places for short stays but my mum says I might go to my family for good.'

'I've been visiting my dad in hospital when he has been ill. I try to do the cleaning in the house.'

'Sometimes I row with my family. I get bored at home.'

'I row too. My mum gets upset so I try to make it up with her quickly.'

'If your mum dies you need to stay at home to look after your dad. My dad likes me helping.'

Women's Group: Mill Hill, London
(Transcribed extracts from discussion)

(iv) Dance, song and poetry

Short life story

When I was a child I liked to dance. I liked to dance to ballet music. My sister came along with me to the dance classes but she never joined in. I was very happy to dance on my own. Up until the time I was sick I used to dance once a week.

As a result of being ill I became dependent on a wheel chair and I could no longer continue to go dancing. I had been dancing for a year when I stopped it. Although I am in a wheel-chair, it doesn't prevent me from dancing and I like to dance when I have the opportunity.

When I was a child I used to go horse-riding, and we would ride around a ring which was good fun. I loved to go swimming and play games with the other people who were in the swimming pool.

I used to go to an ordinary Catholic primary school. But because I moved somewhere else I had to stop going to the school and I felt sorry because I left it. I liked to practise piano at the school. I used to sing with other students in the school.

I like handicrafts and sports. I used to go to church a lot once. Our local priest would come and collect me and both of us used to go into church together. I know all my prayers, and the words of the Mass, and my religion was very important to me. I haven't been to church for a long time due to some family problems, but I often say my prayers and I pray for everyone.

Wanda: A Social Education Centre in London
(Interpreted from signs)

We can sing

It was the 19th November 1987 when we started. We started first at a Gateway Club as a singing group and then Jayne suggested we formed an independent choir.

We are not stupid, we're not daft and we can sing. We are not loonies or nutters. Another word is mental and that's rubbish too. Anyway, the choir decided to show people how good we can be. In eight months we have performed at an ATC fete, a hospital carnival, Bedford River festival, the Bedfordshire Competitive Music Festival where we were awarded a distinction mark of 85, two social/musical evenings we've arranged ourselves and a multi-cultural music festival at John Howard in Bedford.

To get helpers in would be a mistake because they would get under our feet and they'd get on top of us. They might order us about and get bossy, and they'd get away with it as well. They get too big-headed. We're quite happy as we are because it's nice to meet other people and we like to be independent. We also have a music group connected to the choir. That meets on a Tuesday. The group is for non-choir members. The choir members help the others and use the group for extra practice.

The New Era Minstrels
(Line drawing by Meg).

Pam: *I enjoy myself coming to the choir. I like to sing on my own at the Westbourne Centre. I'm singing tonight at the John Howard festival. One day we might be famous and go on telly.*

Janet: *There are so many people on the choir members' committee:*

Tina Mason (Chairman), Pam Todd (Vice Chairman), Graham Ward (Secretary), Janet Umney (Treasurer)
Linda Keep, Linda Lindley, Elaine Duke, Andrew Webb

We get together to discuss what we're going to do and where we're going to perform. I think it's good to be able to entertain other people and see how they feel about it.

Linda: *I quite like the choir. I think it's doing very well.*

Ray: *I enjoy coming to the choir, I think its really good. I enjoyed singing my solos in Michael, row the boat ashore.*

Eddie: *I like the choir better than going to the Pentecostal choir because I have got used to it.*

Elaine: *I like the choir because next year we might win a cup or something but we don't know where we'll put it if we do.*

Lee: *I like the choir. I like the noise of it. I'm so happy about it.*

Alan: *I like what I do plus the fact I like the people. I like the songs we're singing. I don't mind doing concerts because I feel if I didn't I'd let Jayne down. I feel nervous but then everybody does.*

Graham: *I like what I do on the committee. I like singing, I like doing committee work – anything. I enjoy helping to organise the choir. The more publicity we get, the more bookings we'll get and that's good for us.*

Meg: *I love singing because it calms me down and it's lively and bouncy and great fun especially when it's in tune.*

The New Era Minstrels, Bedford
(Extracts from group discussion, plus dictated individual comments)

I feel I've found my niche

I feel I've found my niche
At last, helping disabled people
With their lives
To live their lives.

But here my life is way down
Deep in the pits
Not revving ahead at all,
Like I used to.

Reaching out to comfort some people
Is my goal in life,
Even though it may take time;
And it's like climbing a steeple.

Reaching for new heights
Is my goal in life;
But just now I'm heading
For my lowest ebb.

'One in Four' is a programme
About - and presented by
Disabled and handicapped people
And how they came to terms with life.

And the programme also features music and songs,
Included in its content are music and songs,
Which is very good.
And here is one contented viewer.

Sandy Marshall, Thomas Fortune Work Centre, Glasgow
(Self-typewritten)

Moving on

(i) A new home

I did not like where I had been living

I did not like where I had been living. I had been there a long time and I needed a change. I was living in a large hostel and I was having a difficult time with my girlfriend.

I asked my social worker about moving and we made a list of possibilities. I visited other places and moved to a new flat last December. I am very happy there.

Now I have started a job as a caretaker's assistant in a school. I like it very much. I work two hours a day and walk home to the hostel in time for tea.

It is important that people listen to what you say.

George: A Social Education Centre in London
(Dictated)

Tommy Goard.

My new flat

I have moved into a flat
at Coventry Cross,
Bromley by Bow.

I'm there on my own.

I've got one bedroom,
one kitchen, one sitting room,
and one bathroom.

I've got a 3-piece suite,
a bed, a few pots and pans,
and a bathroom stool.
I've got disco lights
and a television.

I've got a cooker.
The gas people have to come
and set it up for me.

There is central heating.

I've got carpets, a tea pot
and an electric kettle.
I've got a few posters
up on the wall.

I like the flat.
I like to be by myself.

Tommy Goard: Tuesday Reading and Writing Class, Tower Hamlets Gateway Club, London
(Dictated)

(ii) Persuading others

Jenny and Margaret's story

WE MOVED INTO OUR FLAT ON DECEMBER 1ST 1975. WE RENT IT FROM
SOCIAL SERVICES. I HAD SOME FURNITURE OF MY OWN WHICH WAS
MY MOTHER'S. AND MARGARET HAD SOME THINGS OF HER OWN.
AND THE REST WAS PROVIDED BY THE COUNTY COUNCIL. // AT
FIRST OUR SOCIAL WORKER VISITED US EVERY DAY. SHE WENT
SHOPPING WITH US AND HELPED US SETTLE IN. WE DID HAVE SOME
PROBLEMS WITH SHOPPING AND WITH MONEY. JUST AFTER WE MOVED
IN I HAD TO GO TO HOSPATAL BECAUSE I HAD ULCERS ON MY LEGS
//

My name is Jenny. I am 47. My friend is 36. I met Margaret at a small hostel about 13 years ago. When we got to know each other, we realised that we both wanted to move out and to live in a flat. We went to a training centre but this did not help us much, but staff at the hostel helped us a lot.

Gradually we learned to shop and cook and look after ourselves. We lived in a flat attached to the hostel for about a year. This was quite hard because the hostel was so close, and it was tempting to eat in the hostel and easy to spend time in the evenings there.

We moved into our flat on December 1st 1975. We rent it from social services. I had some furniture of my own which was my mother's, and Margaret had some things of her own and the rest was provided by the county council.

At first our social worker visited us every day. She went shopping with us and helped us settle in. We did have some problems with shopping and with money. Just after we moved in I had to go to hospital because I had ulcers on my legs, and Margaret went back to the hostel for a while.

Until recently we had the same home help since we first moved into our flat, which helped an awful lot. She is our friend. Our new home help visits us once a week, mainly to help with shopping. Our social worker (our third one since we moved into the flat) also visits us once a week and mainly helps with our money. We all like to save up and go on a shopping spree about once every six months.

Sometimes me and Margaret get fed up if we spend too much time together. We try to do different things apart as well as together. We are busy and we have a lot of friends. We have been on holiday together by ourselves to Torquay. We stayed in a hotel and went on day trips. We are going to the same place this year. The staff and guests were very friendly and helpful.

I used to go to an adult training centre a couple of times a week. I don't go now because I do lots of other things. I am now a volunteer at a local club for people who have had strokes, and I spend one day each week there.

Some of my family live quite close and I see them every now and again. We have been to two family weddings recently. I like to sing and I belong to the choir at my church.

Margaret does not go to the centre and spends quite a bit of time at home doing the washing and some cleaning and shopping. She says she enjoys doing it. She also goes to some classes each week. We both go to classes at college. We have done classes in cookery, dancing, typing, and Margaret was in a group which made a video about the local area.

We feel proud of what we have achieved. Many people did not think that we could do it. That we could actually move out of a hostel and live in a flat by ourselves. We have been here for over ten years now. We like being independent. We have had our ups and downs but we manage alright. We would not want to live anywhere else.

Jenny Trim: Highbridge, Somerset
(Handwritten)

Our wedding day

'Getting married – that was the nicest thing of all...'

Chris: I used to go to work a bit untidy before I met Sue. Gradually I changed. I used to live with Bill. He used to help me out a lot – he was like a father to me. And then I met Susan. Then we gradually got talking. Then she asked me out. I couldn't believe it at first! I said yes.

I used to take Susan down Bill's. I used to take her into a cafe and buy her dinner. I used to take her home by bus sometimes.

And then, after four years, I asked her to marry me. She said yes. We got married on June 6th. Bill was our best man. Jeannette, Bill's friend, made us a wedding cake.

Sue: My mum said we could get married as long as we could find a flat. John, Mrs Tipping and my parents have been marvellous. And Chris has been a good husband to me.

We had a big meeting about us getting married. They said: 'Would epileptics like you want to get married?' We said we'd give it a go. Things have turned out very good. I know we won't have children but we still love each other.

I like it at home but it was squashed. I wanted to move out to give mum that extra room.

Chris: It was a bit lonely before I met Sue. I wanted to get married but I couldn't find a girl.

Sue: *I'd always wanted to get married but I thought nobody would have me!*

I was as calm as anything right up to getting to the Church. I had two lovely bridesmaids, Kerry-Ann and Angela, who I went to school with. My nan paid for half my wedding dress. I had sequins, flowers, a veil. The dress was beautiful. Coming down the aisle there were all those people. I didn't expect so many. My father took me up the aisle. That was really nice.

I went in as Miss Susan Hirons and came out as Mrs Susan Virgin.

Chris: I wasn't nervous at all. After it was over, I thought – blimey, I've got a wife now! I couldn't believe it.

Sue: *Mrs Dixon did all our flowers. They were gorgeous. Uncle Terry drove the cars and helped with the disco.*

My dad done the disco and all the music. We had to start the dancing off, so people could follow us onto the floor.

Linda and Bridget did a lovely reception. Mum and dad paid for everything! I'll never forget it. Sausage rolls, chicken legs, cheese and pineapple, peanuts.

We cut the wedding cake between us. That was most important. People were taking a lot of photos of us. Cameras everywhere.

We had plates, dishes and cups from the rally people. Dishes from Derek and Judy and other things. We had a chicken to put eggs in. Bill gave us £20 towards a bed. Mrs Tipping gave us a picture. I had a cookery book from the night school people. I felt terrible leaving my evening class.

After the wedding we were tired, exhausted.

Chris woke up at five o'clock on our wedding night and made a cup of tea. He said, 'I can't sleep! I'm too in love!'

Our honeymoon was one of the first holidays Chris ever had. We went to Cherrytree in Yarmouth to stay in a caravan.

Chris: It felt a bit strange.

I felt miserable – I don't know what it was.

Life has changed a lot since we got married.

We realise what we got to pay out for bills – electric and gas. We do our own shopping. We feel more independent.

We help each other out.

Sue: It's nice having our own flat. We keep it clean and everyone says how well we're doing.

Chris does the gardening. We take turns with the cooking.

We have not had an argument yet.

It's nice to be married. I would say to anyone else – try it!

Chris and Sue Virgin: Dunstable
(Tape transcript)

Rebuilding lives

What happened with my life in the world

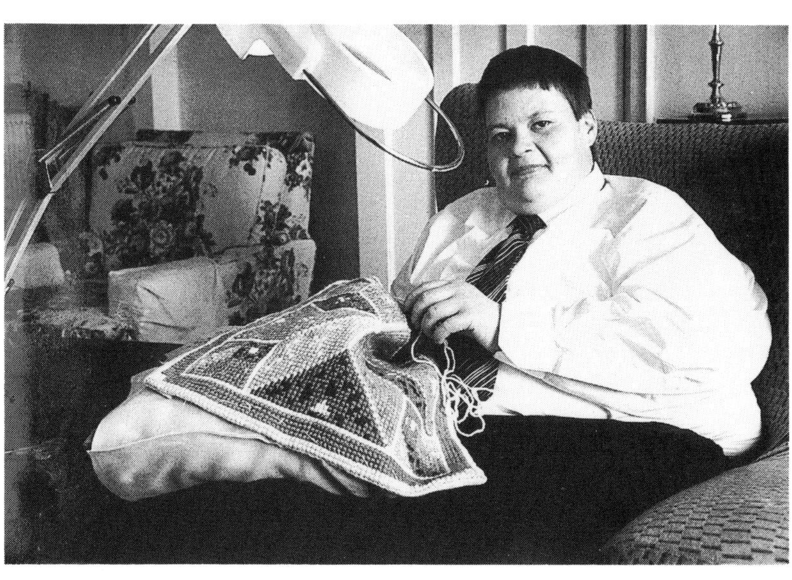

Huw Redwood.

My name is Huw Redwood, I'm 23 years old...I was born normal, as a normal baby...I'm living with my parents...I have got two brothers and one sister but now they are married...

I started to put on weight when I started to take some food from my mother. Also I started to take a nice cake that we were going to have for tea. My father found out that I'd taken the cake because he found a bit of it under the bed. He sent me up to bed. On that day it was a nice day. My sister went to get some ice-cream off the ice-cream man. My father hit me on my bottom. I was getting overweight. I went to my mother's school when I was five years old. I started to take food from the other boys and girls at my mother's school.

Months went by, I put on some more weight. So I went to the Children's Hospital, as an outpatient...When I was eight years old I went into the Children's Hospital to get the weight off me...

My disease became so bad that I could not walk at all. I started to be very overweight before I had my trouble with my legs. I started to eat even more and got fatter; my weight became 20 stone. But while I had such trouble with my legs I reached the weight of 30 stone.

I had to start having trousers made for me; I could not get into any ready-made trousers. I had a lot of leisure time when I was ill as I could not go out to work. I began to do a lot of puzzles, especially jig-saw puzzles, at home. I made one 3,000-piece jig-saw for a local social club. The jig-saw is now on the club wall. I also decided to play darts more often and do more rugs.

Before I had trouble with my legs I used to go to the local social club meetings and parties regularly. In 1979, at the club Christmas party, I was very ill; I had to be taken home from the Christmas party. My mother and father were out at the time. Two social club helpers could not take me upstairs to my bedroom so they had to take me in the front room. Mrs Edna Ward[1] had to call my doctor but my doctor could not come, another doctor came. His name was Dr F. Evans; he gave me some sleeping pills. After Dr F Evans went away there was someone at the door; it was Mrs Hetherington, the club leader, come to see me. Mrs Edna Ward and Mrs Hetherington had to make a bed up for me in the front room as I could not get upstairs to my bedroom.

[1]All names in this account – except the author's – are fictitious.

The next day my mother moved me to another downstairs room. Mrs Hetherington phoned up my mother to ask how I was. When it was almost time for bed I fell off my chair. I could not get me up. I called my mother to help me but she could not get me up. I had to stay on the floor until the morning. My mother stayed away from work to look after me; she phoned the doctor to ask him to come to our house to see me. The doctor would not help my mother to help me up; in the end he did help my mother because my mother told him to help me. The doctor phoned for some ambulancemen to come to help me; he only gave me some medicine. Two men came to our house and tried to get me off the floor, but they could not, so they phoned the police station for some more help. One policeman came to help them to get me off the floor. The three men managed to lift me off the floor and put me in my chair. After they had got me into my chair they asked my mother to bring my bed downstairs to me, and when she had done so they helped to put me to bed....

I had to stay in bed for one week, they made me better. By that time I was very unhappy because I was very ill, also overweight. Last year I went to my bedroom to kill myself; but I did not do it in the end because if I did it, it would make my mother and my father very unhappy. That's why I did not do it in the end. So my mother and my father started to look for some help; they did find help...

By that time, after my bypass operation, I was down to 19 stones - the weight keeps coming off me all the time. I went to the swimming baths with the social club every Sunday from 5 p.m. until 6 p.m.. I sent a letter to Val Croft; she sent a letter to me, which is what happened since I saw her. When it was my birthday I had a card from the social club; also I had a present as well as a card. I told them thank you very much for the card and present indeed. The present was a box of sweets; I ate them when I did some more rugs at home. I did two rugs for my sister-in-law's child and my sister's child to hang upon their walls. My father took them to work to get some orders.

My father took me to work to see my friend. I also went to see my girlfriend to ask her to marry me; she told me 'Yes'. I told her that I am having an operation to take some fat away. Christmas is here soon. I am going to have two parties: one at the social club; another one for my mother because it's her 60th birthday this year. I found that I could go under water about six feet at the baths...

I'm hoping to have a Disabled car; so I can go anywhere without going in my mother's car. While I have not got a Disabled car, I still go with my mother anywhere I like to go in her car. I would like a Disabled car because soon my mother will be too old to get me anywhere because she would be too old to drive me there. That's why I would like a car. Also I would like a Disabled car because whatever happens I would not drive any car at all. The cars that you can get from car shops, I would not drive them without some things to be added to them, which things are for Disabled people like me.

Huw Redwood: Staffordshire
(Edited extracts from self-typewritten account)

Stefan Dubery.

I can, I will, and I'm going to

I have been alive 19 years,
Have caused my family many tears,
In my childhood I was stupid and wild
Couldn't control me although they tried,
I left school a work scheme started
Wasted time money soon parted,
A lucky break a job my way came,
My life became serious not a game,
Stupidity it claimed my life once more,
It shook my family to the core.
Asleep in its back seat, the car took a smack,
My head received a hefty whack.
Darkness came, wouldn't go away,
Floating above myself, three months to stay.
All the while family prayed and wept,
A long time mum at my bedside kept.
She didn't give up, stayed calm and strong,
Always saying her grandad's song.
You can, you will – and you're going to.
I heard it and at last came through,
Another chance given, a long way to go,
I'm making progress, a little, very slow.
Sometimes I give up, is it worthwhile,
Mum listens with patience and a smile,
Making me think life's precious, I am alive,
To reach my goal I'll struggle and strive.
I will do it, I have God and mum on my side,
If I don't, I know at least we three tried.
There must be a reason for being still here,
As death came to touch so very near.
It's up to me to make it all worthwhile,
And be rewarded by mum's special smile.
I take life at a much slower pace,
No chance of running yet, to join the race.

Of my young days I don't feel good.
Can't go back I would if I could,
But my future's important and new,
What matters most is to myself stay true,
I will, I can and I'm going to.

Stefan Dubery: Leeds
(Handwritten)

Building again

There is nothing to stop you from building again -
when all of your castles have crushed,

There is nothing to stop you from dreaming again -
when the things long worked for have smashed.

There is no law to stop you from wearing a smile,
though perhaps you are crying inside
There is never a reason for losing a grip -
Or your nerve - your faith or your pride.

There is nothing to gain by repeating your woes
into every listening ear -
For pity, and sympathy won't get you far -
Though it may be so kind and sincere.

Get on with the job of rebuilding your life -
It's so useless to sigh, or complain
The best thing to do - is to start out anew -
Pluck up courage, and then try again.

Jeannie Miller: Tower Hamlets Institute, London
(Self-typewritten)

Doreen's story

First memories

We lived in Wallsend. And they were fighting. My dad was fighting with my mam and I got a cup on my head. And I've been run over when my brother wouldn't go to the butcher's. He went to a party. I dashed across the road. I hurt my hands, my legs and my neck. I had a collar on my neck. That was when I was 13. It'll be 19 years this March. I was let home the next day. It was just the shock. I was carried out the ambulance by my dad. I couldn't hardly walk.

My brother used to be a bus-driver. He's married now. My brother got married and now he's divorced. He's a free man you see.

School

I used to go to Whitley Bay School, then St Aiden's...I used to wag. I didn't go to school. Didn't like school.

Doreen Young and her husband, George.

The hospital

I moved to Northgate. I was 20. I had a bairn...a baby. He died. Used to be on Ward 8. It was alright in the hospital. Used to work in the printing department. I used to work on the machine making those Makaton type things. Selotaped them down on the back of them. Put them in boxes and then sent them away.

It was a mixed ward...lads and lasses. Food came on trolleys...bread, tea, sausages, breakfast like...I used to run away. People were getting at us, pushed us down the stairs, the staff and things. I used to go to Newcastle and all those places. You'd get put in your nightie. Felt awful.

I used to be on Ward 19, the hostel ward. Used to have their own rooms there, downstairs like. It was alright. We'd take turns at washing the dishes...I used to help the staff get the people up and get a bath. I had to mark them off. I used to do reports – the night reports – to say if you ran away or if you were going home. They'd write it in the report book. I used to take it upstairs. Used to run away, I did. Ran away from Ward 19.

I used to be on Ward 11, the locked Ward, as well, and on the management Ward and on 20, 22...I ran away from Ward 11. I used to be on Grades. See if you ran away you'd get docked. Was there five grades? I used to be grade 3. I got put down to grade 1...I didn't run away from 20...didn't run away from 22. I never been on 10. Been on 13 when it was mixed and I ran away from there.

George and marriage

George used to come on 19 to help me with the reports. Somebody asked you (to George). Heather, remember her? She blew up Ward 8 with a matchstick. She used to cut herself. She used to set a match on the curtains. We went to dances. I was on the ward then getting the baths. Used to watch you getting a bath in case you got scalded. Heather asked George. George been going with Pat A. He asked me to go with us and I make up my mind and I says, 'Yes'. We went to the community centre. They play records...

We used to go home to see our Brenda, George's sister, every fortnight. We'd go out...Had a party. We used to go out have fish and chips and a Chinese meal.

We got engaged together, then we got out. We got work together, then we got married...About three years ago at Morpeth Registry Office...All my family was there and George's and some of the nurses from Northgate. Ken was there and Paul K. with the two bairns. They had tea with us.

We got this flat. George went down the doctor's and he asked Janis, and we got it off the council. Then we got the keys. We're going to move. Getting a house...got a garden, bit of a lawn. We've got it. We're moving 24th June.

Doreen Young: Newcastle
(Tape transcript)

Self-advocacy

The story of my life

Ronald Lewis.

I went to Harperbury Hospital in 1946 as I was 11 years old. I was in Harperbury for eight years to 1952, before going to Brighton from there for one year...An older woman got me to do knitting. I said: 'Only women do it' but she told me: 'No, men do it too'. So this was very good for me and I have made a lot from 1952 to 1988. Now I never stop...

I came to Leavesden in 1953 as I was 18 years old. I went to most wards as I have been around for 35 years and have seen more and more people. This is my home till I kick the dustbin...

I joined the club in Watford which has toys, and pay five shillings a week from 1964. This was how my typing started, with a children's typewriter which cost £8. I had to buy two more in three years. In 1974 my first typewriter cost £10, and my second cost £36.18 from Uxbridge in 1978. It is 10 years old in July 1988 and still working. Now you know this was a good way for making you good at words...

I now belong to a group called the self-advocacy group set up by Bob Gates and Dave Lewis just over two years ago. It started with 14 people and now we have 30 people. In the last year we met every two weeks as meetings.

We did a conference in 1987 and made about £300. About 200 people from hospitals and homes went on the long weekend that we had. It was very good.

R. D. LEWIS

Ronald Lewis (now 53 years old): Leavesden Hospital, Abbots Langley
(Extracts from self-typewritten account)

About self-advocacy

When I joined the class the group was about self-advocacy skills, but it was not a self-advocacy group.

We went up to London to share our self-advocacy skills. The course was called, 'Helping your self-advocacy group to grow'. We learnt about People First of London and Thames.

When we got back from London, I said to the group that we would not be a self-advocacy group unless someone from the group took over. The group then asked Sue (the Adult Education Tutor running the group) to leave the room while we talked about it all. It was decided on the vote that I should be chairperson and Shirley secretary. The tutor (Sue) stayed with the group for a while as an adviser.

I felt I had had enough tutoring and one day when Sue (the tutor) said we should do something, I said, 'No, we don't have to do what you say'. After a while it was decided that Sue (the tutor) should leave the group. Now we meet and we have a new adviser who is quiet and doesn't keep talking like Sue!

Since Sue left we got a vice-chairperson and a treasurer. We have talked about rules that should be in the group. They are:

1 No smoking in the group, only at break time.
2 No roaming round the building.
3 No distracting the driver on the transport.

Self-advocacy is important in the group's life and I have a lot of meetings to go to now. I am willing to go and talk to other groups, to talk to anyone who wants my services.

About myself

The changes in my life in the last few years have been that I was at Hortham Hospital in Almondsbury and then I was at Brentry Hospital. Before it, I was in a hospital in Liverpool. I've been in hospital since 1955 when I was about 11. It affected my mother more than it affected me. She was upset having to leave me behind. It wasn't so bad taking me, but when the Sister said, 'You have to leave him now', she got upset. I lived there because my mother couldn't manage me and my brother on her own after my father died.

There are more bad things than good things about living in the hospital. You have to be told what to do in hospital and you call people 'Nurse' or 'Sister'. You rely on the food being dished up to you and I don't like it. When I was young in hospital, we always had to go to bed early. I didn't agree with that. If I'd still lived with my father I wouldn't have gone to bed that early.

I moved to Brentry Hospital and now I live in a hostel in Southmead with eight people. I share a room with somebody and I'd rather have my own room. In Brentry I lived with about 10 people in a dormitory. I left there in 1987.

I think you are treated better in the hostel, more like an adult even if you are not looked upon as an adult. They are charge nurses and nurses and I have the strange feeling that they think they are the ones that know better. I think I know best because I am the person. I want to live in a flat with someone else. I think I could manage, but I might run into difficulty in budgeting and might need some help with that. I think with two of us we could manage. I'm not saying quite easy, but adequate to look after a flat.

Peter Stevens: Bristol
(Tape transcript)

Anita's story (Part 2)

Well, the Manager turned the meeting round, it was supposed to be about me attending, but when it came down to it what he was on about was that I been offered a place in the sheltered housing and workshop at Cramlington.

And I said I didn't want to go because I was not told that me name had been put down by the social worker, and I didn't want to give up this security so as to share with three other people who I didn't really know. And I might not get on with.

I lost all control of the meeting and I broke down, and like me social worker took me out and told me to pull meself together, and I went back in and the Manager turned around and said: 'You don't want to go'. I said: 'No, I don't and I don't see why I should give me security up', and he was really nasty after that. And then the Deputy Manager said: 'Oh, I think we'll suspend her for three months', and the Manager said: 'Well, what do you think about that decision?' I said the decision was taken before this meeting.

And like I stayed away for four months, and I went out and I told them that I wasn't going back and it's the best decision I've ever made. I've been talking to some of the people who go there now and they hate it, I mean its just the management's attitude.

Well, I first got involved with Skills for People when I was asked to give a presentation at the Newcastle Voluntary Forum and the Newcastle Partnership...that was the start of me involvement with them...I was doing voluntary work at MENCAP at the time, but I was unhappy there because they had residential workers and they were all putting on us and getting at us, and on a lunch-time they'd have their lunch and leave me downstairs on me own to have me lunch.

Now, I felt really out of it so it all came to a head when the District Officer was on holiday and Roy Bradshaw the Divisional Officer was there and I said: 'Roy, I want to leave', because the day before I was really upset because they were trying to make us scrub floors, and to me that was not on because they'd made a mess of the floor.

I waited a while and then I started as a volunteer for Skills, and I used to go to the office and help out and I still go and help out now, but I go out and about now. I done some advocacy courses – I actually taught one at Aycliffe – and I've helped put on a self-advocacy course at Prudhoe Hospital. I've tried to involve consumers and I'm helping out with the latest one, and I've been down to Nottingham where I met Ian Pickering and Ian Pearson and I helped start up the Nottingham Advocacy Network. Well, I helped start that up and I was asked, on the strength of that, I was asked to go and lead a workshop in Derby with one of the other volunteers, Phil Parkin. And I mean the amount of work that I've done, I mean I've done presentations to home helps, I've done presentations to the CQSW students at the Polytechnic, and I've done presentations to graduate social workers at the Newcastle University. So the range is so varied.

(What do you think self-advocacy does for people?)

Well, it's certainly for me; it's helped me to stand up for me rights and it's helped me to be more confident, and I'm not frightened of confrontation now.

I mean, at one time I would sit back and take it, but now I won't. I'm also involved with Gateshead Council for the Disabled; I've just been re-elected on to the Executive Committee for the second time and I'm involved with another group in Newcastle which is similar, run on similar lines, it's called InterAct. It's been going for quite a while, it's a group of disabled and abled-bodied people – it all started off socially like meeting in the pub and then there were different things. And now we have offices in the house, which is in Newcastle, and I've been on the third management committee of that. But that isn't as good as the others; I mean, I was on the programme committee. At one stage I was on that many committees, I had to give one up. And I've been on a management committee which is a group of all kids who like to do work with people like meself, and other disadvantaged groups you know.

They've actually made a video of me when I was on the Gateshead Co-ordinating Council, and I've seen it twice since they shot it. Some of it's done down at the ATC, and other people who've seen it said mine was the best one.

(You said that self-advocacy helped increase your confidence, it helped you stand up for your rights. Could you tell us a little bit about how it does that? How does it help you do that?)

Well, I really can't explain it, but it just helped me to be more confident about these things like rights and responsibilities, and it's helped me like put them into perspective, and I mean for all I've told them I've never actually been on a self-advocacy course, it's as I got more involved I got more and more confident because at one time I was really shy and I just wouldn't say boo to a goose, but now I'm very, I mean I don't mind confronting people.

I was in a conference in Gateshead last year, and one of the people who works for Social Services was sitting and he was laughing at us. Well, I knew this bloke fairly well so I just turned around and said to him: 'Look, don't you laugh at me'. I thought that'll teach you for laughing at us. I only got five minutes' notice that I was wanted to stand in for someone...

(So it's the actual involvement and responsibility it gives you that gives you confidence and helps you do things?)

And assertiveness.

(What is assertiveness?)

Well, being sure, knowing you're right and just being really really confident.

Anita Binns: Newcastle
(Extract from tape transcript)

Chapter Nine
Three life histories

In this final chapter of contributions we present three short autobiographies. These are longer accounts than most in the book but we felt they were so vivid and made such compulsive reading that they deserved their own space. But there are also other reasons for including these longer life histories. These accounts convey the major changes and transitions in their authors' lives in terms of both them as individuals and as part of the social and historical context in which they found themselves. Ronnie, for example, found himself sent away to institutions and a mental deficiency colony partly because his father was 'in and out of hospital because of gas from the war'; Alan was advised not to sit the 11-plus examination because of his epilepsy. As such these accounts bind together two themes in this book. On the one hand, the assertion of a sense of self and individuality; and on the other, the impact of social forces upon identity and opportunity.

They represent, in a more rounded and continuous way, a variety of personal characteristics like humour, anger, determination, reflection, wisdom – aspects which the shorter passages in the rest of the book sometimes miss out.

These longer accounts also provide the reader with the opportunity to get much closer to their authors, to feel and understand their thoughts and actions in term of their own pasts. At the same time, the fact that these stories are converted into the written word creates a certain space between the reader and the author. This space is important, for it provides the reader (without learning difficulties) with the opportunity to drop her or his preconceptions or assumptions about the author, and approach the story more freely.

These three life histories represent only a part of the spectrum of experiences of people with learning difficulties. It is no accident that all three authors are men. The ways the men and women have told their stories in this book have been different. Women's stories have tended to be told in terms of their relationships to others – their parents, friends, boyfriends or husbands – where they as individuals have not featured quite so centrally as the three narrators here. (Longer accounts of women's lives appear in Chapters Three and Four.)

In addition, the three men here, unlike some of our other contributors, have few direct communication difficulties. Nevertheless, their histories, and the struggles and issues they raise, contain experiences common to the lives of many people with learning difficulties: Ronnie's and Robert's childhoods in institutions and hospitals, and the struggle to break away; Alan's and Robert's attempts to break free of the definitions and limitations imposed upon them by others, combined with their recognitions of their own capabilities.

Each author also articulates the turning points in his life and the insights that these experiences have brought him. Robert, for example, says:

> 'One day, I remember talking to a man in my ward who had been in hospital for 39 years. I remember thinking that life wouldn't be worth much if the same happened to me. I began to think about a flat of my own, a job, a girlfriend, how I wanted those things for myself'.

Ronnie reflects on the past 30 or so years living with his sister

> 'We've had our ups and downs, but we've got over it. Same as, we have a grouse together – if you don't have rows it's not a bloody family. You might as well say it's not a family at all! There isn't a family in this world what doesn't have rows, but we get along alright with each other'.

These insights, along with others in the rest of the book, are not rare or unusual, but stand as testimony to the need for those not labelled as 'handicapped' to open their eyes, ears and minds.

Contents

Ronnie Gaukrodger's life history

I was born down Woolshops in Halifax, on March 13th 1931, then we went to live up Haley Hill when I was about five.

My sister Florence went to school at Haley Hill, and I went to Quarry House at Northowram when I was a little boy of seven years old, and I didn't like it – I was always running away. The teachers used to say:

> 'Why do you always run away from us, Ronnie?'

Well, all they taught us was gardening and looking after animals, so I told them:

> 'I don't like looking after animals – I want to learn to read and write'.

The teachers used to say:

> 'If you run away again, you'll go to the headmaster!'

And so, next day I ran away again; came home at night-time.

The police were used to taking me home at one or two o'clock in the morning. My father used to be angry. My grandad, my sister and my father used to be out looking for me all over the place – they didn't know why I did this. I did it for a good long while – I wouldn't go to school at all!

I kept running away so many times that the police got fed up of taking me back home.

When I used to run away from Quarry House School, when they used to bring me home, well, I used to diarrhoea me pants – well, I smelt bloody rotten. Phew!

> 'Ee! This lad needs washing down, Mr Gaukrodger, get him in the sink and wash him down. He's messed his pants again. I know he can't help it, because he's been out in the cold. He should have come home, where it's warm. He'll have to go away, and that'll be the end of it!'

My dad was in and out of hospital because of gas from the war; there was no one to look after me, so I was sent to a place called Monyhull Colony, the other side of Birmingham – after I'd refused to go to Quarry House.

I was there a few years and I left when I was 16 years old. I was sent to a school, a right big school, and lovely school in the hospital. I was in the infants class, playing with the sand and bricks, and all this and the other.

When I got to about ten or eleven, I went into another class, and they learned us to read and write the best way they knew how.

Every morning, when I went there to school, we had to go into a big hall, all in our separate classes, and we had to say a prayer and do some singing.

They used to learn us to do concerts, shows and other things. The teacher in our class said:

> 'Now, we are going to get a show up, and we can show it to everybody that's in this home'.

So we did a pantomime – *The Three Bears* – for Christmas. Some did dancing in between the acts. I did the *Sailor's Hornpipe*; three of the girls did tap dancing. We all did a share of every little bit between the acts.

To finish off, we all sang a very nice song, a very sweet song, *Land of Hope and Glory*. It was lovely, and where the show came off, it came off lovely, and then we went home.

The committee and important people from other towns used to come and see our shows.

When we got home, the nurse says:

> 'Right, come on! Get your hats and coats on, we're going for a walk'.

So, we went for a long walk. We went round the barracks, round the aerodrome, round another barracks, round another aerodrome, 'till we went nearly dizzy.

We came back, and were just alright for tea. We weren't allowed to talk at table. When they were eating they used to swear at the nurses, call them all sorts, and they were only little toddlers – you wouldn't think they could swear at nurses – used to tell them to beggar off out!

When we sat down, the nurse said:

> 'Think on! NO TALKING at the table!'

So, we all had our tea...

> 'I'll be in the kitchen – if I hear any of you whisper, I'll be out on you at once!'

So, we all sat round the table, and I started talking. Well! The nurse just came and pulled me in the pantry, and walloped me on the back of me earhole; and she wasn't satisfied with that! She threw a basin at me, split me head open – on the same place where I'd slipped off the see-saw at Sibden Hall, Halifax. She split it open again...well, what she said to me was:

> 'Think on...you don't say anything to the doctor when I ring him up – because a doctor will have to come, you'll have to have some more stitches – if you dare say anything to the doctor, I shall get you when he's gone!'

Well, I was very frightened. I couldn't say anything. All I could say was I'd slipped down and caught us head somewhere on a corner of a table or where it's sharp.

Then, after tea came bedtime – we'd get ready for bed at about six o'clock, after we'd had a drink of cocoa.

Some used to say: 'WHAT...cocoa AGAIN! When are we going to have something different? It's ALWAYS cocoa, cocoa, cocoa – every after day and every after night!'

We used to get browned off with seeing cocoa; then one night we got a bowl of soup and a slice of bread. Six o'clock we all went to bed, no talking, we were all sleeping.

We used to go to the pictures, what we called the Maypole – *Flash Gordon, Tom Mixing Cement, Buck Jones* and *Kit Carson* – all them, and serials, and then we'd go back and tea used to be out – four slices of jam and bread on your plate, and after they came round with a slab of cake which were so thick you couldn't get it in your mouth!

Some little kiddies used to nearly choke with it, it were that thick!

I'd get on to the nurse about it:

> '"Why don't you cut it smaller? Their mouths are too small".
>
> "They've got to learn to eat such stuff", Nurse used to say.

On the sports field we used to do things with the school. The teachers used to have us all in this big hall to practise songs to sing on the sportsfield; we'd march on to the field, they had their own brass band all that, the brass band played the tune we had to sing, and we all sang it.

We were all in various groups from infants going up to High School, and we all sounded very good.

The Lord Mayor and Mayoress and some more committee people used to be there, and then just after, when the sports were finished, they scrambled pennies on the ground for the kiddies to pick up and put in their pockets.

When we'd gone back in the ward, the nurses would come round and ask:

> 'How much did YOU get? And how much did YOU get? What do you want with the money you've got?'

She'd tell you how much you'd got on your card. If you wanted sweets or drawing books, or anything like that, you could order them. They'd take the money off your card and then they'd bring you your stuff.

After the sports we went to a dance. I used to dance with two or three girls – I can't name any of them, because I've forgot all of them; it were a very long time since I were there!

I used to do the Palais Glide, Waltzes, Tangos, all sorts of dances, every dance you can think of, and that's how I learned to do my dancing, in that place.

When it came to Sunday morning, we all had to get up to put us suits on, and Nurse'd say:

> 'Wash at back of ears, wash inside your ears, wash at back of neck, wash at...'

Some of us used to pull funny faces, as much as to say:

> 'Get away! Who's doing t'job?'

If you hadn't done it properly, she'd send you back to wash yourself all over again; then she'd send you, all in twos, outside and we'd walk in twos up to church. Into church we'd go – there were Ward Two, Ward Three, Ward Five, Ward Seven, Ward Eight, Ward

Nine – it went up to about thirteen wards – there were men's side and women's side, and they were all in the order they'd come from the wards. Then they'd take us back to t'wards.

I was there two years when the War started. Once, during the holidays, the nurse said:

> 'Well, we'll take you for a walk'.

All of a sudden, the air raid sirens went!

The Nurse said – 'It's far too late to get back to the Ward, we'll have to dive into the ditch'.

All the other children dived into the ditch, except one little boy. He'd have just stood in the middle of the road, crying – so I just ran out and got him, and dived in the ditch and pulled him with me, so when this German plane came over he couldn't see anybody.

It went over, and all it did were try to shoot some of the farmers hid behind carts – there were millions of carts to camouflage the fields – the animals used to hide behind the carts when there was an air raid.

There was a head male staff man, they called him Mr Jones – he had hands as big as dinner plates!

> '"Now then", he said, "Who'd like to make a show?"'

So, at once, I said: 'Me!'

He asked me what I wanted to do, and showed us how to go on and how to do it.

We did a Western, like a cowboy scene. I had my leading lady – a little girl of five years old – we used to hold this big sixpence up – I'd made it out of strong cardboard, and it were round and marked on.

We'd sing *I've Got Sixpence.*

Then, after a while, the nurse came -

> 'Oh! The doctor wants to see you, Ronnie – I think you're going nearer home'.

Me dad wanted me near home.

The doctor told me I was going back to Halifax for a while, until there was a vacancy at Doncaster. The doctor said:

> 'I don't know how long you'll be there, you're going to St John's Hospital'.

I was there two or three months, then I went to St Catherine's, Tickhill Road, Doncaster where I stayed until I was 24 years old. I went to a school there, and I didn't like it; because all I learned was how to look after pets such as rabbits, guinea-pigs and white mice; or they'd take you for walks – well!, you can do that at night-time, and have an hour or two on the playing fields after tea; you do enough walking at night-time.

Tuesday nights we used to go to a whist drive; we'd play whist and then we'd come back for supper, and then watch TV for a bit, before going to bed.

Then up next morning and off to school again – I ran away, so they brought me back. Another lad, he ran away with me.

Then Dr Allen came:

> '"Now, what did you run away for?"
>
> "I don't like that school, I want to go somewhere where I can learn something."
>
> "Where would you like to go, Ronnie?"
>
> "I'd like to try the brush shop."
>
> "All right! I'll give you a trial in the brush shop."'

The first brush I made was a scrubbing brush, then from a scrubbing brush to a nail brush, then from a nail brush to a hand brush, and then a bath brush.

The smallest brush I did on that table was a tooth brush.

Then when I'd learned all those brushes on the table, Mr Hanson, the attendant who used to be with us, asked me what I would like to do next. I said:

> 'Well, I'd like to learn on the pitch pan'.

So, I went on the pitch pan – did sweeping brushes, guard brooms, hand brushes and cocoa fibre brushes. I did every mortal pitch pan brush you could think of – even chimney-sweep brushes.

I learned every brush that were in the place, and then went from brushes to baskets. I made shopping baskets, and first-baby nappy baskets and laundry baskets – hampers, fishing baskets, cots, chairs – all sorts – every sort you could think of.

Then I started toy-making. The staff used to do the pattern, and we cut them out and assembled them. We used to have someone to paint them all.

We did ducks what quacked, and rocking horses. After Christmas were over, and we weren't doing toys no more, we did baskets again; then all the brushes that were in the shop, we could do.

I learned a lad there how to make baskets, and he's in Halifax now, he makes his own baskets, and I teached him. He'll tell you himself. His name is Peter Ackroyd, he's got his own business. He makes his own baskets and sells them.

Then we did brooches out of perspex, and then I came out of that shop, and I went into the joiners' shop to clean up after the joiner, when he'd finished.

I'd help him carry wood around to different wards, then he had repairs to do. After, we'd go back to the shop and I'd sweep up, and then it was time to go back to the ward for our tea.

It wasn't as bad as Monyhull Colony, in that place at St Catherine's. It was a lot better; you could talk a little bit, but not too much talking – you had to get on with it just like anything else, because there were other things going off at night-time.

Same as, Monday night we'd go off whist-driving, then Tuesday morning we'd get up in the morning about six o'clock, breakfast at seven, and out to work about eight, back to the joiners' shop.

I was in the joiners' shop for two or three years, then I went into the mat shop. I did cocoa fibre mats there, then after two years I went on to cobbling. The first thing I did was repairing them. If any new shoes wanted doing, we had to do the upper and from the upper we had to do the top piece, cut the other piece out, put it round, and then the sole underneath. Then another sole underneath, and then the heel. I don't think I could do it now; I haven't got the patience I used to have then!

Then I went on the farm. We used to start about nine o'clock on the farm, because we had a very lot to do. The first job, as soon as I got there, Mr Beastall, the farmer there, he said to me:

> 'Ronnie, you go and collect the eggs. There's a big basket there. I want you to go round the boxes and collect all the hens eggs for me from the hen huts. You don't have to go inside, just lift the nest box lid up on the outside'.

Well, there were about six huts to go round, and I picked all the eggs up. After I'd done that, he said:

> 'You'll have to go and clean them out now'.

So I cleaned them out and put fresh sawdust in, and when I'd done that he'd say:

> 'Right, Ronnie, you'll have to clean the pigs out, that's your next job'.

So I used to turn the pigs out into the yard, into like little pens in the yard, while I cleaned out the sties.

I used to swill the sties out, disinfect, then wash the troughs. After that, I used to boil the swill – go round the wards with a bloke and the swill cart, empty the swill bins and bring it back to the farm and empty it into a big hopper, and we used to boil it all up and feed the pigs.

Feeding time used to be about dinner-time; but before then we had summat else to do.

The farmer said:

> 'Right! Ronnie, you'll have to go out in the field, take two horses out and plough the field'.

So I said, 'Righty-oh! I'll do that; I'll take the horses out'.

I went to the field and ploughed it, and when it had got nearly about dinner-time, I thought:

> 'Well, I'd better go, that swill will be ready now'.

The farmer used to stop there and keep an eye on it while we were out in the fields.

He'd say, 'Well, Ronnie, turn the tap on'.

And it used to run out into the troughs and it used to feed all the lot.

When it was empty we'd have to swill the big boiler out ready for next day's feeding time.

Next day, we ploughed the fields and got the potato fields ready. We planted acres of taters, corn and everything!

As the corn was growing, we had to do some haymaking, and then came time to cut the corn and wheat; then there was sugar-beet bashing, where you get two sugar beets, pull them out of the ground, knock them together, clean all the muck off and just lay them down. You have a chopper in your hand, chop the sugar beets off, and then you fill the cart up.

Farming today isn't like it used to be when I did it. I used to have a pair of horses when I were farming. I'd drive them into the fields, plough the fields and then sow the seed from baskets – put the basket on me head and scatter it out on the fields with me hands, sowing seed for corn. When the corn was ripe we used to cut it and do the harvesting, and each day, when we'd done, we went back to the farm and he said:

> 'Let's count you all to make sure you're all here – right! Get in two's, we're going back to the ward now'.

He followed behind on his bike. Some went to Two Ward, and some went to Three Ward, and we all went back to our own wards.

We had us tea, and then it happened to be Wednesday night – Dance Night! So we were all getting poshed up, getting a shave and wash again, getting dressed up, our hair combed back, looking nice for our girlfriends at night.

We did Palais Glide, we did Tangos, we even did Rumbas and Foxtrots.

They played all Victor Sylvester and Edmundo Ross dance tunes. After dance were over we went home and watched telly while we had our supper. Then they'd say it was time to go to bed, so we went to bed.

Next morning we'd get up and have us breakfast. They'd say:

> 'Is everybody ready? The farmer's come for you'.

The staff used to open the door with keys and he used to count us out.

Same at night- or dinner-time, when they used to count us in and out.

If we went out at night-time, when we were busy haymaking or corn-cutting and we had to work over; then they used to count us out again and count us in, when the farmer used to come for us.

When I'd been there so many years, I met an intelligent patient there. He used to do his own concerts. Well – we made kettle drums out of milk tins. We made summat like knockers on top, turned out of solid wood. Made us own drum sticks, and we'd make a concert up.

He did a medley in between, I did the *Sailor's Hornpipe* dance, and then after a bit, when something else had been on, I did the sword dance, then tap-dancing.

Well, I learned this song so it would be something to sing at the end of the show. It were a very good show; they all come – the committee, and all the high people from every mortal town in Yorkshire – all the high people.

Me dad came to see me once; he says:

> 'Well, Ronnie, I've told your sister she's to get you out of here – she says she's got to have a man behind her first, before you can come home'.

Well, I were in there until I were 23 years old, then the doctor wanted to see me. He said:

> 'Well, Ronnie, you'll be going home soon on licence'.

I said, 'Ooh! That's good!'

He told me, 'You'll be going on licence for twelve month, and if you're good while you're on that twelve month you get your discharge papers to say you've nothing to do with us at all'.

Well before that I used to go out on Saturday afternoons, we got 7/6d a week, and I always saved a bit to spend on a Saturday down at the market.

My brother-in-law, what's died, the Ukranian one, he had to see me first, to see what he could do, and then I could be on licence.

So now I went home for the day, on a Saturday. I set off from Doncaster at six o'clock, went by bus and got into Halifax for nine o'clock.

I went up home, up to Clarence Street, where they used to live:

Well!...They'd moved!...

I'd no idea where they'd gone!

Someone said they'd moved up Pellon Lane, so I cut across the road at Gibbet Street, out through one of the streets, and came out at Pellon Lane.

I asked someone where Bangor Street was, and the man said – 'Just go on there, and it's the end street'.

So, I knocked on one door and asked:

> 'Do you know where me brother-in-law lives, and me sister?'

He said, 'Who are you?'

I said, 'I'm Ronnie! I've come home for the day!'

He said, 'Oh, aye! They live just next door'.

So I thanked him, and knocked next door.

When my brother-in-law came to the door, he said:

> '"Ronnie! You haven't run away, have you?"
>
> "No! I've come home for the day! Does it look as if I've run away – I'm all dressed up?"'

So, he goes to the bottom of the bedroom steps, and calls my sister, because she was still in bed at that time -

He called: 'Flora!'

> '"What?"
>
> "Your Ronnie's here!"

"Oh!...He hasn't run away, has he?"

"Oh no; not the way he's dressed up – you can't tell him!"'

So, she comes downstairs in her dressing gown; she says – 'What are you doing here?'

'I've come home to see you!'

My brother-in-law says, 'Oh! He's alright, he's alright for coming home. Anyway, I'll be working when your sister comes for you'.

Three weeks later, I came home on the Friday.

My sister got me out of there, and she's been very good to me – very nice to me – and she's looked after me ever since I came out of them places.

When I came home, my sister took me down to Powell Street to see a probation officer, and get me a job.

The first job I had were road-sweeping for Halifax Corporation. When I'd learned all that I went on to dustbin wagons, then a swill wagon, then to paper wagons, then a gulley wagon, then back to a refuse wagon where there were just two of us and the driver. We did Warley and other farm areas, and I like it there.

There were so many wagons I could talk about – I've had about 19 jobs while I've been in Halifax.

The second job I started was at St John's Hospital. We started at seven in the morning, and finished at half past five. I was in the kitchen, doing the veg, tatties and cabbages, and marrows and carrots and all that.

We had a weekend off once in a blue moon, and the wage was poor – working seven days a week, with a break once a fortnight.

Matron used to come round and inspect the tatties and the carrots...if she used to see a black speck on your carrots or tatties, she used to say:

'You can go through them all again until they're spotless!'

So, we used to have to go through them again! Then she'd come back and have a look, and say:

'"Right! Why can't you do them right in the first place, without having to do it again?"

"Well", I said, "I thought I'd cleaned them all. I cleaned them in the machine – you've got a machine there – that's supposed to do all the work!"'

She said – 'It doesn't do everything – you've got to peel them all and take the eyes out. How would you like to eat taters with their eyes in?'

I said: 'Well! Blame your bloody machine; not me!'

I got browned off there, so I started to work at Whitaker's Brewery.

I was working in the barrel shed, washing the barrels out. We went down in the cellar, and we'd fill them up with beer, same as Four X and bitter, and Old Tom.

They used to have two barrels, just round the back, for the workers. You could have a pint of Old Tom, or a pint of Four X.

We used to go round there when the gaffer wasn't coming! The gaffer said:

'You can drink a pint of beer...as long as I don't see you'.

After I'd finished at Whitaker's Brewery, I started at Candema, up Pellon Lane. We did dehydrated food – cabbage, carrots, tatties – we used to boil them; then when they were half-cooked we used to spread them on to trays. Then they went into the dryers when we had put the time down. Say it was a quarter to eight, we had to put down '7.45', and when they'd been in an hour one way we'd taken them out, turn them round, and push them back in again and put the time down.

When they'd been in long enough, the girls used to come round and scrape the vegetables on to big trays, and they used to have to mix them together – potatoes and carrots and such.

When they had dehydrated cabbage they used to have a machine to re-fill these tins, press the cabbage down, and when it was full enough a lid used to go on and the machine fastened it on. We used to put six tins in a box, then we got ready and went home.

After I'd worked at Candema, I got a job down at Sowerby Bridge, because I lived down there.

I started at Morris's Mill, in the warehouse, taking the wool bags and weighing them, and stacking them up in their orders.

Then we'd go in to the other part of the warehouse and sort wool out, and when the wagons came we used to have to unload them.

I worked there for so long, and then I started at another warehouse place, where you put wool down a draughter, where it used to go through into the next place where there were two men treading it into bags which they used to skewer up.

Then I went to Atkinsons, piece-carrying. I was there two or three years, then I went to a firm where we made lollipops and all this and the other.

I worked there for a few years then I went to Whiteley's at Slitheroe Bridge, where they did car parts, and I worked there for a few years.

Then I left there and I started at Butlers, on days; then when I'd worked on days for a bit I went on nights.

I'd worked on nights for a while when I had my stroke.

Well! That beggared it.

I had my stroke in 1980 – I had to go into hospital – I was in the Halifax General Hospital for a month until they could get me walking again, but I'm very glad I can walk again a little now.

The first centre I went to was down Fountain Street in Sowerby Bridge, and then I got to know of another place in Mytholmroyd, where disabled people met in Mytholmroyd Community Centre, so I started going there on a Wednesday. Then they got their own place at 1 Greenhill, Mytholmroyd, and they call it the Calder Valley Club.

I still go there every Monday to Thursday, and usually do my drawings on Mondays, Tuesdays and Thursdays. The members get picked up in the Calder Valley Club mini-bus, and then they take us home again about four o'clock. We have our dinner made for us, and I enjoy it all very much.

I used to go to the Stroke Club on a Tuesday, but this year (1987) there was an art class going on at Calder College, Todmorden, so I went to that instead.

This autumn I will be going to a cookery class at Hebden Bridge, and I go to evening classes at Bermerside too.

I've been to all kinds of classes – reading and writing, newspaper headlining and all sorts.

Sometimes I've been to the Queen's Road Community Centre and we do all sorts there – going out on days when the teachers think of somewhere to go.

When I go to the Queen's Road Community Centre, they send a taxi to take me and bring me home again.

I think it's very good for people to be able to go to places like the Stroke Club, Bermerside, Queen's Road and the Calder Valley Club.

There's everything going on for you at these places and it's all very interesting. It gets you out of the house, and you see all sorts of different people and do different things.

I do all kinds of drawings, mostly with felt pens, and people like my drawings. They think they are very good.

I've lived with my sister ever since she got me out of those places.

We've had our ups and downs, but we've got over it. Same as, we have a grouse together – if you don't have rows it's not a bloody family. You might as well say it's not a family at all! There isn't a family in this world what doesn't have rows, but we get along alright with each other.

We've got a video. We buy films in our turns and we watch the TV, and then after we've watched TV we go to bed. Then next morning, probably the lad'll go to work, and I'm waiting to go out to my classes or the club, and it helps pass the day on, and then after we'll come back home. Then we start again.

When my sister got me out of that hospital, she was very happy to have me home. I always went to work and paid me board – paid me food money and all that.

Sometimes, when we go out shopping, we go and have us dinner together in a restaurant, and then after she may worry about having to get the bus home.

I say, 'Oh! Beggar buses – what do we get me Mobility Allowance for?'

So we go home by taxi, because it's a lot better for me with me bad leg.

Well, I'll never forget what my sister has had to do for me.

Some of the the places I've been to were bad, and some of them were good places.

So, now I'm at home with me sister, and she likes it, and we have our fallings out but we soon get back together again, and that's it.

Well, that life story should be good 'un for me. It's very hard to remember so much at once.

That's all now, from Ronnie.

Ronnie Gaukrodger: Queen's Road, Community Centre, Halifax (Tape transcript)

Alan Jones's life story

Chapter One

As a baby there were no signs of me having any illness until when I was about five months old. I was in my pram when a neighbour passed by and looked in my pram and saw me convulsing. They just thought I was cold so they knocked on my front door to tell my mother I was shaking with cold. It was fortunate that in the flat above there was a person who had medical training. My mother called him in panic and he said straight away that it was a *grand mal* epileptic fit, and from that day I have been taking tablets.

It must have been really hard for my mother because my father left her at about the same time. That meant that she was left with herself and three sons. I know one of them was working but that didn't compensate for much; it meant my mother had to work hard. My family have always been good to me.

Then I started school but I was told by doctors at Great Ormond Street Hospital not to run around, as that would make me dizzy, avoid excitable games and to try not to knock my head as it could create problems. I took to school as I liked the teacher. Her name was Miss Hayward. I will never forget after a while she announced she was getting married and her name would become 'Mrs Cornwall'. I don't know why but it upset me. I assumed she would become a different person but it surprised me when she was still the same understanding person.

Then I moved up to the junior section where I was told to be careful as the children had a slightly more aggressive nature, but I coped fairly well and teachers said I was average at most subjects. In those days I had one epileptic fit every couple of months or so.

By this time other children used to be very rise-taking and this used to really hurt me deep down. I used to worry an awful lot about this as they never done this to other children.

Then I was coming up to the age of 11 and the 11+ exam that decided whether you went to secondary modern, comprehensive, or grammar school. In talking to the doctors at the hospital, I happened to mention I was concerned about my inner feelings and how I would cope with life in these surroundings and what I wanted to achieve. Then the doctors said: 'Why don't you just go to a secondary modern school and not take the exam? We will confirm this with the Education Committee and you won't have the endless homework, or any other problems that have been troubling you'. I thought they would know better than me so I took them at their word and settled for secondary school. Anyhow, when I finally moved on to the new school I was very surprised as it was not a bit like I had thought.

Chapter Two

The children were far more savage towards each other, and more hostile. Then I found out that, as I hadn't taken the exam, I would naturally be classed not as slightly above average intelligence like my primary school had classed me, but below average. They assigned me to the lowest class in the school. There were 39 children...

My mother complained and she said she felt it was so unfair that I wasn't given the chance to try to widen my horizons, so the headmaster said he would put it to the teachers and let me know. The next thing was a couple of days later the headmaster said he was glad to say the teachers felt I was in the wrong class, so they moved me up two classes and the teacher was far more understanding. If he felt I was getting very friendly with the wrong crowd he would call me back at some time to tell me, if he thought it might lead to trouble in the future. He was considerate towards most of his pupils. He knew I was very good at mathematics and would encourage me to widen my knowledge and give me extra homework.

But still some of the children called me names: 'Jonah' was a common name because my surname is Jones, and that didn't worry me at all. It was when they called me names like 'fitty' or' floppo' or 'sparky' because I had these *grand mal* fits, that it really hurt me. At one stage I said to my mother I wouldn't go to school, as I was afraid of what they might say, so she went up the school to see the headmaster and he asked when my next hospital appointment was. My mother gave him the date, and he said he would tell the school not to make fun of me or he would punish them, and not to mention to me what he had said. As I didn't know about this, I wondered why nobody had called me names for ages – not that I wanted them to.

Then about a year later I was talking to one chap and he mentioned something regarding epilepsy and he said: 'Sorry, I wasn't meant to say that', so I said: 'Well you're not the first', and he said: 'What, aren't you going to report me?' I said: 'What for?' He said: 'Being rise-taking', and I said: 'No, what made you think that?' He said: 'The headmaster said he would punish anybody who done that'. I said: 'Don't be daft, they've never worried before', and went to call another boy who was a prefect. The prefect said: 'You weren't supposed to know'. Then they told me all about it; by this time I was aged about 14.

The school said they thought 'O' levels or GCE exams were out of the question, and what did I plan to do when I left school? I was undecided, then the hospital asked me the same thing next time I went to see them. As I had always been mad about cars I assumed that anybody could possess a licence at the age of 18, providing they had passed their test, not realising that this didn't apply to people with epilepsy. So I said to this doctor: 'Well, what I intend to do is just get a job doing anything for three years, then get a job driving when I have passed my driving test'. He looked me in the eyes and said: 'That is one thing you will never do, you will never drive'. Well, being sentimental at heart, I burst into tears. He said: 'So you might as well get that idea out of your head'. I wanted to know the reasons. I thought: 'You hard man'. Obviously since then I have looked back and recognised how right he was to be so direct in telling me, though I must say it hurt at the time.

Chapter Three

So at 15 I left school and the labour exchange said they would do their best to get me some form of employment, and I was so pleased. But I had such a job trying to make a start in life, and couldn't find a job for a couple of months. Then the labour exchange said I might stand a better chance if I registered myself as disabled, so I agreed and a couple of months later they said: 'We think we have found a job suitable for you'. When I went into details it was working for F. W. Woolworths and Company in Dalston, with a view to becoming what they called a redcoat so's to advise people at what counters different items were available. I said I would do this as I was sick and tired of being at home doing nothing.

The manager said I had the biggest counter in the shop and if I needed help to ask the supervisor, but also I alone had to keep the stock cards up to date a couple of times a day and display all the stock myself. After a couple of days the other staff thought how well I had taken to the job and even the manager remarked that I was always busy doing something. The reason for that was, being that it was an electrical counter, it wasn't as busy as let's say the food counter. But I was on six weeks' trial, and I was coming to the end of my fifth week and I had a customer come in every day for the same item and that was two children's night-lites. They were made of candle wax. Friday was always a busy day, as people got paid, so I thought I would save that woman waiting – I would put her goods in a bag at the side of the cash register.

Anyhow, at lunch-time it was getting busy and in walked this old lady. I just said: 'Hello, you want two night-lites, dear?' And she gave me a mouth full of verbal abuse. Well I was dumbfounded, the worst part being that the manager was standing about three yards away so naturally he came over: 'Anything wrong, dear?' he said. 'Yes', she replied, 'it's him what is the matter'. He asked so she told him: 'Is this true?', he asked. 'Yes, I was only trying to stop her waiting about'. 'Well', he said, 'I'm afraid the customer is always right'. 'Well, not in this case', I said. He said: 'I'll have to give you your notice next week'. Even the other staff admitted it was wrong. They went as far as asking the union steward to investigate it, but she had no luck either, so I had to leave.

Then, after about another three months, I managed to get a job in a chemical wholesalers putting the stock up on the shelves. I accepted the job and you really had to work for your money in those days. It was about £6 per week. After about six months I was asked if I would work in the despatch for a couple of weeks. I agreed, then the charge-hand in the despatch asked if I would agree to work in that department full time. He said: 'I will get you a rise, that's if you like the work of course'. I was really pleased because it gave you more scope because you weren't under the watchful eye of the directors all the time.

I can see now why the charge-hand wanted me in the despatch because the staff he already had were very lazy, they would let work pile up and still sit there picking out horses and going out putting on bets. But I would even work through my tea-break just to help get vans on the road and even out this heavy backlog of work created by others. But I liked being busy; you had a laugh with some of the drivers. Some would also be rise-taking after I had an epilepetic attack. The chap who was most rise-taking, his name was Sid Watkins, made out he was so brave. Once I was taken ill and they had to call an ambulance as it was a bad attack. The next day I saw him, he tended not to want to say much and I always ask after a fit if it was worse than before so I asked him. He replied: 'Don't ask'. I said: 'Why?' He said: 'You put the fear of Christ up me yesterday. After convulsing you laid so still I thought you was dead. I kept thinking of it last night all evening'. So I replied: 'It's not such a joke as you make it out to be'. He said: 'Don't do that again'. I said: 'If I had my way I wouldn't do it in the first place', and he didn't take the rise no more, maybe the odd remark.

I was happy there, then redundancy came and after working there seven years they said to me: 'You've nothing to worry about because you're the best worker we have in the despatch. What we will do is pay the other staff off as they were all due to retire within about a year. The charge-hand wants to go out driving and you and Georgie Drew will be put in charge of the despatch and answer phone calls'. Well, I had been doing that for seven years and it meant I would get a pay increase. Then they came to me about a week later and said: 'Sorry, change in plan'. The management said: 'It is too much of a risk having one out of two staff with epilepsy'. I said: 'Why?' They said: 'Well, let's say that Georgie was off sick and you were taken ill, there would be nobody to take care of you, no one would know. Now Georgie wants redundancy money and what we suggest is that we let the shop steward have the job'. I said: 'But he retires in six months time and he has never done the job before, he's always been a checker'. They said: 'But he has got 50 years' service behind him so we'll have to make you redundant as the firm thinks one man can do the job'. I said: 'He's only hanging on for his service pay', and once again I was out of a job. And as I had been made redundant the firm paid me about £100 so I couldn't go straight on to benefit. Once again I was waiting about just idle.

Chapter Four

Then, after about two months, I was offered a job in a sheltered workshop for Remploy and Company. It was the job of assistant storekeeper and stock controller. It was a salaried staff position – I would be mainly book-keeping, crediting, ordering some parts, issuing off parts to the factory floor, then balancing in my record with the accountant's record to see if they differ in any way.

When I first started, the head storekeeper and myself really worked well together, but he moved on to a better job and that left his position open. They were thinking of offering me the position, then along came this little whizz kid who bluffed his way into the job. He made out he could do the job if given the chance, which was rubbish from the start because he was so bad at keeping records. I had to teach him how to deduct totals correctly, but the management thought he was so good they wouldn't hear a word against him. He kept making out they were my errors; alright, everybody makes mistakes, but he made far more than me. Then stock started going missing. When I mentioned this to the accountant he kept saying: 'Well write it off as faulty components'. But it was always the same items that went missing. Then they sacked the accountant because he was fiddling the books.

Then I started getting slowed down in life owing to having to take so many drugs for epilepsy. I was taking 17 tablets daily, so Remploy contacted the Maudsley Hospital to ask if I was worried about anything, and if so, is there something the hospital could do to remedy this? The hospital replied that they could keep me in under observation for a few weeks but that would be my choice. The next time I attended the hospital the consultant approached me, telling me what had been said between Remploy and the hospital. Being afraid of losing my job, I replied that I couldn't accept this brain scanning because my job would be at risk as I had no more sick leave. The consultant then said: 'But Remploy have said they would give you the time off, they have assured me of that'. So I said: 'I will confirm it and let you know'.

The manager said that was correct. He assured me if I was away from work a year it wouldn't matter; as long as I came back a new man, my job would still be open for me. I never got that information in black and white, I only had it by word of mouth, but I had always got on well with the manager and I trusted him.

It turned out I was in hospital about eight weeks. I kept phoning them to tell them how I was progressing, and they kept saying don't worry. Then one week before coming out of hospital, Remploy wrote to me informing me that they had filled my position and my services were no longer needed. It had turned out that the manager, who gave me the assurance regarding my job, was leaving and a new manager taking his place said that as a friend of the storekeeper, who was a labourer in the factory next door, was willing to accept the job, and as they didn't know how long I would be in hospital (even though I contacted them to say I was coming out of hospital within days), they just said: 'We'll pay you a couple of hundred pounds'. I said: 'What, for nine years' service, and for seven years I have also paid a private pension of four pounds per week extra, and you have the cheek to offer me a couple of hundred pounds and no employment at the end of it all?' Well, you can imagine that undid all the good the hospital had done.

I appealed against it. Then I was told that they had reconsidered and I was entitled to more than that, so they increased what they had offered me by three times the amount. And since that day I have never done a full-time job.

I have done voluntary work because I feel any disabled person who wants to start work nowadays gets no incentive, especially if it is a hidden disability such as epilepsy. Any employer can say things like: there is machinery in the place of work, and should the person have a seizure they would be a risk to themselves and the company. I think people are afraid of losing some or all of the benefit they have been used to, and for that reason I feel some don't bother to apply for work. I know how they must feel as I have felt this way myself. Nowadays I attend a day centre in Archway to help pass the time. I have taken up voluntary work. Also I re-assembled medical records for a health centre in Archway and I work for Islington Disablement Association. I don't really see any hope for the future now apart from voluntary work.

Alan Jones: Tower Hamlets Institute
(Produced on a word-processor)

Robert's story

I remember feeling different from other children since I was seven years old. I just couldn't keep up with them. I didn't have any friends as I didn't know how to make contact with other children. When I was a child, I was a problem for my family because I used to misbehave a lot. I was full of nonsense and I was always fighting. When I was six, I went to a special school and I was there until I was 12.

When I was 11 and a half I remember my mother taking me to the doctor. After that, I was told I had to go to the hospital (Lynebank) as a day patient for two weeks. I remember feeling that things were going to change, and I remember thinking that I was going to hospital because of my bad behaviour.

At the end of the two weeks, I was told that I was going to stay in hospital for good. They didn't tell me why. I suppose it was because my parents couldn't cope with me. The only thing that I can remember about the hospital is that they let me do arithmetic. I didn't do this at my previous school. I remember being very upset because I found arithmetic difficult and I couldn't cope with it. My mum and dad didn't visit me often at the hospital. That made me angry. I was also angry because nobody let me do anything that I wanted to do. I used to run away from the hospital, most of the time during the night.

I stayed in the children's ward until I was 16. I was then moved to a men's ward. The good thing about this ward was that they taught me how to behave and how to control my temper. Also, they encouraged me to do things for myself and I used to enjoy this very much.

Later on, I started to work in the hospital's metal workshop. I used to enjoy this type of work very much. I don't really remember anything else happening during this time. Six months later I moved into a hostel for mentally handicapped people. I was excited about it. However, I didn't stay there long because life at the hostel was the same as life in the hospital. Nothing had really changed. While I was at the hostel, I got a job in a bakery. This job was special because I got it and I wasn't like everybody else. I had to give up this job when I moved back to my native town to stay with my parents. I soon managed to get another job, pushing trolleys at the local supermarket. I remember being annoyed, because I used to earn £20 per week and I had to give my mum £15 a week for board. I didn't think this was fair. Also, I wasn't allowed to go out and enjoy myself, and my parents and I couldn't get on at all. I had no choice but try to be sent back to hospital, so I did something wrong at the supermarket and was sent back to Lynebank without limit of time.

I was sent to the secure ward. After a while, I decided to try to settle down and get things right. My parents hardly visited me, but my uncle from Glasgow used to come and see me often.

Eventually, I was allowed back to work in the metal workshop. My instructor was good to me. He used to teach me how to grind and how to measure, etc. so I would be able to get a job one day. He also used to give me a lot of attention and I felt that he was helping me to gain confidence.

After a while I ran away again. I ended up in England. I ran away because I felt I was never going to leave the hospital and I didn't want to spend the rest of my life there. However, they caught me and brought me back. The hospital told me that no matter how many times I would run away, I would always be brought back. I then realised that running away was not going to get me discharged from hospital.

After 18 months, they moved me from the secure ward to an open ward. I settled quickly there and I began to behave myself. One day, I remember talking to a man in my ward who had been in hospital for thirty-nine years. I remember thinking that life wouldn't be worth much if the same happened to me. I began to think about a flat of my own, a job, a girlfriend, how I wanted those things for myself.

Eventually, with the help of a nurse, I came off the compulsory order and became a voluntary patient. I then decided that I would leave the hospital as soon as I felt ready. I didn't discuss my plans with anybody except the workshop instructor. He told me a gentleman he knew was going to visit me to discuss the possibility of a job with his firm – an apprenticeship as a sheet-metal-worker machinist in Cowdenbeath. I was taken on a three months' trial. I thought to myself: 'This is the beginning of my plan'. I did this job for seven months. I then had to leave because I couldn't cope with the 10-hour shifts. Also, they didn't pay me enough for the work I was doing. During this time, I made a decision – I was going to leave the hospital, do things my way and of my own accord without anybody telling me what to do and how. The first person I broke the news to was my brother. He was not amused. He told me I was a 'so-and-so'.

On the Friday night, I told the nurses I was 'resigning'. They soon phoned the doctor. He told me that if anything happened, I would not be allowed back in the hospital. I was prepared to take the chance. On the Saturday morning, I packed my bags and walked out. I went straight to the area where I used to live, knocked at doors, and eventually I found a place to stay. It was with an elderly couple. They told me I could stay with them for as long as I needed to. I never told them where I came from, but the next morning the man offered to take me by car to collect my belongings, so I had to tell him I had been in a hospital for years. He didn't seem to mind. I lived with this family for three months and, for the first time, I felt free. I left because of a disagreement. While I was away visiting my uncle, they interfered with my belongings and I didn't like this. I moved into digs and stayed there for two and a half years. During this time, I made a friend. He was good and sympathetic towards me. I was feeling fed up with being unemployed. I felt I was just drifting, so one day I walked into the Job Centre. The girl at the desk told me that if there were no vacancies on the board, there was nothing she could do for me. I told her I wanted a job and to tell the manager of the centre that I wanted to see him. He saw me and, as a result, offered me a job at the dockyard as a labourer. My workmates at the dockyard accepted me straight away. I settled in my new job quickly and I felt I was 'fitting in'. I was still wanting a house of my own, so I contacted the welfare people and the social worker helped me to get a council flat. I went to tell my mother straight away. I was laughing on the way, because she had told me many times that I would not get a job or a house. My mother was over the moon about the news. My dad offered to paint my flat and my workmates scrounged around for bits of furniture. I felt great when I moved into my flat. My own place at last! I was 24 years old.

I lived in this flat for six years but the area was beginning to get rough. I also wanted to move nearer my family, so I applied for a house transfer. The social worker gave me a lot of help and support over the years, but I was disappointed that my parents rarely visited me at the flat.

Anyway, after a while, I got a new flat in a nice area. I have been here nine months and I'm very happy. I got promotion at the dockyard. I now work in the store and I enjoy my job. I also made a lot of friends at my workplace and I play pool with some of them. I also go to Country and Western concerts, and I'm a voluntary helper at the local youth club for mentally handicapped teenagers. I'm totally independent and I'm enjoying myself. All I need now is a girlfriend. I don't have any more contact with the hospital. I used to visit, but they discouraged me because my visits unsettled the patients.

Robert: Dunfermline
(Dictated)

Conclusion

The conclusion is in three sections:

- Main themes.
- Implications for research.
- Future research.

First, we look at the main themes which have emerged from the book as a whole. These are not confined to chapter headings, as often they cut across our arbitrary divisions.

Secondly, we look at some of the research issues raised by this project. We look, albeit retrospectively, at this book as an example of innovatory and open-ended research, and describe the processes involved in enabling people to participate in it. Although we set out to produce an anthology rather than undertake a research project, nevertheless this book, as a collection of people's work and histories, fits within a research tradition. And behind each contribution is another story: the account of how it was told and recorded. The methods used by intermediaries to enable people to tell their personal stories have their roots in qualitative research. We link the research issues raised here with issues raised elsewhere in related fields.

Finally, we reflect on what has emerged from this book both in terms of research methods (and processes) and in the future directions of further study and research.

Main themes

At this stage, one might expect to pull out of this anthology a series of themes around the topic of 'what it's like to be handicapped' or 'the experiences of people with learning difficulties'. And yet one cannot do that. People's 'stories' range far and wide, but they are not primarily about handicap. Though their differences, as others and they perceive them, cannot be minimised, and their different life experiences (of special schools, centres, hostels and hospitals) are ones we have not shared, yet the themes that emerge are universal. Our contributors have written about their lives and, in so doing, have written about life itself.

We imposed a structure on this anthology. The chapters reflect major themes that struck us during the early stages of reading and selecting the material contributed. But there are other themes which are interwoven throughout, and which emerge regardless of our imposed structure.

The book is in many ways about identity. This is a key underlying theme. The contributors addressed this issue from two angles: personal and social identity. Personal identity is sought, and found, through having a past; experiencing a sense of belonging; being loved and valued; being seen as and treated as an adult; and valuing one's self.

Social identity is sought through adopting social roles, achieving a valued status and acquiring useful skills or accomplishments. In this context, contributors wrote and talked about having girlfriends and boyfriends, getting married, acquiring 'proper jobs' and more money, having their own home, being a carer of other people, improving their reading and writing skills, and learning to drive.

A sense of identity is not easily achieved. People with learning difficulties are faced with obstacles at every turn. Their stories witness their battle, often life-long, to overcome these obstacles and find a sense of self. The battle theme is a strong one and permeates the anthology. The battle is both against outside forces (often well-meaning parents and carers) which deny adulthood, and internal learned prohibitions (particularly the internalised barrier to parenthood). The struggle finds expression in the search for, and celebration of, autonomy, freedom and independence.

Much of this anthology is about relationships and the love, joy and despair that those relationships bring. Contributors describe their feelings – there is much talk of love, but also of hate and anger. There is sadness through loss – a theme captured time and time again. But throughout the book there is insight and wisdom about people and relationships that belies any notion of handicap, and there is many a turn of phrase which simply captures a treasured moment or a new awareness.

Key themes: some examples

To provide many and varied examples of the three main themes, and the interlinked but numerous sub-themes, would be to rewrite the book with different chapter headings! We are offering, therefore, only a minimal selection of examples around the main themes.

1 Identity

Personal identity

• Having a past

'Grandma was short and grandpa was short and he had a moustache and he was a shepherd who looked after sheep...My grandma made old-fashioned wine...She used to put her washing up on a pulley in the kitchen, up to the ceiling. My mum used to do that and help grandma with the washing...I used to go out with grandpa sometimes to look after the sheep...'

(*Eleanor Mary Hearn,* Chapter Two, p. 41)

• A sense of belonging

'I love my mum and dad very much because they are my family. They love me too because they had me as a baby.'

(*Susan Bonshall,* Chapter Three, p. 65)

• Being loved and valued

'I am very happy with my wife because she is a very kind wife. And because I love Margaret.'

(*David Marsh,* Chapter Four, p. 95)

• Being seen and treated as an adult

'College is different...I am older and more mature, and that's it. Everybody has helped me to get more mature – staff and other students.'

(*Colin,* Chapter Seven, p. 156)

• Valuing one's self

'When I told my mum I was in a women's group she said I was a girl. I said I was a woman. Now she knows I was right.'

(Women's Group, Chapter Eight, p. 173)

Social identity

• Having girlfriends and boyfriends

'Boyfriends are important to me. My boyfriend has got lovely blue eyes and nice black hair. He is very tall and handsome, with a lovely personality. I love him a lot. I hope we will be together for the rest of my life. My boyfriend is special to me. He is the best boyfriend in the world and I want the world to know it.'

(*William Brinson Centre,* Chapter Three, p. 81)

• Getting married

'My mum said we could get married as long as we could find a flat...I know we won't have children but we still love each other...I'd always wanted to get married but I thought nobody would have me!'

(*Sue Virgin,* Chapter Eight, p. 181)

• Acquiring 'proper jobs' and more money

'What I really need to do over the next few years is get a job. I need practice at interviews...I need a job where I can get good money so I can support Diane when we get married.'

(*Andrew,* Chapter Six, p. 131)

• Having one's own home

'Last year I decided I wanted to have a home of my own so that I could have more freedom...my own home at last...my own house...I am very glad I decided to get my own flat...I am much happier now in my own home.'

(*Doretta Adolphine,* Chapter Four, p. 94)

• Caring for others

'My mum died when I was small so now I look after my dad. I can't leave home because he needs me.'

(Women's Group, Chapter Eight, p. 175)

'I do voluntary work with a playgroup and in sheltered housing for old people...If I had a job I would like to work with children.'

(*Wilma Rhodes,* Chapter Four, p. 107)

- Improving reading and writing skills

'My name is Gerry Cleary and I came to Kirkdale Centre because I couldn't read. The woman in the dole office, she started me off to come up here like. She said: "Would you like to learn to read Gerry?" and I said: "I would". She said, "I'll phone up Kirkdale and fix a time for them to see you".

I feel more happier now because I can read a bit and I never could when I was young...'

(*Gerry Cleary,* Chapter One, p. 31)

- Learning to drive

'I'm hoping to have a Disabled car; so I can go anywhere without going in my mother's car. While I have not got a Disabled car I still go with my mother anywhere I like to go in her car. I would like a Disabled car because soon my mother will be too old to get me anywhere because she would be too old to drive me there. That's why I would like a car.'

(*Huw Redwood,* Chapter Eight, p. 186)

2 *Personal struggle*

- Obstacles: from without...

'I can't get married. I'm not old enough yet....I can't drive. My mum won't let me...she won't let me move away by myself.'

(*Ros,* Chapter Three, p. 86)

'They are charge nurses and nurses and I have the strange feeling that they think they are the ones that know better.'

(*Peter Stevens,* Chapter Eight, p. 191)

- and from within...

'Staff can have children. People like us need help.'

(*Women's Group,* Chapter Eight, p. 175)

'Women with a handicap can't really go out.'

(*Women's Group,* Chapter Eight, p. 173)

- The search for autonomy, freedom and independence

'I'm there on my own...I like the flat. I like to be by myself.'

(*Tommy Goard,* Chapter Eight, p. 179)

'Now I'm in a nice flat. I do everything myself.'

(*Sarah Hunt,* Chapter Four, p. 102)

'It was a good idea to move away from my foster parents. I am more independent now.'

(*Eugene Lynch,* Chapter Six, p. 132)

'We feel proud of what we have achieved...a flat by ourselves. We like being independent.'

(*Jenny Trim,* Chapter Eight, p. 181)

'I felt great when I moved into my flat. My own place at last! I was 24 years old...I'm totally independent and I'm enjoying myself.'

(*Robert,* Chapter Nine, p. 215)

'[Self-advocacy] it's helped me to stand up for me rights and it's helped me to be more confident...(and assertive) being sure, knowing you're right and being really really confident.'

(*Anita Binns,* Chapter Eight, p. 192)

3 Relationships

- Feelings

'I've got a lot of love for mum. She's part of my life...'

(*Linda Collins,* Chapter Three, p. 63)

'And I fell in love when I met her...'

(*Robert,* Chapter Three, p. 83)

'We never fall out...I think it's true love. Sandy helps me put my coat on every night.'

(*Jean*, Chapter Three, p. 81)

'My friend is Janet. We like writing up notes. I like looking at her face...'

(*Florence,* Chapter Three, p. 77)

'I have a best friend; she helps me do things. Best friends are closer to you; you can speak to them openly.'

(*City Lit,* Chapter Three, p. 78)

'I dreaded to go out in the playground; I was frightened inside and it was all bottled up...I then was filled with outrage...'

(*Brenda Cook,* Chapter Two, p. 45)

'I went red with anger, I was fuming...I felt terrible, I felt like slamming someone.'

(*John Symes,* Chapter Seven, p. 150)

'When dad was drunk I felt bad inside...I was frightened, there was nothing I could do...My tummy's going funny. I get angry...'

(*Alan Marshall,* Chapter Seven, p. 153)

- Loss

'When my grandmother and grandfather died I was upset, and when my mum and dad died, I felt awful...I started to cry. I sat down and cried...I was much too upset to do anything...I felt very awful.'

(*Eleanor Mary Hearn*, Chapter Four, p. 98)

'When they came and told us my mother had died it nearly broke my heart.'

(*George Mustard,* Chapter Four, p. 106)

'I went upstairs and saw him lying there dead and I was really shocked – I couldn't believe it...My mum...died suddenly... I felt terrible. I thought she was going to get better – it was another shock.'

(*Vera Stone,* Chapter Four, p. 100)

'My brother has left home now. There is just me and my mum at home. I miss him. The house is quiet now.'

(*Dawn ,* Chapter Four, p. 97)

'My aunty is dead and my uncle too...I'm sad, I miss them...I cry in bed.'

(*Pearl Chilcott,* Chapter Four, p. 98)

'When my friend died I stayed quiet for three weeks.'

(*City Lit,* Chapter Three, p. 79)

- Insight and wisdom

'My dad and mam split up. I was eight when they split up. It's all in my record book. My story's in my record book in the hospital. That's my story. It affected my speaking. When I get excited I'm stuttering too much.'

(*Jackie Heyworth,* Chapter Four, p. 108)

We've had our ups and downs, but we've got over it. Same as, we have a grouse together – if you don't have rows it's not a bloody family. You might as well say it's not a family at all! There isn't a family in this world what doesn't have rows, but we get along alright with each other...So, now I'm at home with me sister, and she likes it, and we have our fallings out but we soon get back together again, and that's it.'

(*Ronnie Gaukrodger,* Chapter Nine, p. 207)

- The turn of phrase

'You have to know me as I am.'

(*City Lit,* Chapter Three, p. 79)

'My dad...had a smiley face.'

(*Pearl Chilcott,* Chapter One, p. 22)

'Later on I started doing man-like things like laying the table before mealtimes...'

(*G.E. Wilkins,* Chapter Two, p. 59)

'I can't remember what it was like to be a child. Everything is the same. I feel the same. But as a grown-up I can have a baby.'

(*William Brinson Centre,* Chapter One, p. 31)

'Dyslexia is pain when my eight-year-old daughter says: "Mum, how do you spell..?", and I pretend I am deaf because the hole in my head is letting the letters fall through again.'

(*Kathleen Oakley,* Chapter Seven, p. 156)

Implications for research

(1) The book as an example of 'research'

We take as our starting point the fact that this book has an impact at two levels. On one level it is an anthology – a moving and vivid collection of people's work and personal stories. But on another level it can be seen as an example of qualitative research, and it is that aspect which concerns us here.

This venture was not set up as a research project. We set out to produce an anthology. But in so doing we addressed many 'research' issues to do with enabling people to give personal accounts of their lives and experiences. The anthology project took on, over time, aspects of a research study. It had to. We were venturing into relatively uncharted territory. And what we found on the way may well be of value to those who want to follow our path. This is, in a sense, our 'story'.

We start with a 'how it was done' account. The book did not just happen. People invested time, effort, enthusiasm and personal belief into making it happen. This is partly an account of the methods used in enabling people to tell their stories. It is not a scientific account. It is the story of a piece of 'research' which is both untidy and imprecise. And there are dilemmas and doubts which make it a very human story too.

The 'how it was done' account follows this sequence:

- the role of the editors
- the role of intermediaries
- an evolution of ideas
- the Editorial Advisory Group
- personal reflections
- dilemmas
- social recognition.

(i) The role of the editors

You read earlier, in the Introduction, about the editors' role in *setting up* the project and making contact with intermediaries and contributors. We move on now to our involvement in the actual project itself.

The editorial role in the actual 'telling' of stories was, in most cases, limited to one personal visit where contact was made with individual contributors. Most visits were carried out by the two anthology editors over a six-week period. Visits were made at all stages of the story-telling process, often at the preliminary thinking-about-it stage or at the very beginning of the work, but also at various points during the production of materials. Many people waited for the visit before they started. Others got work under way at once, and were then happy to share what they had done already when their visitor arrived. A few people were already engaged in similar, though localised, projects and their work was seen during the course of its production. A handful of intermediaries already had work in hand from related projects and sent this in for consideration; in those cases, personal visits were not undertaken.

The personal visits to individuals, groups, families, establishments and organisations proved invaluable. A 'one-off' visit of this kind had to achieve several aims: to inform people of what we were looking for, to engage their interest and enthusiasm, and to encourage them to take part. A visit from someone connected with the Open University seemed to rate as a special or different event in people's lives, and an atmosphere of interest and excitement usually prevailed. Contributors seemed to welcome this link, they seemed to feel personally involved and that their life and their story mattered. There is dignity in being listened to and taken seriously. An anthology of their 'stories' offers people a real and long-lasting sense of personal dignity.

The visits helped secure people's commitment to produce material for consideration for the anthology. The idea of a book captured their imagination and interest. An initial potential problem for the editors was: 'Will there be enough material to make into a book?' Later on that problem receded and was replaced with another one: 'Will there be room for all the material submitted?' The degree of interest sparked off from all corners of the country suggested that our problem would be having too much material rather than too little. This possibility was raised in discussion with contributors during visits. The point was made that probably there would not be room for everyone's work and that decisions would have to be made about what to include. It was with this in mind that an Editorial Advisory Group was set up. An account of their work is given below.

The anthology editors kept diaries throughout the project so that a chronological account was compiled. The diaries logged how contributors were located and described what happened during visits. The diary account was written after each visit. In addition, a tape-recorder was used, where possible, to record contributors' names and their introductory statements about themselves and, in most cases, photographs were taken. The tape-recorder sometimes proved an intrusive companion, stopping conversations rather than enabling them to take place! The camera did not have an adverse effect as people seemed to enjoy having their photographs taken. Most of the written diary accounts were supplemented by tape recordings and photographs. The recordings and photographs from these visits do not appear in the book. They helped us keep track of the many people we met on our travels, and helped us put faces (and voices) to names when contributions began to arrive.

The story behind the story sometimes emerged during visits, the 'real' story confided or revealed at a personal level which differed from the story eventually submitted for consideration. This presented us with one of the dilemmas dealt with later; do we reveal the story behind the story?

The following is an extract from a diary account of a visit to a social education centre:

11 May 1988

Sue (our intermediary) is an enthusiast! She has already got the Life Stories Discussion Group interested in taking part. But word has already spread around the centre and other people have decided to take part, working with their keyworkers. As I sat chatting to Sue, a handwritten note was passed in to her office, saying 'Linda has decided she would like to meet the person from the Open University'.

In all, she has about 15 people interested, including people with quite severe handicaps. Indeed the discussion group is made up of people who have exhibited problem behaviour, as a way of helping them come to terms with angry feelings, find an understanding of them – and channel them into an acceptable outlet. It's also an interesting project, which deflects their energies elsewhere.

In discussion, Sue mentioned her Women's Group. She thought they would be keen to take part. They tackle issues of importance to women generally: roles, relationships, sexuality, pregnancy, rape etc. This is the first offer of a contribution from a women's group! One tends to assume that all people with learning difficulties face similar problems. Yet there are obvious gender issues which could well be aired – and which would lead nicely into other parts of the course.

Sue thought that today's group would reflect on key themes:

- relationships
- moving out
- teasing

There is a general air of excitement about contributing to a book, especially one that is likely to influence staff. Several possibilities emerged – group projects, using role-play and video (video stills might be submitted) and individual contributions including interviews with keyworkers, painting and photography.

Because of the large number of possible contributors, people were seen in two smaller groups. In the first group John, a keyworker, joined us.

Group 1

There were no tape-recorder rebels today. Everyone said something. A young Asian woman, who actually uses Makaton signs (and for whom English is a second language) bravely kicked off. I had difficulty understanding Jasoda but she persevered and Sally (another group member) translated. When asked if she had ideas about what she might contribute, Jasoda said 'rabbit stories'. This was treated with disdain by Sally, who said the idea was too 'babyish'.

Not many other ideas were forthcoming. Sally, in particular, was fascinated by the idea of a book, and would like to show it to her 'nanny'. (She lost both parents at an early age, and acquired a nanny who is very important to her.) She was keen on an adult contribution, and ran through items on her weekly list of activities...

(ii) The role of intermediaries

What was the role of the person 'on the spot' in relation to the story-telling process? The editors saw intermediaries as enablers or facilitators. They knew the contributor and had regular face-to-face contact. Their task was to enable the contributor to tell, draw or write his, or her, own story. But what did 'enabling' mean in practice? Did it involve active help and encouragement in developing ideas for stories? Did it involve interviewing skills? Would a tape-recorder help? Or should words be written down as they were dictated? What about someone unable to speak?

In practice, enabling meant using a variety of helpful strategies. In several instances, contributors were able to write or type their own story in their own words. Others produced their own pictures or photographs, and wrote poems. But most people were helped in some way with their story telling.

We asked our intermediaries to let us know how they had helped in the story-telling process and we received a variety of replies. The following are some examples:

- 'Most of the stories were initiated by a few questions from an instructor, although the substance of all of them is derived from the clients themselves.' (ATC instructor)
- 'I started with asking about their earliest memory – and prompted by asking short questions to link their trains of thought, but being aware of not putting the words into their mouths. As far as possible, I tried to record everything they said in their own words.' (ATC instructor)
- 'The group were left on their own with the video camera running. With the exception of the editing of a few repetitions, the discussion was transcribed word for word.' (ATC instructor and college lecturer)
- 'He couldn't speak into a tape-recorder, so I did. He told me the story and I spoke his words on to a tape. Our secretary transcribed the tape, and he and I have checked the wording.' (Social work student)
- 'Some of these pieces are language experience exercises, i.e. dictated by the student to the tutor and taken down in exactly their words. This is a technique we regularly use with beginner reader/writers – it helps their reading when they read back their own words.' (College tutor)
- 'Stories are not corrected for spelling, grammar, punctuation, etc. Students wrote what they felt and wrote in their own words. The idea is to encourage them to write expressing themselves freely in the form they are comfortable with.' (Adult Education teacher)
- 'He wanted to write a story to "get it off his chest". He wrote the story over two weeks. The first part is factual, but for the second I encouraged him to write about what he did, which as you will read is quite revealing! He wrote this without help.' (Outreach worker)

- 'The first section of this piece was transcribed following a discussion about all aspects of the choir. The ideas were put out by everyone and individuals were asked to put them into clear sentences which were approved of by the group before being written down. The named pieces were from people who wanted to make their own comments without group intervention. Some of them set up interview roles and asked for their answers to be written down.' (Choir leader)
- 'Using signs and sounds, she created the meaning of this account which was written fully by a helper. She listened to the drafts until she agreed with the final version. Dad picked the title.' (Father)

The two most detailed descriptive and explanatory accounts are provided by John Swain, a consultant to the Course Team which produced K668 *Mental Handiciap: Changing Perspectives.* The commentaries were compiled with the help of two different colleagues, who were also involved in the interviewing process.

(a) Robert and Ros's story

Commentary by John Swain and Paul Lawrence (Lecturer in a college of further education)

'The philosophy behind this project appealed to us both from the outset. It seemed to us to be a means of promoting the voice of people with learning difficulties. Nevertheless we had some reservations:

- We were not sure how to begin to get Ros and Robert's story. They obviously could not write it down for themselves. We felt they would need a lot of help to tell their story, but we also felt there was a great danger of it becoming an interview i.e. if we weren't careful (or perhaps however careful we were!) it would become our story rather than theirs.
- We were also not sure whether Ros and Robert's story was what was required for the anthology. It seemed, in a way, too 'ordinary'.

The following are some of our main thoughts after collecting the story:

- We felt that Ros and Robert had talked freely. Paul, who knows them well, felt we had gained a valid view of them and their story.
- There were unforeseen problems in transcribing the story. Ros had poor articulation and also talks with a strong Geordie accent! Secondly, we felt that the heart of Robert and Ros's story is the strength of their relationship, but this is inadequately conveyed in their words. There is a close mutual intimacy between them. They hold hands, put a hand on the other's knee or round their shoulder in a very natural way. As they talk there are many exchanges of glances between them, looking for or giving support and reassurance. They remain physically close and as they talk they even seem to move in synchrony.
- Our main problem was completely unforeseen. There were times when Robert and Ros became so involved in their discussions they seemed almost to forget we were there. In

one way this seemed good. Our misgivings about it being an interview were overcome in that we were truly listening to Robert and Ros's story. However, there were times when we felt that we were listening in to a private domestic conversation. Ros and Robert were no longer telling their story, they were discussing very personal matters between themselves. At its worst it felt like voyeurism. For example, when Ros brought up the early troubles they had in their relationship (when she caught Robert with another girl), we eventually intervened as both she and Robert were becoming quite upset as they re-aired past grievances. The problem was exaggerated, of course, by the fact that this was to be a story which might be published. But who were we to intervene? We were left with a dilemma.

- We were also left with a strong impression of a very close couple who had built an intimate loving relationship without many of the opportunities that most young couples their age enjoy.'

(b) Stories by Doreen, Jackie and Anita

Commentary by John Swain and Jean Ollerton (Staff trainer: Regional Health Authority)

'We collaborated in collecting these three stories, and found the process challenging and in many ways problematic. With each story we took the following steps.

1 Jean made the initial contact with each person. She knew them all through their involvement with the Skills for People advocacy/self help group and felt they would be interested in the anthology. She explained what was involved and asked if they wished to participate.

2 We visited each person in their own home. John gave a second explanation about the anthology and what we would be asking them. Each person was also told that they could stop or withdraw at any time they wished.

3 Each story was taped to be transcribed later. The intention was to ask open questions, following rather than leading, and use reflection to help the person tell whatever story they wanted to tell.

Many questions arose for us. Our central concern was that we wanted it to be the person's story, told in their own way and covering what they wanted to cover. We also wanted to be open about the process and feel confident that each person knew why they were telling their story and what would happen to the material. These questions of ownership and control were crucial and for us the central issues out of which other questions arose:

- Was the use of special visits with a tape-recorder the best way to collect stories? In some ways we felt this was an unsatisfactory method. We felt Doreen's story, for instance, was somewhat disjointed. Visits over a long period of time could have elicited a fuller and more fluent story. Such an approach, however, would have raised other difficulties. At what point does 'telling your story' become observing and prying by the other person?

- Was our conception of 'telling your story' and our visit generally shared with the person with learning difficulties? On the one hand, we felt fairly sure that each person wanted to tell us their story. They were certainly all very welcoming and enthusiastic. On the other hand, it became increasingly obvious that there were major differences in perceptions about our visits. For Doreen, for instance, our visit seemed to be a very welcome social event. Once the tape-recorder was turned off, she seemed to become more relaxed and began to ask John questions. She turned the tables on us and listened to 'John's story'. Doreen also used a much more common and in some ways much more effective way of 'telling her story'. First, she got out her album and showed us pictures of events and people in her life (with comments such as, 'that's our Alan' and so on). She then showed us round her flat, showing us and talking about some of her possessions. It was 'a story' which could not have been presented in a book (and probably Doreen would not have wished it to be).
- Did the stories cover what the person wanted to cover or what we wanted to hear? As interviewers, we found it very difficult not to get drawn into the story and ask about particular things that interested us. When we listened afterwards to the tapes, we were struck by how easy it is to talk the person down tracks they might not necessarily have gone down. Anita talked quite openly about 'Turner's Syndrome', for instance, but would she have included this in her story unless she had been asked directly?
- Finally, we had not expected one very welcome outcome of our involvement in this project. The people who told us their stories have been very proud of their involvement. They have spoken about it to other people as something they were not only pleased to have done but as a real accomplishment. They have told and had published stories about themselves and, like most people would, they see this as a highly valued thing to have done.'

(iii) An evolution of ideas

The information sheet initially sent out to individuals, organisations and networks said the anthology would be a collection of stories 'by and about the lives of people with learning difficulties'.

At that stage, it was thought that:

- existing, published material would be included
- stories could be written by people with learning difficulties, or *someone else*
- 'stories' included short or long contributions, in written form or on tape; as narrative accounts, poems, pictures, or photographs
- some new material, specially produced for the anthology, would probably be generated through our nationwide appeal for contributions

- the anthology would include work by and about people with mental handicap ('learning difficulties').

Many of these ideas changed during the course of the project. The editors were influenced by the people they met, and their stories. Our thinking changed through our involvement in a project initially of our own making. The project later took on its own identity and gathered momentum as other people became involved in it and shared its ownership. We became partners in a nationwide joint venture. This book is in effect the work of its contributors, and the people who worked alongside them.

The size and scale of the response to our initial appeals surprised us. The idea of an anthology of people's lives was greeted with enthusiasm. We had struck a chord with people and had tapped a rich vein of experience and energy. It became apparent very early that we could compile an anthology of 'new' material; based mostly on stories produced specially for it but also including some existing related but unpublished work.

It also became apparent that the anthology could be compiled entirely from work contributed by people with learning difficulties themselves. We did not need stories *about* them, we could use their own stories. And this included people with severe and profound handicaps, and people with little or no speech. Enthusiastic and innovative intermediaries found ways of including people through role-play, group work, drama, video- and tape- recordings, Makaton signs and computers, as well as by more conventional dictated or written stories.

The term 'people with learning difficulties' is ambiguous. We used it originally to mean people with the label of mental handicap. Most of the contributions are, in fact, from people with that label. But our first contribution was from someone who described herself as 'dyslexic' and who felt, therefore, that she had very real 'learning difficulties'. Her vivid portrayal of her own life experiences shifted our thinking. Thus the anthology now includes contributions from others who feel they have learning difficulties, not on account of innate learning disability, but because of a physical condition which has proved disadvantageous within the existing educational system. Contributors include, therefore, people with epilepsy and people with physical disabilities. Their experiences are vividly recorded in these pages and they link with the experiences of those more usually known as 'people with learning difficulties'.

(iv) The Editorial Advisory Group

At an early stage, it became apparent that we would not be able to include all contributions. To help us in the selection process we set up an Editorial Advisory Group, whose members were themselves people with learning difficulties.

At the first meeting with our Editorial Advisory Group we broached some of our dilemmas:

- *Do we include pictures that some people might regard as 'childish'?*

  'Yes, people have different ways of drawing.'
- *Would our readers want to read about people's 'ordinary' days?*

  'I find them interesting, but I don't know if my social worker would. I can ask her.'
- *Do we tell the 'story behind the story'?*

  'No. Use the story that is sent to you.'
- *Do we indicate the (sometimes great) effort that has gone into the telling of a story?*

  'Yes.'
- *Do we correct and 'improve' unpolished handwritten stories, or do we present them as they are?*

  'I would rather have my story presented nicely.'

The guidance we received was straightforward and helpful. This enabled us to make a preliminary selection of material for inclusion in the first draft of the anthology.

At a second meeting, we were able to share some of our selected material and obtain comments and advice about editing and presentation. We raised a number of issues with the group:

- *Is it OK to use the word 'stories' to describe people's contributions?*

  'Yes.'
- *What did you like?*

  'All of it. It's really good.'
- *Have you any suggestions about layout?*

  'Mix up the sad stories with the happy ones.'
- *Sometimes people make spelling mistakes, but at other times they use words in an unusual way – what should we do? Correct everything? Leave everything?*

  'Correct the spelling mistakes but keep the unusual words because they make the stories more interesting.'
- *Did anything strike you personally about people's lives?*

  'Yes, I know what it feels like to have epilepsy. I have to take tablets. Most people don't know what it's like.'

  'Ronnie says he had "cocoa, cocoa, cocoa every night". It was like that at my school.'

  'Wilma remembers being fostered as a child. That must have been awful.'

Again, we received invaluable advice. We acted on this advice in our final editing.

What struck us most in this discussion with our Editorial Advisory Group was the high level of interest and enjoyment that people gained from reading about the lives of other people. We knew already that contributing to this anthology had brought interest and enjoyment to many. Now it seemed that contributors' words, ideas and experiences would in turn bring pleasure to their *readers*, especially perhaps to people with learning difficulties.

(v) Personal reflections

The compilation of this anthology has stretched everyone who has taken part. The work involved for contributors and intermediaries has sometimes proved arduous and taxing. It is not easy to tell one's story. It is not easy either to be the person who helps that process along. Several people who meant to take part have not been able to do so. Sometimes this was because time ran out or ill-health intervened.

It seemed, too, that what had appeared to be a good idea in principle sometimes proved unattainable in practice. As one intermediary explained after the event: 'I began to go ahead with two particular men from Dickens Ward who have some speech, but it has been very difficult and extremely time-consuming. I could easily write things out myself but I know that is not the point and you want to hear from the people themselves...now I have a slightly more realistic view of the effort and time needed to produce something'.

The editors themselves have found their involvement difficult and time consuming. One editor's six-week visiting programme entailed 40 visits, meetings with over a hundred contributors and journeys covering thousands of miles. Tiredness crept in. And doubts. There have been doubts from the outset. Could this project be done? Would we collect enough material for a whole book? Would people's stories prove interesting? Would we have endless accounts of 'ordinary' days?

One main source of doubt was our lack of direct control of the project. We did not have direct links with contributors. We had to rely on people to contact us with invitations to visit. During our visit, we had to fit in with whatever class, group or family activity was planned for us. And after we left, then what? We had no further control of events. We had to wait for contributions to arrive. We did not know what, and how much, to expect.

The following diary extracts from one of the book's editors chart these personal doubts and misgivings during her arduous six-week visiting programme.

(1) 'The end of the first day of meeting people. As always the reality is more messy than the neat principles and strategies drawn up in advance.

- The noise factor

How audible are my recordings? I've visited a centre and family today both with a lot of background noise and activity.

- Lack of preparation

Contributors have not been prepared in advance. How much do they understand?

- Shifting content

Content shifts around a lot. I keep forgetting to go through my checklist.

- Pressures on me

I have to remember to use my tape-recorder and camera. And justify their use.

I'm only taping the bits where people tell me who they are and what they might do for the book. And I'm not taking individual pictures, only group shots. No objections yet either to the tape-recorder or the camera, though I am using them quite sparingly.'

(2) 'My third day. So often people have not been prepared in advance. I have to explain each time. It probably has little meaning for contributors, though perhaps staff get something out of my explanations. Maybe my visits are as much for the intermediaries as they are for the contributors, to get *their* commitment, and to make them into good interviewers.

It's hard to say how it's going! (Though colleagues keep asking.) Or what might emerge. It's a process of capturing people's imagination and commitment. But I have little control over what happens next. I can't *do* the interviewing. I have to rely on a series of (enthusiastic) intermediaries, who are willing but how able? They are getting minimum preparation. More of an adventure story than a 'research' project!'

(3) 'Looking around that room (noises, unco-ordinated movements, dribbles..) I couldn't imagine *anyone* could be involved in anything called "drama" It didn't seem possible. And yet other people could see potential there that was lost to me...'

(4) 'The ward was fairly grim. Some ambulant, but severely handicapped, men sat or wandered in the dining space. In the office was a container full of toothbrushes! (Are they doled out?) The attitudes were grimmer. Permission? To speak to us?'

(5) '"I didn't know you were coming!" He was angry. He sat down so we had to bend or crouch to speak to him (he's deaf). He avoided eye contact. He said Martin ("the sociologist") had mentioned the book to him "but I never answered him". He was adamant. He had *not* agreed and he had *not* expected us. He felt that we'd intruded, singled him out and made him look small.

It *was* an imposition. It was a mistake to button-hole him in front of everyone. Perhaps we should write and apologise. The sad thing is that he probably would be good. He has a good command of language and an extensive vocabulary. Perhaps he'll change his mind. But maybe he shouldn't!'

(6) 'Robert and Rodney, from Dickens Ward, were in O.T. for a Movement Class so we were "introduced" (barest flicker from Rodney, no recognition from Robert). Still their voices should be heard. Or if suppressed, that suppression should be recorded.

Peter didn't get involved in any of this. I wondered what his feelings were. Does he dissociate himself from people with very severe handicaps? I thought he might act as go-between or at least advise us about how we might proceed. But he didn't offer, and we didn't ask.'

(7) 'What they hadn't done was realise the main purpose of my visit; i.e. not just to meet them and have lunch but to meet

would-be contributors. This meant that three of the seven were not in and the rest, though around, had to be found and invited in.

The room was not ideal. We had to borrow it from another group, and people kept coming in. However, through contributors were not forewarned they coped well with a stranger armed with a tape-recorder...'

(8) 'This group didn't like the tape-recorder much! It silenced them, particularly three men who made a fuss and conspicuously remained (almost) silent. Whilst respecting their right to do so, I doggedly persisted with the idea, especially as the women appeared to be co-operative and I knew they were always active in their video sessions. I'm afraid I manipulated them and eventually group pressure brought two of them into the session, and even the third contributed his name and where he lived.'

(9) 'When Simon returned with coffees, he confessed he'd done nothing so far - had not even mentioned the book to people! I reiterated what it was about, but it seemed beyond their understanding. He had had only one idea; taking them on a trip to the zoo and getting individual accounts afterwards. This didn't seem promising to me; his idea not theirs, and an organised trip to boot. I threw in ideas that other people had had and he perked up (the group continued to look bored).

It was only after I had left and had started my long walk back to the station that I remembered my camera. For the first time I'd forgotten to take a photo! That more than anything indicates how uninspired I felt by this visit. Simon was enthusing by the end: "How exciting!", etc. But they haven't actually done anything yet. And will they, I wonder? My first failure.'

(10) 'A wet Monday in south London. Tired and decidedly jaded. Three hours by car from Milton Keynes and a full five minutes to negotiate reception ("I can't think *who* you mean..."). I walked into the room and was greeted by the tutor. The students were all working on computers.

This was a third-hand contact, who thought we were producing a book for teachers. She hadn't told the class I was coming. Her suggestion was that I drifted round the room chatting to people as I went, sort of Princess Di style. That didn't seem right.'

(11) 'My heart sank when she said she hadn't actually done anything yet, and perhaps I could explain... Could I really lift myself for the 35th time and say: "Thank you for asking me to come. It's really nice to be here. I expect you've heard of the Open University?" Well, I did because I had to. But it was an effort.'

(12) 'No visits today (bliss) but the anthology continues to dominate my life. Two contributions arrived in this morning's post and left me feeling even more depressed and dispirited:

- A poem written on behalf of a married couple. It's not their words at all! and it rhymes.
- A few lines only from Andrew. Where is his "real" story? My visit was much more interesting. This short piece conveys nothing about the person I met...'

These doubts were very real and pressing. We didn't know for sure, at any stage, how it was really going. We had to trust that people's interest and motivation would carry them, and us, through. Most visits were encouraging and optimistic, some were inspirational. And much of the material, when it came, was in fact full, rich and varied. The anthology was on its way.

The doubts are included here because they were significant features of the process. No project of this kind could run smoothly from beginning to end. We were all venturing into unknown and uncharted territory. Who knew what we would find (if anything)? A slick presentation of the process and neat compilation of materials would mislead. This was a human story after all, and human doubts were never far away.

(vi) Dilemmas

In compiling this anthology we faced a number of dilemmas. We discuss them below around three main themes:

- promotion vs acceptance
- the story behind the story
- people with 'learning difficulties'?

(a) Promotion vs acceptance

On the one hand, we were concerned to promote 'positive images' of people with learning difficulties; to record their achievements and give an indication of potential which often passes by unrecognised. This includes potential for independence, empathy, creativity, self-expression and self-awareness. On the other hand, however, an anthology which merely compiled 'achievements' would miss the point. It would be in danger of begging the question of what 'achievements' are.

Within the pages of this book are works of art which please the eye immensely, and there are poems and stories with an insight which touches the soul. By any criteria these are major achievements of self-expression and communication. But there are also descriptions of events in people's lives which are neither dramatic nor touching. They are mundane and ordinary, like the major parts of many of our lives. Yet they are still representative and significant.

Similarly, there are accounts and drawings which appear, at first glance, to be slight and rather inconsequential but which, in fact, represent for the author or creator a major step in a communication with the outside world. This applies, for example, to someone who has no speech and little muscle control but has strung words together on a computer. It also applies to the person who, whilst refusing to speak to most people in his everyday life for six years, has 'spoken' in this book through a painting.

All this starkly revealed the extent to which, in spite of efforts to the contrary, the compilation represents our own and especially our intermediaries' choice of what work is representative. For example, many of our life-stories came to us illustrated by the authors, or narrators. Some of these illustrations were what we might describe as 'child-like', featuring people with large heads and hands, but others were abstract designs and some showed extreme technical competence.

It occurred to us that if we had asked our colleagues in the Department of Health and Social Welfare at the Open University to submit illustrated stories of their lives, that their drawings also would range from the 'child-like' to the imaginative and competent. And probably only those whose illustrations were imaginative and competent would want their efforts shown to the outside world. In the end, however, we followed the advice of a member of our Editorial Advisory Group who said: 'If that's what they've sent you, I expect that's what they want put in the book'.

The issue raised above about contributions appearing *at first sight* to be no major achievement posed a second set of dilemmas.

(b) The story behind the story

The issue here was whether we should let the contributions speak for themselves or whether we should add background information about the contributor which would put the account in a very different light. Two examples have already been given above where it seems helpful to contextualise what might otherwise appear to be rather ordinary and indifferent pieces of work.

But the issue can and does run deeper than those examples. Some of the more bland descriptions of people's lives in fact hide a great deal of pain and suffering. Ought the reader to know this? Perhaps it is more significant simply to say at this point that we know this to be the case, and to begin to ask why it should be that some contributors clearly did not choose to write about their pain and suffering in their accounts of their lives. (Although it is also clear from the many accounts of death, and of fear and oppression, that some did.)

One answer is that from many of the accounts it was clear that the expression of hurt, pain and suffering during the contributors' lives had been discouraged and indeed, in many cases, had been a cause for further punishment. Clearly it would be unhelpful and unconstructive to expect people in such circumstances to plumb, and to give expression to, feelings of sadness, loss and despair unless we could also guarantee full support in coping with such feelings.

A second answer suggests that, for our contributors, as for most people, self-respect and dignity are crucial principles of survival. One does not want to be seen solely as a 'victim' but as someone who can maintain some modicum of contentment in life. The presentation of self to the outside world in terms of a balance between surviving it and being ground down by it, is difficult, though some of our contributors have managed this (see especially the life histories in Chapter Nine).

We chose, in the end, not to reveal the story behind the story. Contributions were left to speak for themselves.

(c) People with 'learning difficulties'?

We have veered away from a rigid definition of 'learning difficulties'. Some of our contributors have learning difficulties because of physiological differences of the brain, whilst others, through social circumstances, found themselves sent away at an early age to special schools and then to mental deficiency colonies. Others were simply denied the potential for learning and communication because of their severe physical handicaps or by some characteristic, like epilespy, which posed too great a challenge to the existing educational services.

The advantage of having such a broad catchment of 'people with learning difficulties' is that it shifts the 'problem' away from those people themselves to the problem of what constitutes 'ability to learn' (or 'intelligence') and towards the question of how such concepts as 'learning difficulties' are created by society and its institutions of education and work. On the other hand, in using a broad definition, there is a danger of losing sight of, or of minimising, the very specific difficulties which some people with severe and multiple handicaps do have.

We have tried to make sure that the compilation represents the broad range of learning difficulties. We have also attempted to ensure that our contributors represent different age groups, as well as class, ethnic and regional background, and an even gender balance.

(vii) Social recognition

This anthology brings to its contributors the reward of social recognition. Being a published author or painter is a valued social role. This is a rare enough experience for most people, but for people with learning difficulties it is virtually unknown. We know from our intermediaries, and from meeting some contributors again personally, that this social recognition is highly valued. It has given people a sense of achievement, and one to be proud of.

We contacted, via intermediaries, every contributor whose story appears in this book. We asked intermediaries to go through every story with each contributor to check the contents and presentation, and make whatever changes were necessary both to our commentary and to the story itself. This process led to several changes:

- the inclusion – with pride – of full names rather than just first names
- the submission of many authors' photographs
- a clearer account of how some stories were told and written, and the effort involved
- agreement that extracts of original handwritten, typewritten or word-processed accounts could be included in the text.

In returning completed checklists, and annotated texts, many intermediaries commented on the rewards that publication has brought to contributors. The following examples illustrate how social recognition brings with it a sense of personal identity and affirmation of self:

> 'You can have no idea as to the effect on these three students of your decision to publish their work. It is one of the best things that has happened in their lives – they feel affirmed – their excitement and joy knows no bounds.'

> 'One member of the authors' group expressed the feeling of the group when he said he felt proud to be included.'
>
> 'I may say everyone was very pleased with their contribution and very keen that people should know what it (institutional life) was really like.'
>
> 'Everyone was highly delighted with the results of their labours. Many thanks for giving the students the opportunity to be part of this wonderful collection of work.'
>
> 'I telephoned just to say how thrilled we all are that "Our holiday" is going to be included in your project...I'm so excited about your project. The work is wonderful, isn't it?'
>
> 'The students were delighted to see themselves in print.'
>
> 'All the writers have asked me to send their thanks, love and best wishes.'

There is, however, another side to social recognition. It brings with it public exposure and some of its attendant dangers. Some contributors have requested that their family names are removed, so they cannot be identified. One person, delighted to be included but fearful of the possible consequences, has deleted references to an abusing step-father.

Social recognition for authors may mean exposure for the people (and the places) in their lives. Some real names of centres and hostels have been deleted at the request of intermediaries, and some authors' names have been reduced to first names only also at *their* request. Whilst we regret these changes we have, in all instances, respected everyone's views. In any case, such changes cannot diminish the overall impact of this anthology.

(2) A wider research context

This book is rooted in the qualitative research tradition. It is a compilation of people's subjective experiences. Contributors describe their own social worlds and what these mean. People look back on their past lives and they describe who mattered to them then and who matters now. They describe their innermost feelings. In so doing, they are coming to understand their own experiences and themselves. We are involved in that process. As researchers, or as readers, we can empathise with our authors, and begin to see their world as they see it and feel it.

Qualitative research is an umbrella term. It includes, for example, what we can loosely call the 'life histories approach' and what, again loosely, we can call the 'participative approach'. This is a distinction we make for convenience; in practice, there is much overlap between the two approaches.

In the mental handicap field, there is currently considerable interest in finding novel and effective ways of enabling people to convey their subjective experiences; through sensitive interviewing, for example, or through 'being there' and experiencing the rhythm and the content of people's days at first hand. This book links with these various approaches and makes a contribution to their further development. We will look briefly at each of them in turn.

(i) Life histories

We use the term 'life histories' to include autobiographical accounts of varying length, depth and style. In that sense the book is a compilation of life histories, as all accounts are told from the participant's point of view.

In the 'life histories approach', the researcher wants not only to find out how people view their own worlds but to enable them to give their own detailed account of it. It is likely that participants are people who do not usually have a voice. The work involved is detailed and painstaking. Researcher and participant spend a lot of time together talking about life now, recalling past events and reminiscing about how things used to be (Plummer, 1983).

The life histories approach has something in common with *oral history* and *reminiscence*. Again oral history involves remembering and recalling, and often involves people who traditionally are neglected in history books; for example, working-class people, women or people with mental handicap. This is history 'from below' (Humphries, 1984). Reminiscence entails reviewing one's life, making sense of past experiences and valuing personal achievements. It can be an uplifting experience, giving people a sense of self-worth (Coleman, 1986).

This book makes an important contribution to giving 'a voice' to people with learning difficulties, and providing a means for that voice to be heard. Other collections of people's work and lives have appeared in recent times. The situations of some women with physical disabilities are vividly described by the people themselves in an anthology edited by Jo Campling (*Images of Ourselves*, 1981). There is minimal editorial comment there, as it was strongly felt that 'the contributions speak for themselves'.

A second recent example is a compilation of children's work, edited by Helen Exley (*What It's Like To Be Me*, 1981). The children who contributed to the book all had disabilities: 'The basic idea was that this was to be *their* book, entirely their own words, entirely their own drawings, saying what disabled children themselves really felt'. The compilation of words and pictures, though moving, is not depressing. The editor herself, expecting sadness, found the editing of a 'genuinely happy' book a profound experience.

A third example involves the autobiographies of two people with learning difficulties, collected and compiled by Bogdan and Taylor (*Inside Out*, 1982). These are detailed life histories. The stories are themselves revealing. But so too is their context. The researchers also discuss the impact on themselves of their involvement in the *process* of collecting these stories (through close contact with the two people concerned), and in their growing awareness of the *wider meaning* of the lives and experiences of Ed and Pattie. The editors found they were learning not only about Ed and Pattie and their lives but, through their involvement and growing understanding, they were learning about themselves.

(ii) Participative research

This book is itself a study of participative research. In its compilation and in its presentation, it involved a set of principles which are in evidence in related types of research:

- it is a 'grassroots' account; it is by people with learning difficulties themselves
- it is an example of a 'bottom-up' model of research, or 'research from the underside'
- it values people as participants or partners in the research process
- the research story itself is told
- the impact of the experience on the editors is revealed.

A grassroots account

Peter Beresford and Suzy Croft, in *Whose Welfare?* (1986), discuss their participatory approach to research. They avoid the traditional research tendencies to regard and treat people as research 'objects', or to study them as 'clients'. Instead they value 'grassroots views', and set out to find them by involving people in the research structure, process and outcomes.

A bottom-up model

Bob Holman (1987) distinguishes the 'top-down' model of traditional research from the 'bottom-up' model which he advocates. The top-down model involves researchers and researched. The former call the tune; they design, implement and report their studies of the latter. In a bottom-up model, the 'investigated become the investigators' (Holman, 1987).

Partners in research

In this anthology, people were involved as participants or partners. They told their stories – the book is a collection of their work. 'Giving a voice' to people often entails their greater participation in the process, and a move towards a closer research relationship with them as partners in a collaborative effort. This point is well made by Ann Oakley, in describing the principles of feminist research which she adopted in her interviews with women (1981). She describes the non-hierarchical relationship that she developed with participants, and her own personal involvement in the process of enabling other women to discuss their experiences with her.

Telling the research 'story'

This anthology also tells the story of the research process. This is still unusual, though there is some acknowledgement of the value of researchers describing the process, and their involvement in it. Clare Wenger, for example, says that 'doing research is itself a social act and is itself of sociological or anthropological interest' (1987). Sandra Harding makes the point that in 'the best feminist analysis' the research process itself is open to scrutiny.

Personal impact

The collection, compilation and editing of this anthology, and the personal link we established between ourselves as editors and many of our authors, has had an impact on us. This we have explored and revealed. This links us with the other editors we have featured here (Campling, Exley, Bogdan and Taylor) who have commented on the impact of their work on themselves as people. Qualitative research is about people's subjective experience of their worlds. Whoever sets out to find and record this experience is inevitably involved personally in the process and with the people. There is then a second set of subjective experience which deserves a place in the overall account; that of the researcher.

(iii) Research involving people with learning difficulties

There is a growing literature on qualitative research in the mental handicap field. Increasingly, researchers are using interviews and other methods specifically to find out the viewpoints and experiences of people with learning difficulties. This anthology has links with this developing area of interest and makes its own contribution. The intermediaries who enabled people to make their contribution here used various techniques, including interviews, video and interpretation of meanings through signs.

Some of the issues involved in using interviews with people with learning difficulties are summarised by Flynn (1986) and Atkinson (1988). In particular, such interviews require an informality of style and approach on the part of the interviewer. It helps if time is spent in gaining people's confidence and establishing trust between interviewer and interviewee. In their research, for example, Jahoda *et al.* (1988) spent time with people (prior to interviews) informally in clubs and other leisure settings, getting to know them and gaining their confidence.

The 'naturalistic' approach used by Edgerton and his colleagues makes personal contact between researchers and people with learning difficulties a central issue. In their approach, researchers become part of everyday life; not setting up formal interviews but being with and talking to people within their usual daily context. This approach involves researchers in people's lives and, in so doing, encourages conversation and confidence, and opportunities to observe. The researcher is personally involved not only in many everyday events and activities but, inevitably, in a relationship with the people s/he is interested in. (See Edgerton, 1967; Edgerton and Bercovici, 1976; Edgerton, Bollinger and Herr, 1984.)

The relationship between researcher and participant is also central to Julie Wilkinson's 'being there' method (1990). The 'being there' role meant being with each of her research participants in all walks of their lives, and *experiencing* their lives as far as it was possible to do so. This is a good example of 'bottom-up' research. The people themselves, their lives and experiences are central. The researcher shares temporarily their lives and fully their experiences and, in capturing these at first hand, gives a voice to people who are rarely heard.

Further research

We set out to produce an anthology, and this we have done. But we have also learned a lot on the way about the processes involved in enabling people to tell their stories. We summarise here our new knowledge, and the gaps that still remain in our knowledge. We cover two areas: *research methods* and some possible *future directions* for further study.

(1) Research methods

This book confirms, in its range and richness, that people with learning difficulties do have stories to tell – and welcome the opportunity to do so. But there is more to telling one's story than simply having that opportunity. The processes involved in enabling people to share their experiences with others are complex and still need further exploration. We have only skimmed the surface.

We have, however, identified some areas of interest from our own experiences and the experiences of our intermediaries. These are areas we have only just begun to address here and which still need more work:

- the relationship between the researcher, or interviewer, and the story-teller
- the methods used in the story-telling
- issues of ownership and control
- the story of the research itself

We comment briefly on each of these areas in turn.

(i) The research relationship

The discussion, reflection and revelation take place within the context of a relationship. People talk more freely when they are at ease. But who puts them at their ease? Is it someone they know well and see regularly? Or someone they do not know? Is it easier to tell one's story to a familiar person, or to a stranger? Can inner pain and despair be revealed to someone close, someone who has to be seen again afterwards? Or is a stranger a safer person to confide in?

The researcher's *role* probably has a bearing on how these questions might be answered. Someone in an everyday position of power, influence or control over a potential story-teller may not be the person to share pain with. On the other hand, the stranger, like John Swain with his special visits and tape-recorder, was left wondering if he got a full or a partial account. He felt he needed longer; more time to spend with people, allowing a story to emerge not only through words but through the various documents of life considered important, such as photographs, letters and personal possessions.

The researcher has a personal impact on what happens. The familiar person, who knows there is a story to tell, all too easily engages in revealing that story. (The transcript of the interview with 'Susan' in Chapter Seven is an example of that process.) But even John, the stranger, found himself involved in people's stories, asking questions on what he was interested in rather than, as he had intended, always using open-ended questions and encouraging reflection, to allow the person's story to emerge fully.

(ii) Methods

Various methods were used by intermediaries to enable people to tell their stories. These are outlined on pp. 225–8. In order to elicit the individual's account, some sort of discussion or interview was necessary, using whatever prompts, questions and comments seemed helpful. This raised, however, several issues to do with the uses, and limitations, of interviews with people with learning difficulties:

- interviews can easily become *question-and-answer* sessions, with the interviewer inadvertently guiding the responses
- *whose story* is it then – the interviewer's or the interviewee's?
- it is tempting to ask *leading questions*, especially when one knows or suspects there is a story to be told
- the interviewer's personal interest might be evoked and a *direction* imposed on the interaction
- the account which emerges cannot easily convey the *interactions* which occurred and the *non-verbal* communication which was witnessed (this can be important in a one-to-one interaction, but becomes even more illuminating, and complex, when couples and groups are involved).

(iii) Ownership and control

People who wrote their own stories for this anthology retained ownership of presentation and content. Most people, however, worked with an intermediary. Although great care was taken to enable people to tell what they wanted, and in the way they wanted, nevertheless the issue of ownership remains real and unresolved. When an intermediary helps to elicit the story, interprets the meaning and then converts it into words, there is the likelihood that ownership, if not lost, is at least shared and possibly transferred. This does not invalidate the process, or the outcome, but the area of participation in, even initiation of, research projects by people with learning difficulties themselves remains one for further study.

(iv) The research story

We have included here the story of our involvement in the production of this anthology. We have included some diary extracts, shared our dilemmas and described our personal responses. This is, as we discussed earlier, relatively rare in research accounts. We think it's important. Hopefully, any subsequent research which builds on our experiences here will also include the stories of those projects. Only by describing the difficulties, as well as the findings, can knowledge about research methodology be shared.

(2) Future directions

We list below the areas that we have begun to find out about. We now know a little about each of these issues, but there remains still the challenge to learn more. The contributors to this book have set the agenda for further research. This list summarises what we found out; it also indicates what still needs to be discovered.

1. We learned something about people's *sense of self*: their identity in terms of who they are, their pasts and where they came from, and where they feel they belong. Identity persists in spite of (sometimes) negative life events and experiences – but we don't know why or how
2. People described their *class* origins and awareness – 'My father was a baker'. 'Dad was a headmaster'. 'My dad was a first-class bricklayer'. But we still know little about what the effect of these origins has for future lives. Cultural identity, too, is important for many contributors, and the experience of racism is articulated by some.
3. We noticed *gender differences* in people's experiences. For example, in story-telling, we found that women's stories involved the relationships that mattered to the author, but men's stories often focused more on a chronological account of life events. What is the impact of divisions of class, race and gender upon the lives of people with learning difficulties?
4. We discovered the *commonality* of people's experiences and feelings – with each other and with us – and, for some, a sense of *difference*: 'I felt set apart from people since I was 12. Even before that.'
5. We were struck by the richness, depth and diversity of people's *memories*. Much social history, particularly of long-stay hospitals, still remains to be told from 'below' and 'within'.
6. We were struck by the range and diversity of the *relationships* in some people's lives. We noted the enduring ties of kinship, and the importance of family life, or family memories, for many contributors. Loss, separation and death were described – as were feelings of sadness. We noted people's insight into the importance of their close friends and partners
7. People stressed the importance of *adulthood* and *adult status*, and described the social markers which indicate and reinforce this stage. An issue for many people was how to be seen as grown up by others, and acknowledged as being no longer a child.
8. Issues of *autonomy*, *freedom* and *independence* loomed large in this anthology. What do these mean, and how are they achieved?
9. We began to see *creativity* as an important means of self-expression, as an opportunity to display technical competence; and/or as a form of relaxation.

10 We noted the value to people of the 'ordinary' and *everyday rhythms* and routines of life.

11 We noted people's *experiences* of pain, frustration and despair, and the ability of some to *express* these feelings. Whilst the experiences were relatively common, the expression of feelings was less so. Are there ways to enable people to talk about the pain in their lives?

12 We were struck by people's will not only to survive, but to move on and gain autonomy. People can and do *struggle* against the odds, and seek to become self-determining individuals. What determines who struggles, and how?

13 We learned the value of the unfolding longer life story, and its potential for *self-expression* and *personal awareness.* People welcome the opportunity to look back, reflect and make sense of what has gone before – and to plan what happens now and later. The individual's own life history emerges as part of a larger social and historical context. Having a past, and sharing it, helps reinforce a sense of self...

We embarked on this project with relatively open minds and a wide brief. We did not know what, if anything, to expect. The result is a wide-ranging compilation of personal accounts. This book tells us much about the lives and experiences of our contributors and does so through their eyes. But this, we hope, is just a beginning. There are many more stories still to be told and voices yet to be heard.

References

Atkinson, D. (1988) 'Research interviews with people with mental handicaps', *Mental Handicap Research*, 1, 1, 75–90.

Beresford, P., and Croft, S. (1986) *Whose Welfare? Private Care or Public Services*, Brighton, Lewis Cohen Urban Studies.

Bogdan, R. and Taylor, S. J. (1982) *Inside Out: The Social Meaning of Retardation*, Toronto, University of Toronto Press.

Braginsky, D. and Braginsky, B. (1971) *Hansels and Gretels: Studies of Children in Institutions for the Mentally Retarded*. New York, Holt, Reinhart and Winston.

Brandon, D. and Ridley, J. (1985) *Beginning to Listen: A Study of the Views of Residents living in a Hostel for Mentally Handicapped People*. London, CMH Publications.

Campling, J. (ed.) (1981) *Images of Ourselves*, London, Routledge and Kegan Paul.

Coleman, P. G. (1986) *Ageing and Reminiscence Processes*, Chichester, John Wiley.

Deacon, J. (1974) *Tongue Tied*, London, MENCAP.

Edgerton, R. B. (1987) *The Cloak of Competence: Stigma in the Lives of the Mentally Retarded*, Berkeley, University of California Press.

Edgerton, R. B., and Bercovici, S. M. (1976) 'The cloak of competence: years later', *American Journal of Mental Deficiency*, 80, 485–497.

Edgerton, R.B., Bollinger, M., and Herr, B. (1984) 'The cloak of competence: after two decades', *American Journal of Mental Deficiency*, 88, 345–51.

Exley, H. (ed.) (1981) *What It's Like To Be Me*, Watford, Exley Publications.

Flynn, M. C. (1986) 'Adults who are mentally handicapped as consumers: issues and guidelines for interviewing,' *Journal of Mental Deficiency Research*, 30, 369–377.

Harding, S. (1987) 'Is there a feminist method?' in: Harding, S. (ed.) *Feminism and Methodology*, Milton Keynes, Open University Press.

Harper, G. and Dobson, J. (1986) *Participation: Report of a Workshop Involving People with Mental Handicaps and Staff who Work with Them*, London, CMH Publications.

Holbrook, D. (1964) *English for the Rejected*, Cambridge, Cambridge University Press.

Holman, B. (1987) 'Research from the underside', *British Journal of Social Work*, 17, 669–683.

Humphries, S. (1984) *The Handbook of Oral History*, London, Inter-Action Imprint.

Hunt, N. (1967) *The World of Nigel Hunt*, Beaconsfield, Darwen Finlayson.

Jahoda, A., Markova, I. and Cattermole, M. (1988) 'Stigma and the self-concept of people with a mild mental handicap', *Journal of Mental Deficiency Research*, 32, 103–115.

Lowe, K., de Paiva, D. and Humphreys, S. (1987) *Long-term Evaluation of Services for People with a Mental Handicap in Cardiff: Clients' Views*, Cardiff, University of Wales College of Medicine.

Oakley, A. (1981) 'Interviewing women: a contradiction in terms', in Roberts, H., *Doing Feminist Research*, London, Routledge and Kegan Paul.

Potts, M. and Fido, R. M. (1990) *They Take My Character* (working title), Plymouth, Northcote House.

Plummer, K. (1983) *Documents of Life*, London, Allen and Unwin.

Ryan, J. (with Thomas, F.) (1987) *The Politics of Mental Handicap. London*, London, Free Association Books.

Shearer, A. (1972) *Listen*, London, London, CMH Publications.

Shearer, A. (1973) *Our Life*, London, CMH Publications.

Towell, D. (1988) *An Ordinary Life in Practice*, London, King's Fund Centre.

Wandsworth Social Services Department (1976) *Project '74: A Research Study in which Mentally Handicapped People Speak for Themselves*, London, Wandsworth Social Services Department.

Wenger, C. (1987) *The Research Relationship*, London, Allen and Unwin.

Wilkinson, J. (1990) '"Being there": a way to evaluate life quality, starting with a person's feelings and daily experience', in: Brechin, A. and Walmsley, J. (eds) *Making Connections*, London, Hodder and Stoughton.

Williams, P. and Schoultz, B. (1982) *We Can Speak for Ourselves: Self-advocacy by Mentally Handicapped People*, London, Souvenir Press.

Index